Black Faces in the Mirror

Black Faces in the Mirror

AFRICAN AMERICANS AND THEIR

REPRESENTATIVES IN THE U.S. CONGRESS

Katherine Tate

PRINCETON UNIVERSITY PRESS

PRINCETON AND OXFORD

COPYRIGHT © 2003 BY PRINCETON UNIVERSITY PRESS
Published by Princeton University Press, 41 William Street,
Princeton, New Jersey 08540
In the United Kingdom: Princeton University Press, 3 Market Place,
Woodstock, Oxfordshire OX20 1SY

All Rights Reserved

Second printing, and first paperback printing, 2004
Paperback ISBN 0-691-11786-1

THE LIBRARY OF CONGRESS HAS CATALOGED THE CLOTH EDITION OF
THIS BOOK AS FOLLOWS

Tate, Katherine.
    Black faces in the mirror : African Americans and their representatives in the U.S.
Congress / Katherine Tate.
        p. cm.
    Includes bibliographical references and index.
    ISBN 0-691-09155-2 (alk. paper)
        1. African Americans — Politics and government.   2. African Americans — Attitudes.
    3. African Americans — Statistics.   4. African American legislators — Public opinion.
    5. Legislators — United States — Public opinion.   6. Public opinion — United States.
    I. Title.

    E185.615 .T37 2003
    328.73′0089′96073 — dc21   2002019846

British Library Cataloging-in-Publication Data is available

This book has been composed in Sabon

Printed on acid-free paper. ∞

www.pupress.princeton.edu

Printed in the United States of America

10 9 8 7 6 5 4 3 2

Contents

E
185.615
.737
2003

033004- gift Donnell

Figures and Tables

Preface and Acknowledgments

THIS BOOK only came about because of the financial support provided to me initially by my former chair, Paul Beck, in the Department of Political Science at the Ohio State University, and by the National Science Foundation's Political Science Division headed by Frank Scioli. Their financial support funded the 1996 National Black Election Study, which is at the heart of this book. I am eternally grateful for this support.

This book will spark controversy. To quote one of the Princeton University Press reviewers, "I expect this work will be controversial and much discussed in the fields of politics, law, and race. Lawyers from both sides of the racial redistricting debate will alternatively cite and criticize portions of this book in voting rights litigation. For example, voting rights lawyers will like and use the findings that show blacks view black representatives more positively than white representatives. However, members of the voting rights bar will also vilify her for presenting data that shows that black support for racial redistricting is weak."

Because there are some scholars who delight in it, I must state from the outset that I don't wish to be vilified by any group, left or right. Yet while I don't court it, I don't shrink from controversy either. I believe in the integrity of my findings. Obviously, I cannot stop persons or groups from selectively interpreting my findings and/or arguments. Thus, I wish to make my own political views plain from the outset so that those seeking to increase the numerical representation of political minorities in government might refer to them. Such references may be used in order to rebut any portion of the book that implies opposition to the extension of the Voting Rights Act (VRA) or that is against its application in case law. Blacks are shortchanged politically by their numerical underrepresentation in Congress. As I argue in the concluding chapter, the extension of the VRA and a meaningful interpretation of it by the courts are short-term fixes for this current situation. At present, it is clear that that the VRA needs to be renewed. However, I ultimately support moving to a proportional representation system. My ultimate position in this debate raises the question of how historically subordinated and marginalized groups fare under different political systems, notably proportional representation ones. This question is one that I am presently working on.

Many colleagues, friends, and family members gave me encouragement and support along the way, and I apologize for not singling each and every one out. I want to acknowledge several scholars whose dissertation committees I served on (now years ago) who contributed intellectually to the project: Valeria Sinclair Chapman at the University of Rochester, Claudine Gay at Stanford University, and David Ian Lublin at American University. Former doctoral students Miki Caul-Kittilson and Kim DeFronzo helped collect additional data for this project, while Stefanie Chambers, Gloria Hampton, and Teresa Todd assisted on the 1996 National Black Election Study. My former OSU colleague and political scientist Janet Box-Steffensmeier gave me tremendous support when I was working on this project as well, especially as I transitioned from my old department (Ohio State) to my new one (UC Irvine). At UC Irvine, I especially want to thank the intellectual support provided to me by Bernie Grofman, a very distinguished voting rights scholar, and Russell Dalton, the director of the Center for the Study of Democracy, as well as UCI colleagues Garance Genicot, Claire Jean Kim, Kristen Monroe, Kevin Olson, and Judy Stepan-Norris. Professors Lucius J. Barker, Paula D. McClain, Morris Fiorina, Gary King, Dianne Pinderhughes, Christopher Parker, Fredrick Harris, Luis Fraga, Mark Petracca, and David Mayhew provided critical feedback on different stages of the book manuscript. The political science editor at Princeton, Chuck Myers, is a wonderful editor and deserves special thanks for making the review process speedy and professional. I appreciated the editorial assistance provided by Linda Truilo, my brother Emory Andrew Tate, and production work by Ellen Foos. I also want to thank Sarah Harrington at Princeton University Press for her help in the production of this book, and especially helping me when I needed it with the book's figures and artwork. Sarah had the dangerous job of trudging to the city's main post office to collect the mail during the anthrax scare when Princeton University's postal system was temporarily shut down. Thank you all!

Finally I need to acknowledge the unwitting support provided to me by my kids. It is commonplace for parents of young children to acknowledge them for having distracted them and caused some delay. As the mother of two preschoolers, perhaps this has been the case for me as well, but the arrivals of Luke and Sophie also forced me to become greatly more disciplined in my professional life and greatly more efficient. Their arrival forced me to make a clean separation of my work life from the rest of my life. Because there would be no more mixing, work felt more like work, and even, at times, became highly stressful and oppressive, but also because of them, the rest of my life was an incalculable improvement over my old life. I thank God and Jesus Christ for these children, and this book is dedicated with great love to them both.

I. Introduction

CHAPTER 1

The Puzzle of Representation

> But, in spite of many centuries of theoretical effort, we cannot
> say what representation is.
> — Heinz Eulau, in *The Politics of Representation*

To THE ANCIENT GREEKS, democracy meant rule by the common people. For very practical reasons, the American political system is not a
pure democracy, but an indirect one. Americans participate in government by selecting others to make decisions for them. How the government actually represents and does the people's bidding is an important
question. Designing a government with limited powers, the framers of
the Constitution sought to ensure government-by-the-people or popular
sovereignty through elections. By granting only two-year terms to legislators in the House of Representatives, the nation's founders arranged
for the quick replacement of lawmakers who failed to live up to constituent expectations. In addition to regularly scheduled elections or popular control, there was the presumption that elected officials could be
trusted to represent the will of the people because government officials
would be drawn from the ranks of the people. A perfectly representative
body would be similar to the general population in race, sex, ethnicity,
occupation, religion, and other fundamental social characteristics.
Through the possession of social characteristics similar to their constituents, representatives could be counted upon to share their political beliefs and interests.

As methods of preserving popular sovereignty, these propositions
have their shortcomings. Winning an election to the U.S. House of Representatives now usually requires at least half a million dollars, and
generally those who spend the most win most often. There are now
scholars who worry that political equality and popular sovereignty have
been undermined by the high cost of winning an election. Thus, an
entire field has emerged devoted to the question of how campaigns and
money have impacted on the American political system. That the U.S.
government is socially unrepresentative of the public — with its members
being wealthier, older, whiter, and overwhelmingly male — has generated
far less concern and little corresponding scholarship. Indeed, most congressional scholars have long assumed and argued that the social back-

ground of legislators has little bearing on their politics. In the opinion of one set of leading congressional scholars, "Must Congress demographically mirror the populace to be a representative institution? Probably not. Legislators from farming districts can voice farmers' concerns even though they themselves have never plowed a field or milked a cow; whites can champion equal opportunities for minorities. Legislators can speak for voters of divergent social rank or life style" (Davidson and Oleszek 1981, 104).

Nevertheless, as the numbers of women and racial minorities winning seats to the U.S. Congress have increased, the question of whether such groups are equally or unequally represented in government has generated some research. For women, scholarship has seemingly reached a consensus that women's political interests have been underrepresented in the past since women legislators are more likely than their male counterparts to address "women's issues" (Swers 1998; Thomas 1994; Darcy, Welch, and Clark 1994). In contrast, the more limited scholarship on Blacks has yet to reach such a consensus.

In this book, I address the question of whether or not the racial composition of government is relevant to the political representation of Blacks. Like women, African Americans have made tremendous gains in holding elective office but still fall short of proportional representation. Constituting 12 percent of the population, Blacks hold about two percent of all elected offices in the country. Blacks make up about 7 percent of Congress — the chief lawmaking institution in the U.S. governmental system — with thirty-eight members in the House of Representatives but none currently serving in the Senate. Today about one-third of Blacks are represented in Washington by Black officeholders. Are these Blacks better represented in Washington by Blacks than the two-thirds not represented by Blacks?

My goal in this book is to present a broad and balanced assessment of the value of descriptive representation for African Americans. A new breed of empirically oriented scholars have pursued this question largely by examining whether Black representatives cast different roll-call votes than other representatives or file different sorts of bills (see Swain 1993; Lublin 1997; Whitby 1998; Canon 1999). However, my book brings substantially more data to this debate. Political representation, as I briefly explain in the next section, consists of three forms: substantive, descriptive, and symbolic. In contrast to previous empirical studies, I consider all three forms in my assessment of the importance of race in political representation.

A second unique and contrasting feature of my book is that utilizing a 1996 national telephone survey of Blacks, I address the question of how important is descriptive representation from both sides of the representative-constituent relationship, uniquely from the vantage point of Blacks themselves. Do Blacks feel that they are better represented in the U.S. system of indirect democracy when their representative is Black? In addition, how does the race of the House representative impact their political behavior and attitudes? In other words, does Black representation in Washington lead Blacks to become more informed about and more active in national politics? And does Black representation affect attitudes that Blacks have about Congress as an institution more broadly? The analysis of survey data allows me to address these critical questions that have been much subject of much debate, especially within the field of minority voting rights. These are questions that have been subjected to fierce debate but without, to my knowledge, much hard, empirical evidence. While touching on the normative components of the debate over race and representation, my book provides hard, empirical evidence as well.

The argument that I will make at the end of this book is that it is the majoritarian or district plurality system that the nation's founders imported from Great Britain that systematically encourages lawmakers to provide descriptive and symbolic representation as much as substantive representation to their constituents. The reasons why all three components of political representation are stressed by American legislators are several. First, lawmaking is a difficult and lengthy enterprise in the U.S. system. At the end of a term, the typical House member can claim credit for passage of only one bill that they sponsored or, more likely, cosponsored. Rationally, therefore, American legislators work hard to convey to constituents that even in the absence of tangible or substantive policy outputs, their views and interests are still well represented in Washington through activities weighted toward the symbolic and descriptive. Second, U.S. legislators are also much less confined by party memberships than elected representatives under different electoral arrangements. Legislators are credited less for what their political party achieves than for what they individually provide for constituents in the American political system as a consequence. As members of geographically defined spaces as well as of political parties, American legislators pursue their own particularized goals, including pork barrel legislation, in addition to their party's ideological agendas (Arnold 1990). Related to this second point is that modern political campaigns are candidate-centered with parties in the background (Aldrich 1995; Wattenberg 1991). House members seeking reelection try to build a record based on personal accomplishments as much as they share the credit with their political party. Candidate-centered campaigning pushes the balance even further in favor of Richard Fenno's "home style," or the concentrated efforts by members of Congress to establish "personal ties" with their constituents (Fenno 1978). Members spend considerable time and resources talking to constituents, providing personal services to constituents in addition to the time that they spend on Capitol Hill doing legislative and committee work. And the campaign materials of House members reflect the strong emphasis of the "personal" over the "political" in fact.

Ultimately I will argue that Blacks are not alone in their strong appreciation of being descriptively represented; all Americans place a strong value on it as it is a component of political representation continuously stressed by members of those elected to the U.S. Congress. Thus, in describing and analyzing the manner in which Blacks are political represented in the U.S. Congress, I provide new insights, broader and more balanced coverage of the nature of representation in the American political system than congressional scholars have to date. Thus, by providing this empirical analysis of how Blacks are represented in the U.S. Congress, I make a significant theoretical contribution to the field of congressional studies in establishing the very broad nature of political representation in the U.S. Congress.

RACE AND THE REPRESENTATION DEBATE

Does the social background and race of the representative matter in a representative democracy? While congressional scholars generally think not, the founding fathers explicitly expressed the hope that their government would be a descriptively representative body. John Adams, a leading architect of the Constitution, explicitly conceived of elected representatives as "a portrait of the people at large in miniature" (Wood 1998 [1969], 165). Still there is a debate over the degree to which the founding fathers truly desired popular representation. Some argue that James Madison intended a government composed of the social elite when Madison wrote in *The Federalist* No. 10 about the role of Congress to "refine and enlarge" public opinion (Wood 1998; Fishkin 1995). Other scholars, notably Robert C. Grady, contend that Madison was a true democrat and his tendency toward elitism was tempered by a strong preference for a government that reflected "the great body of the society, not . . . an inconsiderable proportion of a favored class" as he wrote in *Federalist* No. 39 (1993, 17–18). A review of the Revolutionary debates over representation is not especially clarifying. Even at the time of the nation's founding, according to historian Gordon S. Wood (1998), there was "great confusion" concerning the concept of political representation.

The problem of how best to represent the American people in an elected government was so controversial at the time the Constitution was drafted that it nearly defied political solution. Small states objected to legislative seats based solely on population, which is what large states preferred. The "Great Compromise" resulted in a bicameral Congress where each state legislature would send two senators and the lower-house seats would be allocated on the basis of the state's population. While the conflict is treated as a small state/large state feud, at its core was the fear of democrats who believed that the Senate and presidency were constitutional devices to curb the political influences of the lower classes in this new democracy. As "Montazuma" sarcastically declared in the Anti-Federalist Paper No. 9, "we have designated by the popular name of the House of Representatives. But to guard against every possible danger from this lower house, we have subjected every bill they bring forward to the double negative of our upper house and president." Because senators and the president were to be chosen by the state legislatures or their electors, Anti-Federalists believed they would remain positions largely controlled by the members of the economic and social elite. Federalists wanted a government somewhat removed from the masses, and designed a government that "filtered" citizens' views through the indirect elections of senators and the president (Wood 1998; Fishkin 1995). Anti-Federalists, in contrast, wanted a government closer to the people; they therefore sought frequent, direct elections and rotation in office. Additionally, the Bill of Rights became the procedural mechanism that safeguarded the rights of the lower classes by a government whose Senate would most likely be limited to the social and economic elite.

The division of the national legislature into two houses, while it solved the immediate problem of the balance of power among the thirteen original colonies, did not fundamentally resolve the problem of how elected representatives were to represent the people. The framers left the question of how voters would elect representatives to the states. And in the beginning, only five states chose to use districts, while the majority elected members of Congress through at-large elections. In 1842, Congress passed legislation requiring single-member districts. This move resulted from partisan competition as the majority parties in at-large elections states were electing delegations composed entirely of members from the majority party (Barber 2000).

Thus, the methods of electing representatives would be a source of continuous debate throughout U.S. history. Americans had revolted against British rule because they felt that they were not represented in the government. The British responded that Americans, as subjects of Great Britain were "virtually represented," as are those living in England, since no one was "actually" represented (Wood 1998). Virtual representation claims are elitist. Historian Gordon S. Wood writes that while John Adams had urged that representatives should mirror the people, "in the same breath he had suggested that they must also be 'a few of the most wise and good' who, as the English defenders of virtual representation had implied, would presumably know better than the bulk of the people what was the proper interest of society" (1998, 180). Such claims were naturally challenged; one American leader expressed the view at the time New York was ratifying its constitution that elected representatives need not be the "best sort," but preferably average men with "common sense and an unshaken integrity" (Wood 1998, 180).

Ultimately Republican claims that Americans are a "singular and united people" that lay beneath claims of virtual representation would be contested as fair and equal representation increasingly implied actual representation. Still from 1776 to 1778, American revolutionaries un-consciously — it seemed — embraced the notion of virtual representation because they assumed that people were "a homogeneous entity in society set against the rulers" (Wood 1998, 607). In a few short years following the Revolution, Wood writes, American political thinkers would recognize that their country was one comprised of many political factions. And as such, the political good was no longer a single "entity distinct from its parts" but formed in the aggregation of these combative separate interests. Increasingly, representatives need not possess great abilities, as their role in government was to represent faithfully the will of the people as instructed. Writes Wood, "The representation of the people, as American politics in the Revolutionary era had made glaringly evident, could never be virtual, never inclusive; it was acutely actual and always tentative and partial" (600). For Wood, clearly all of the various factions should be actually represented in government, for at least some of the time. Yet the very principle behind the claim that Americans were virtually represented in English Parliament was used by Americans to dismiss arguments in favor of granting suffrage to Africans, mulattos, and Indians in Massachusetts (183). Insofar as legislators were ultimately pursuing policies that served the interests of their communities and of the nation as a whole, such groups were virtually represented.

Race, when raised as a political problem at the constitutional convention, was only raised with reference to the enslavement of Africans. Even then the matter of race and representation ironically was debated only over whether the Black slave population should be used in the allocation of seats to the slave-owning states to the House of Representatives. Blacks at the time the Constitution was ratified were explicitly and unanimously excluded from the new government as noncitizens, even while the original Constitution did not make direct reference to race. The Constitution, the shining document that sprung from the Declaration of Independence, sided with the slave-owners and enshrined the practice of slavery in three provisions, though, all without mentioning slavery or slaves. Slaves would be partially counted in the state's population, augmenting the political representation of slave-owners in the House and in the Electoral College. Congress was forbidden as well to ban the importation of slaves until 1808. The Constitution also instructed states to return escaped slaves to their slave-owners.

It was on the basis of these three passages contained in the Constitution that Chief Justice Roger B. Taney would argue with the consent of the Supreme Court's majority in the 1857 Dred Scott decision that Black people, even free Blacks, were not U.S. citizens and had no rights under the Constitution. Although many American government textbooks generally stress that slavery "embarrassed" the founding fathers, Alexis de Toqueville's own observations were that few Americans saw the blatant contradiction between slavery — as well as the country's treatment of free Blacks — and democracy. It is truly difficult to imagine the founding fathers favoring a government that included Blacks as elected officials given not only their acceptance of slavery but also the extent of their racial prejudices. At the time he wrote the Declaration of Independence, Thomas Jefferson owned over 200 slaves. Still, Jefferson publicly opposed slavery. James Madison became a staunch abolitionist who saw the enslavement of Blacks as a vile contradiction to a democratic system. Radical Republicans in their effort to create a truly color-blind democracy also advocated Black officeholding, and twenty Blacks, half of whom had experienced slavery, would serve in the U.S. House of Representatives during Reconstruction.

Nevertheless, rather than only the outcome of a terrible compromise, or better still, a capitulation to slave-owners in order to create and preserve the Union, the denial of individual rights and equality to Blacks reflected the illiberal traditions that justified it. These same illiberal traditions that are enshrined in the Constitution have also consigned a majority (women, Indians, Blacks, and Asian immigrants) to an inferior and unequal status for a majority of America's history (R. M. Smith 1997). The claim that the Constitution was and is "color-blind" has blinded liberals to the social and economic inequalities that were either sanctioned by aspects of the Constitution or encouraged. This liberal creed that enshrines color-blindness (or gender- or class-blindness) obscures then how much racial group membership has affected and continues to affect U.S. politics and the distribution of public goods (Phillips 1995; R. M. Smith 1997). And, in fact, outside of New England, many states such as Ohio, as they dropped the basic property qualifications during the era of Jacksonian democracy, added the restriction of race to the right to vote. Even northern states such as New York, Pennsylvania, and New Jersey, which had previously permitted free Blacks to vote, adopted new state constitutions confining the right to adult White males (Barber 2000). Whigs would push for literacy requirements instead of race, but in states where Democrats controlled matters, the party line against Black male suffrage held firm. As historian J. Morgan Kousser (1999) argues, Black voting rights were denied in part as a consequence of intense party competition.

It was the history of state-sanctioned discrimination against Blacks that alerted the courts to the importance of Blacks having the right to elect a "candidate of choice," and implicitly, therefore, the importance of Blacks' descriptive representation in elected legislatures. Without this history, their numerical underrepresentation in government never would have won judicial protection and remedy. The initial case validating the importance of creating opportunities that gave minorities meaningful opportunities to elect one of their own to government involved multimember as opposed to single-member legislative districts. In *White v. Regester*, Blacks and Latinos argued that multimember districts in Texas were used to dilute their voting strength, therefore denying them their Fourteenth Amendment rights. In 1973, the Supreme Court unanimously ruled in favor of the Black and Latino plaintiffs. The basis for declaring the multimember districts unconstitutional was vague, but notably included the state's history of discrimination against minorities. Seven years later, however, in *City of Mobile v. Bolden*, the Court would rule that election systems that are shown to discriminate against minorities are only unconstitutional when minorities can show that they were purposefully created with a racial animus against them. After testimony was offered about the history of discrimination in Alabama, however, the case was remanded. Racial intent was proven, and the Black plaintiffs prevailed in Mobile. (Yet proving racial intent was costly, and the legal standards for proving it were vague, making such intent very difficult to effectively establish in courts [Kousser 1999].) Thus, voting rights activists in response to *Bolden* successfully pressed for modification of the 1965 Voting Rights Act in 1982 (Pinderhughes 1995). The modification expressly prohibited voting procedures that afforded minorities "less opportunities than other members of the electorate to participate in the political process and to elect representatives of their choice" (Davidson and Grofman 1994, 35). Minorities could never be fairly represented in government, in other words, as long as the electoral system was biased against them.

The 1982 amendment of the Voting Rights Act unleashed a furious controversy. On the one side, political conservatives such as Abigail Thernstrom (1987) argued that using the act effectively to force states to create minority-majority districts violates the principle of colorblindness and fairness. This was also the argument used by Associate Justice Sandra Day O'Connor in the 1993 *Shaw* ruling against a North Carolina plan that had sent that state's first two Blacks to Congress since Reconstruction. Liberal supporters countered conservative critics of the Act by applying the same logic of racial fairness, arguing that without it Blacks and Hispanics would never have won election to Congress in the South in the first place. Voting rights activists like Frank M. Parker (1990) have pointed out the inherent racial bias of a system that perpetuates White political domination and the necessity of drawing minority-majority districts to overcome that racial bias. Still others, such as Lani Guinier (1994), have rejected majority-minority districts as a short-term fix, supporting instead the more radical solution of moving from a single-member plurality election system to a proportional representation one.

Complicating the debate have been the arguments developed and advanced by Carol M. Swain in her award-winning *Black Faces, Black Interests* (1993). Drawing a distinction between descriptive and substantive political representation, she asked if Black elected officials were necessary to advance Black political interests? The question was both legitimate and timely. In the 1992 House elections, Blacks gained a record number of thirteen new seats in Congress, largely through the U.S. Justice Department's enforcement of the 1982-amended Voting Rights Act. Including the District of Columbia's nonvoting delegate, this brought their number in the House to thiry-nine in the 103rd Congress. No longer could the question of whether Black elected officials were necessary for Black political representation be dismissed or evaded by voting rights liberals who had stressed the "paucity" of Black elected officials, and especially in the South, as the primary justification for the racially gerrymandered districts. Blacks were now serving in Congress from five southern states that during the twentieth century none had previously served: Alabama, Florida, North Carolina, South Carolina, and Virginia.[1] Were these Blacks representing their Black constituents differently than did whites? Based largely on case studies of thirteen black and White House-members, the study concludes that blacks did not need to be descriptively present in Congress for black citizens to be fully represented in government. Further still, Swain argues that Blacks' push for descriptive representation undermines their substantive representation in Washington.

THE PUZZLE OF REPRESENTATION

Does race matter in the political representation of Blacks in Congress? Obviously the answer depends on how interests are represented in Congress. Although the issue of political representation remains of enormous interest to political theorists, interest in this topic among congressional scholars has lagged. In the 1970s interest shifted from a focus on political representation to congressional elections (see Mezey 1993; Fiorina 1974; Mayhew 1974). The study of elections still remains one of the hot areas of research in congressional studies.

Since the theories of Edmund Burke in the eighteenth century, congressional scholars have pointed out two different styles of political representation: delegate versus trustee. Delegate representatives try to reflect in their representative role the views of their constituents, while those acting as trustees serve by relying on their best judgment of the issues. Rooted in his republicanism, Burke strongly believed that representatives should represent the country, not constituents nor districts. Not surprisingly, early surveys of legislators found that they did a little bit of both. The issue is not a dead one. It was raised quite seriously during President Clinton's impeachment hearings as some of his critics felt that members of Congress should disregard the president's strong showing in opinion polls and vote according to their "conscience." A survey showed that members of Congress thought that while they should behave as trustees, they nevertheless acted as delegates since that is what they thought the public wanted (Davidson and Oleszek 1981).

Since Burke, political scientists have made a distinction between the focus (nation vs. constituent) and style (delegate vs. trustee), as both are implied in Burke's view on the role of the elected representative. Often times, a two-by-two typology is presented to establish the four types of legislative roles elected officials can assume (Miller and Stokes 1963; Thomassen 1994), but the roles are each best depicted as single dimensions as shown in figure 1.1. On issue after issue, legislators move between a trustee role and delegate role, in pursuit of national or particularistic goals. After all, as legislators strive to bring back "pork" to their districts, they also participate in making national policy. Elected representatives fall somewhere on this two-dimensional space. In the United States, however, the idealized form of political representation is the instructed-delegate version, where representatives are not independent, but constrained by elections, and strictly obey the will of their constituencies. Moreover, as much as Congress along with the president makes national laws, its members pursue their own particularized goals as representatives of geographically defined districts. Legislators' efforts to represent districts as well as individual constituents make the U.S. system of government somewhat unique. The accumulated evidence, nevertheless, suggests that even this typology fails to show adequately the full role that members play in the U.S. Congress. U.S. legislators are also opinion leaders even if the normative view casts them as electorally

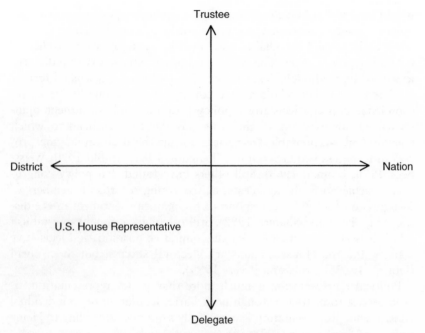

Figure 1.1. Style and focus of elected representative.

constrained agents. Groups within districts are also represented in the activities of members in addition to the district and the nation as a whole.

The role of the elected representative is but one conceptual component; another is the way in which constituents are actually represented. In 1967, political theorist Hanna Pitkin's seminal work held that citizens are represented in elected government in three ways: descriptively, symbolically, and substantively. One is descriptively represented when the representative belongs to your social or demographic group. Representatives substantively represent their constituents through the realization of their political needs. Descriptive representation devoid of any substance impact is "symbolic." She concludes by discounting the value of descriptive or "pictorial" representation. In the end political representation is best achieved when legislators act "in the interest of the represented, in a manner responsive to them" (209).

The initial empirical work that emerged generally ignored symbolic and descriptive representation in favor of a model of representation that was purely instrumental. Warren Miller and Donald Stokes's seminal article published in 1963 searched for "congruence" between constituents' beliefs and the legislator's voting behavior, and subsequent studies would interpret political representation as policy responsiveness or congruence. Policy congruency, for good and bad, would become the elusive "Holy Grail," the chalice used by Christ, in empirical studies of political representation. The Miller and Stokes study was roundly criticized for its methodological shortcomings, which are discussed further in chapter 6. Other scholars have concluded that a one-to-one correspondence between legislators' policy positions and constituent opinions need not exist on all the issues, as the constituencies to which members are accountable are varied, and as the decision-making process in Congress is quite complex (Kingdon 1981; Arnold 1990; Weissberg 1976; Froman 1963). Still others have found that policy congruence is achieved in the aggregate, as the voting records of members of Congress do faithfully correspond to the majority sentiment in the district (e.g., Page and Shapiro 1992). Still others have sought to establish a link between constituency service, committee position, and legislative activity and the House incumbent's electoral success, but to no avail (Fiorina 1989; Fiorina and Rivers 1989).

Political representation is much more than policy representation, or even service to districts through pork barrel legislation or to individual constituents. Representation is powerfully symbolic, according to Heinz Eulau and Paul Karps (1978). As they note,

> By emphasizing only one component of responsiveness as a substantive concept, they reduced a complex phenomenon like representation to one of its components and substituted the component for the whole. But if responsiveness is limited to one component, it cannot capture the complexities of the real world of politics. . . . How else could one explain that representatives manage to stay in office in spite of the fact that they are *not* necessarily or always responsive to the represented?" (60–61).

For Eulau and Karps, constituents were symbolically represented through "public gestures of a sort that create a sense of trust and support in the relationship between the representative and the represented" (1978, 63). Congress is loaded with acts of symbolic representation. Politicians routinely push for policies that they know won't ever become law (Edelman 1964). Legislators vote for legislation that won't ever be implemented (Pressman and Wildavsky 1984). The average citizen, however, does not understand that certain resolutions (simple and concurrent), for example, don't make law and are unenforceable by law. However, because 200 or more such symbolic resolutions are generally passed in each Congress, there must be political rewards and tactical advantages associated with them. Symbolic legislation is also a byproduct of the American legislative structure, where members are elected to represent geographic communities in addition to their parties and constituents. Empirical examination of how members of Congress symbolically represent their constituents, and the electoral and political significance of symbolic representation is still a fledging field that has only recently taken off (Chapman 2002). This said, symbolic representation is one important reason why blacks need to be descriptively represented in the U.S. Congress.

Since Pitkin's seminal work, a new group of political theorists, stimulated by the voting rights controversy, have begun to assert that descriptive representation, something Pitkin herself discounted, is an important form of political representation. A number have pointed out the importance of representatives "standing" for social groups (Young 1990; Phillips 1995; M. S. Williams 1998). Taking this a step farther, Melissa S. Williams (1998) argues that fair representation must include descriptive representation for marginalized social groups in legislative bodies. As the American system of government functions as a deliberative democracy, marginalized groups must take part in it (Phillips 1995; Mansbridge 1999). Such groups, these theorists contend, must be free to define their interests and defend them publicly. Any other form of political representation short of descriptive representation might result in the neglect or dilution of their interests. Many women believe that the issue of sexual harassment was not initially taken seriously because there were no female members on the Senate Judiciary Committee at the time of Clarence Thomas's confirmation to the Supreme Court. Not only will such groups now be heard in legislative chambers, but the process in which policy is worked out might become more discursive and consensus-oriented (M. S. Williams 1998, 146–47).

These electoral mechanisms, psychological and structural, however, failed to work as theorized for Blacks in the one-party South and were generally weak in the nation's two-party system (Frymer 1999). When the interests of minorities are defined as outside or contrary to those of the community, then legislators can safely ignore them. Blacks' political history, Williams contends, justifies the perception among Blacks that Black representatives are more trustworthy representatives than are White legislators. Whites can win trust from Black constituents, of course, but because of history, they are necessarily going to have to work harder at establishing that trust. Congressional scholar Kenny Whitby writes that "[h]aving members of Congress who share the sociological attributes of the electorate is a powerful symbol of representation" (1998, 6). Descriptive representation remains potently symbolic to Blacks today. It represents their inclusion in the polity, the progress achieved in America's race relations, and their political power in the U.S. system.

The battle between Black and White legislators in South Carolina over the state's Confederate battle flag illustrates the continuing significance of symbols. This flag flying over the South Carolina Statehouse symbolized White supremacy and Southern resistance to the Union, although its supporters maintained that it represented "heritage," not hate. The flag was hoisted over the state capitol only in 1962, however, during the peak period of Southern resistance to the Black civil rights movement. The National Association for the Advancement of Colored People (NAACP) in its efforts to force the White-dominated state government to remove the flag sponsored a boycott aimed at the state's tourism industry, a measure, according to media accounts, that was draining millions of tourist dollars from that state. Seeking a compromise, in May 2000, Governor Jim Hodges backed a bill removing the flag from the dome of the statehouse, but allowing a smaller one to be flown on a thirty-foot pole in front near a monument to soldiers of the Confederacy. This compromise legislation failed to satisfy the NAACP, which has vowed to continue its boycott. The NAACP president, Kweisi Mfume, a former member of Congress, in fact, singled out and criticized the ten black state lawmakers (out of thirty-three) who had voted for the compromise legislation.

The war over racial symbols in South Carolina plainly demonstrates that symbols matter not only to Blacks but to many Whites as well. A few months earlier, South Carolina finally agreed to recognize Dr. Martin Luther King, Jr.'s birthday as a state holiday, but only as part of a compromise bill that created a state holiday called the "Confederate Memorial Day." To ignore the role that elected representatives play in symbolically representing their constituents and to examine only the substantive legislative products is to miss a very critical component of how constituents are actually represented in the American political system.

Finally, Congress is an institution with historical and momentous weight in American politics, and not simply because of the collective output of its members as agents of the public. Rather, members of Congress carry great influence for the actions that they take as individual actors within the "public sphere." This public sphere, as conceptualized by David Mayhew (2000), represents the public consciousness. As means of pressing upon the collective consciousness, members have a wide array of activities to consider that cannot be adequately captured by the Constitution's description of the legislature's functions. "With the member's job," Mayhew writes, "goes a license to persuade, connive, hatch ideas, propagandize, assail enemies, vote, build coalitions, shepherd legislation, and in general cut a figure in public affairs." The member's capacity to influence collective outcomes and possibly transform society through issue preference formation is far greater than his or hers ability to make laws. The presence or absence of Blacks within the Congress, within the U.S. Senate, therefore, has far greater consequences than textbook treatments of Congress generally suggest. It is not simply a problem of whether electing Blacks can cost parties' their majorities, but significantly more than this. Members of Congress possess a "power of one" in addition to their contribution as one of 535. This broad understanding of Congress elevates the problem of Black political representation as citizens are not only represented through the enactment of public laws. Constituents are represented through many more activities than bill initiation and roll-call votes.

POLITICAL REPRESENTATION: THE VIEW FROM THE BLACK ELECTORATE

As the quote at the beginning of this chapter suggests, the concept of representation is elusive. Like power, it may elude all efforts toward a precise theoretical definition. Constituents are represented in everything that legislators do in their formal capacity as elected representatives. Members of Congress engage in three principal, interrelated activities: (1) constituency service, (2) policy-making, and (3) reelection. Out of all of their activities, members substantively, symbolically, and descriptively represent their constituencies. Constituents are substantively represented by legislators in the form of policy initiatives, votes on policy, and in the form of constituency service. They are represented in activities below the floor level of Congress, not as visible to the public (Hall 1996). At the same time, constituents can also be represented symbolically. They are represented by the "position taking" that members of Congress engage in, as described by David Mayhew (1974). Symbolic representation gives voice and recognition to the goals and values of a key interest and social group. Substantive and symbolic representation are not mutually exclusive categories but can overlap. And of course, Black legislators providing substantive representation provide Black constituents with both. Of the three forms that political representation can take, which activities are recognized and valued most by constituents?

Public knowledge about Congress is abysmally low. Ordinary citizens do not and cannot be expected to follow the legislative voting history of their representatives in Washington, watch their floor speeches on C-Span, and learn about the interests from whom they receive donations or the lobbyists with whom they lunch. Empirical work in congressional studies has generally focused on elections, not representation. Important determinants of the congressional vote are political party and ideology. For sure, political party is an important element in evaluating one's elected representative and in congressional elections (Miller and

Stokes 1963; Erikson and Wright 2001). In low-information congressional elections, party presents a clear choice. Some revisionist work established the importance of ideology and issues in congressional elections. Alan Abramowitz's analysis (1984) shows that ideology was a force in the 1980 and 1982 House races. The more liberal the voter was, the more likely the voter was to vote Democratic. Erikson and Wright (2001) show that the member's ideology independent of political party is consistently linked to the vote decision in the House elections. Candidates whose ideologies are too extreme for their district generally are punished at the polls.

While the evidence suggests that party and ideological records of members do matter to their poorly informed constituents in elections, Richard Fenno's detailed case studies establish that members of Congress emphasize their personal qualities as much as, and perhaps more than, their policy stands. Reading Fenno's *Home Style*, one is struck by how much members of Congress stress their "descriptive" representation of constituents when in their districts. Fenno quotes one congressman telling his audience, "I am not exactly one of you, but we have a lot in common, and I feel a lot like you." It may be that with most members of Congress socially so unlike the population, members work very hard at identifying with their constituents and connecting with them at a personal level. Samuel L. Popkin (1991) writes about how presidential candidates will eat tacos in Mexican American communities to symbolize their support. Similarly politicians during the campaign will eschew suit jackets to bond symbolically with the ordinary, working person. This effort to identify and bond can be politically costly, as when a *Washington Post* news story quoted then-Georgia U.S. Senator Wyche Fowler telling a Black audience in his reelection campaign that "I'm black — white on the outside but black on the inside." His Republican opponent Paul Coverdell made copies of the story and had it distributed to his supporters at political rallies (MacNeil/Lehrer NewsHour transcript, 11/23/92). Coverdell went on to defeat Fowler narrowly in the 1992 Senate race.

Voters use demographic facts about candidates such as their race, ethnicity, gender, religion, and social origins, as a "low-information shortcut" according to Samuel Popkin (1991) to estimate their policy stands. Voters also use more information, when available, such as party affiliation and the candidate's qualifications, but descriptive characteristics are not simply ignored. The public's inability to follow and interpret Washington politics may in the end give special weight to the symbolic form of representation, and specifically, then, to descriptive representation.

Work by Lawrence Bobo and Franklin D. Gilliam, Jr. (1990) has found that the descriptive representation of Blacks is politically empowering, that is, Blacks descriptively represented are more interested and active in politics than Blacks who are not descriptively represented in government. They contend that believing the system perhaps to be more responsive to their needs and interests when Blacks hold positions of power in government, Black citizens become more politically active. Black elected officials represent a potent symbol of Blacks' inclusion in the polity, inspiring more Blacks to take part in it. Similarly, Nancy L. Schwartz (1988), following a long line of theorists, argues that political representation can be empowering, a vehicle through which citizens become educated and become linked to their communities. If descriptive representation in Washington is found to empower Blacks politically, the case for structuring elections to achieve their descriptive representation is strengthened. This definition of representation is a general one, not at all exclusive to Blacks. I believe that legislators strive in their everyday activities to represent their constituents descriptively as well as substantively and symbolically. Whether constituents value that descriptive representation as well as substantive representation, however, or whether only marginalized social groups value descriptive and symbolic representation more, is an open question that I address in the book's conclusion.

The problem of race and political representation generates a number of complicated issues. People dogmatically fall on one side of the fence, either opposed to the value and all means of achieving descriptive representation in government for Blacks and other political minorities, or in favor. For those readers who already have made up their minds in this debate, I would like to illustrate both the appeal and costs of descriptive representation through the application of a sports metaphor.

With respect to Black descriptive representation, is it enough that Blacks identify with a team and cheer it on to victory on the sidelines, or, to truly take part in the activity, must some of the players on the field also be Black? What happens to Black supporters if none of the players are ever members of their own race? Are they as enthused about the game as supporters whose social groups are well represented on the field? Will they continue to show up at the games even if they receive shares in the team's victories? Will they continue to care if their team wins or loses in events? What if, however, having Black members on the field as players reduces the team's likelihood of winning? After all, as many contend, like Swain (1993), the practice of constructing majority-Black congressional districts reduces the likelihood of other Democrats winning their seats. Some contend that the dozen or so majority-Black districts constructed in the 1990 round of redistricting helped the Republican party become the majority party in the U.S. House of Representatives in 1994. But still, might Black players bring different strategies (and agendas) to the field, and might they seek to achieve different goals that were not apparent before?

In short, is the race of the players salient and important to the many Black spectators in the stands? This is the central question that my study takes up.

OVERVIEW OF THE BOOK

In the first half of the book I consider the question of whether Black members of Congress are different from their White counterparts. Chapter 2 begins by focusing on an elemental but neglected aspect of the question, namely the sociological characteristics of Blacks in office compared to those of Whites. The nature of our system requires that individuals have wealth and education, and that they belong to certain occupations as informal prerequisites for public office. The higher the office, the higher the status demands. Are Black legislators more like the average Black American in terms of their occupation, wealth, education, and gender or more like their White counterparts in the House? If Blacks legislators are unlike their Black constituents on almost every social dimension but race, what is the real value of descriptive representation? Chapter 3 examines their elections to Congress. Certainly, most Blacks in Congress represent districts very much unlike their White counterparts as they are majority-Black or majority-minority in population. Whether the fact that Black members are elected in majority-Black districts gives them a degree of "electoral immunity" is addressed in this chapter. While ample new research has examined this, chapter 4 once again compares the political styles and voting records of Black legislators and White legislators through an analysis of their voting records. A departure from past work, however, is a comparison of Black members' key votes in the 104th Congress to actual public opinion data on African Americans. Chapter 5 addresses the issue of symbolic representation. Representation is much more than pork barrel policies; the representation of Blacks through symbolic legislation is presented as a valued component of how legislators elected to represent communities and groups. Whether Black legislators offer only "symbols" and not substantive public policies that benefit Blacks and the general public is a charge that I also consider in this chapter.

The second half of the book addresses the relevance that race has for Blacks in terms of their political representation. Chapter 6 examines the impact that race has on how satisfied blacks are with their representation in Congress. In chapter 7, I determine whether Nancy Schwartz's claims about the constitutive value of political representation is valid or not. Does representation empower Blacks? Does having Black representation in the House affect the attitudes that Blacks have about the institution? In chapter 8, I examine the link between attitudes toward Congress, political trust, and descriptive representation. Chapter 9 presents my conclusions about the degree to which race affects the political representation of Blacks and the degree to which Congress must socially mirror Blacks to be a representative governing body.

THE 1996 NATIONAL BLACK ELECTION STUDY AND THE 104TH CONGRESS

Much of the data analyzed in this book are from the 1996 National Black Election Study (Tate 1998). The 1996 NBES is a survey of 1,126 African Americans modeled after the 1984 National Black Election Study, the first-ever national telephone survey of a racial minority group (Jackson 1993). The 1996 NBES was designed with an explicit congressional focus. Respondents were matched to their congressional districts through their telephone exchanges and asked to evaluate their House representatives. A total of 252 House districts fell into the 1996 sample, including the districts of 34 of 39 Black members of the House. A description of the sample design and survey is presented in Appendix A.

These 252 House legislators were part of the 104th Congress. This Congress has a special place in history because it was the first Congress with a Republican majority in the House of Representatives in forty years. In fact, Republicans controlled both houses in the 104th Congress. Two Black Republicans were also part of this new Republican majority, J. C. Watts of Oklahoma, a star of the Republican freshman class, in fact, and Gary Franks of Connecticut. Their districts, less than 2 percent Black, did not fall into the 1996 NBES sample, however.

The first 100 days of Republican leadership in Congress were staged for drama. Many House Republicans had campaigned on the basis of a "Contract with America," a policy agenda consisting of ten legislative proposals, such as a balanced budget amendment and welfare reform. Republican candidates pledged to bring these contract items to the floor of the House for a vote in the first 100 days of the new session. President Clinton would veto the Republican budget plan. With House Republicans unwilling to reach agreement, the government would shut down on December 16, 1995 through January 2, 1996. The twenty-one-day shutdown is so far the government's longest one, during which federal workers did not receive full pay and most federal offices and museums were closed over the Christmas holiday (Sinclair 1997, 206–12). This shutdown, writes one journalist, "would in fact survive as the most enduring accomplishment [of the 104th Congress] . . . No other Congress in the country's history had closed down the government for three weeks" (Killian 1998).

This was the political context the 1996 NBES was conducted in. The 1996 NBES was a two-wave panel study in which 1,126 Blacks were interviewed shortly after the 1996 national conventions and the day preceding the November election. Eight hundred sixty-nine Blacks were reinterviewed shortly after the November election. Not only were these Black respondents asked to choose a president, they were voting in a new Congress: the 105th. Republicans would retain their majorities in Congress in the 1996 elections, but by an even smaller margin.

II. Black Members of Congress

CHAPTER 2

Black Members of Congress

ONE WAY TO REPRESENT is to be similar to those one is representing, but the U.S. Congress is far from representative in this respect. As pointed out in chapter 1, Blacks and women are numerically underrepresented in Congress. Today's Congress is 88 percent non-Hispanic White and 89 percent male. But another significant social feature of Congress is the overrepresentation of the economic and social elite. Many of its members are upper-middle class, who previously to being elected worked in law, business, or public service. A significant minority elected to the U.S. Congress are millionaires.

That members of Congress disproportionately belong to the socio-economic elite is not a direct consequence of how Congress was designed. Although Thomas Jefferson, James Madison, and Alexander Hamilton assumed and sought a republican government composed of members from their own economic and social class, they deliberately rejected a "House of Lords." The architects of the American government imposed very few formal qualifications for holding office in the national government. Members merely had to be U.S. citizens for seven to nine years and meet the age requirement of twenty-five for the House and thirty for the Senate. As stated in Federalist No. 57, "Who are to be the objects of popular choice? Every citizen whose merit may recommend him to the esteem and confidence of his country. No qualification of wealth, of birth, of religious faith, or of civil profession is permitted to fetter the judgment or disappoint the inclination of the people." To this bare-bones list, individual states imposed residency requirements and candidate filing fees. States would also, of course, write into their own constitutions laws explicitly prohibiting women and Blacks from voting and holding public office until Congress amended the U.S. Constitution and enforced the political rights of these legally-subordinated groups (McClain and Stewart 1998).

In contrast to the social characteristics of legislators, political party and the demographic characteristics of the district that they represent are far more critical determinants of the legislator's voting pattern (e.g., R. H. Davidson 1969). At the same time, congressional scholars recognize the important role social background, notably wealth, plays in determining who actually runs for elective office in the United States.

Running for Congress takes a lot of money and a lot of time. To defeat a sitting House incumbent seeking reelection in the 1996 election cycle (which few did), the average successful challenger spent more than $1 million (Ornstein, Mann, and Malbin 1998, 78). Many candidates running for Congress start out by using a portion of their own wealth to finance their campaigns. While much of the money for political campaigns comes from PAC donations, more than half is generated through individual contributions. Who donates to political campaigns? Generally, the wealthier do. And thus, it is useful to belong to the wealthier classes and have a circle of friends and acquaintances who can afford to donate. Money begets money. Candidates need to prove their political viability by establishing their ability to raise a lot of money. Interest groups are more likely to contribute to the candidate most likely to win, regardless of the candidate's ideology. It is also a fact that the major political parties will deny campaign funds to otherwise attractive candidates if their campaign organizations are not (yet) sufficiently funded. All in all, wealthy individuals have a tremendous advantage over the average citizen in financing their political campaigns. Time is also important, and here is where owning your own business or firm can facilitate a bid for public office. As the owner, you can determine the hours that you'll work and those that you'll spend on the campaign. And when you're the boss, you don't need to punch a clock, use up your vacation time, or quit to pursue public office.

Even while the background characteristics of legislators is a nonissue for most in the study of Congress, it remains normatively important to the issue of fair political representation for Blacks. Are the Blacks who win seats in the U.S. Congress closer in social background to their White colleagues in Congress, and, therefore, unlike most of their Black constituents? If the answer is yes, then, the argument that Blacks need descriptive representation in government become less compelling. Those advocating descriptive representation often base their case on claims that Black legislators will share the same experiences as the Blacks whom they represent. Such claims are patently less true if, in fact, Black members belong to a homogeneously elite social class. Recognizing that race will still affect their life experiences, economically privileged Blacks still lead strikingly different lives from the Black poor or working class.

In this chapter, I examine the social backgrounds of Blacks elected to Congress during three periods, Reconstruction to 1900, the Civil Rights Era, and the Post-Civil Rights Era. This issue has garnered some previous research (Swain 1993; Button and Hedge 1997). Political scientist Carol Swain in her review of the social backgrounds of Black legislators concluded that Black representatives "share backgrounds quite similar to those of the white males in Congress," except that a higher percentage of Black House members had prior officeholding experience (1993,

86). While my investigation into this matter somewhat corroborates Swain's, I still report key differences between Black and White legislators mostly on social dimensions, such as slave experience, which Swain either glossed over, or those such as marital status, which she simply overlooked. Notably, I find that greater diversity of life experiences is brought into the House not only because of race, but because of gender as well. I find that Black women legislators are remarkably unlike their White male counterparts.

THE FIRST BLACKS TO SERVE IN THE HOUSE FROM RECONSTRUCTION TO 1900

A period lasting from 1863 to 1877, Reconstruction commenced with Lincoln's Emancipation Proclamation and included the ratification of the Thirteen, Fourteenth, and Fifteenth amendments. Of all manner of ways in which liberal Republicans attempted to create a color-blind democracy during Reconstruction, Black political officeholding was perhaps their most radical proposal. Reconstruction and Black officeholding pretty much ended with the election of President Hayes. Hayes would oversee the withdrawal of federal troops from the South. While much of Black officeholding would end once the troops left the region, Blacks would still win seats to Congress from 1878 to 1900. These Blacks were, without exception, all men as well as all Republican.

Slavery, education, and wealth were the most important distinctions that separated Blacks of the nineteenth century from their White counterparts. Most Blacks were slaves until Lincoln's Emancipation Proclamation. Most Blacks were born and resided in the South. Most were illiterate and poor. Early historians would inaccurately portray the Blacks elected during Reconstruction as incompetent and corrupt. While some indeed took part in the rampant corruption of America's "Gilded Age," revisionists would later depict them as remarkable Black men of political acumen and courage. It was, after all, a courageous act to run for public office as a Black man in the South.

Roughly 2,000 Blacks held public office in the South during Reconstruction (Foner 1996). Even though it had been illegal in the slaving-holding South to teach slaves to read and write, more than half of these Black officials were ex-slaves and over 80 percent were literate. Two Blacks sat in the Senate and twenty served in the House during the 41st to 56th congresses (see table 2.1). All represented states in the South, including five states that, after most Blacks were disenfranchised, would not send another African American to Congress for one hundred years.

Of the twenty blacks who served in Congress, ten had experienced slavery, while ten had been born free. All were literate. Robert Brown

TABLE 2.1
Black Members of the House of Representatives in the Nineteenth Century
by State

State	Black Representative	Years Served
Alabama	Jeremiah Haralson	1875–77
	James T. Rapier	1873–75
	Benjamin S. Turner	1871–73
Florida	Josiah T. Walls	1871–76
Georgia	Jefferson Long	1870–71
Louisiana	Charles E. Nash	1875–77
Mississippi	John R. Lynch	1873–77, 1882–83
North Carolina	Henry P. Cheatham	1889–93
	John A. Hyman	1875–77
	James E. O'Hara	1883–87
	George H. White	1897–1901
South Carolina	Richard H. Cain	1873–75, 1877–79
	Robert C. DeLarge	1871–73
	Robert B. Elliott	1871–74
	Thomas E. Miller	1890–91
	George W. Murray	1893–95, 1896–97
	Joseph H. Rainey	1870–79
	Alonzo J. Ransier	1873–75
	Robert Smalls	1875–79, 1882–83, 1884–87
Virginia	John M. Langston	1890–91

Source: *Members of Congress Since 1789* (Washington, D.C.: Congressional Quarterly Inc., 1977), p. 6.

Elliott was perhaps the best educated among them. Although no record of his attendance there exists, his congressional biography "boasts" an education at Eton College in England (Foner 1996, 70). Elliott was born and educated in the North and later moved to South Carolina to establish a law practice in 1868. He served in the U.S. House of Representatives from 1871 to 1874. Six of the ex-slave congressmen learned to read and write somehow during slavery. John A. Hyman's attempts at book reading supposedly so enraged his owners that he was repeatedly sold and by emancipation had passed through eight of them (Christopher 1971, 149). Two, John Lynch of Mississippi and Robert Smalls of South Carolina, were able to receive schooling only after the war.

Elliott and O'Hara were the only ones born outside of region; the rest were native sons of the South.

Many Black officials during Reconstruction were teachers, ministers, businessmen, farmers, and artisans, the latter group consisting of high-status slave trades that required skill and gave them relative independence even during slavery. A few of the Black congressmen were artisans. Both Joseph H. Rainey and Robert C. DeLarge were barbers, while Jefferson Long worked as a tailor. Of the three, only DeLarge had been free, the son a free Black tailor. DeLarge, in fact, had been able to attend a high school in Charleston. John R. Lynch was the slave son of a Louisiana plantation master who remained a slave until freed by the Union army. He worked in the Union army until 1865 when he took up photography as a trade. Lynch served three terms in Congress, where he was its youngest member. Lynch would later be admitted to the Mississippi bar. He would retire, however, from the military, and write books, including one entitled *The Facts of Reconstruction*. Only one of the fourteen Black congressmen began as a laborer. Charles E. Nash of Louisiana, born free, had a public school education. He worked as a bricklayer before enlisting in the Union army. After losing most of his leg during battle, he held a post in the customs house before winning election in 1874 to Congress. After Reconstruction, he served as a postmaster then worked as a cigar maker in New Orleans until his death.

The rest of the Black congressmen either worked in farming or were professionals in law, publishing, or the ministry. Josiah T. Walls of Florida entered business after working for the Union army and obtaining some schooling in the North. After serving only one term as Florida's only Black Reconstruction congressman from 1871 to 1873, he later practiced law and published a newspaper. As noted earlier, Elliott of South Carolina was a lawyer, but he also helped edit the *South Carolina Leader*, which Alonzo J. Ransier of South Carolina also helped edit. Prior to the war, Ransier, a free Black, had worked as a clerk in a prominent shipping house in Charleston. Robert Smalls published the Beaufort *Standard*, another successful Black newspaper in South Carolina. As a twenty-three-year-old slave, Smalls had won his freedom and his family's by piloting a Confederate army vessel into Union hands (Christopher 1971, 38–39). The deed was widely publicized and so daring that the outraged Confederates offered $4,000 for his capture. Richard H. Cain was a minister who also edited the *South Carolina Leader*. Cain had been born free and was educated in Ohio. A convert of the Methodist Episcopal faith, he left it because of the church's segregationist policies to join the African Methodist Episcopal Church. He later rebuilt the Emmanuel Church in Charleston into the state's largest AME congregation. The church operated as his political base. Serving only one term, 1875–77, Jeremiah Haralson of Alabama was the Reconstruction Congress's second Black minister. Haralson had worked as a field hand and had been sold once on the auction block. He was also remembered as a gifted campaigner, using humor to speak out against racism.

In terms of wealth, few of the fourteen men who served in Congress entered politics wealthy or were as financially secure as their White counterparts. Here is where I sharply diverge from Carol Swain's conclusion that

> In financial terms, too, black members of Congress [during Reconstruction] were quite well off. Only one black representative had an estate worth less than $1,000, while five had estates ranging in value from $5,000 to $20,000—very respectable fortunes for the time. Black Congress members in the nineteenth century, therefore, fit the standard profile of quality candidates. Just like white members then and now, these black legislators were not socially, economically, or educationally representative of their constituents (1997: 85–86).[1]

My examination of the twenty Black House-members is consistent with Foner's overall conclusion, that they generally lived off their congressional salaries and were hardly financially secure. According to historian Eric Foner, the wealthiest of the Blacks elected during Reconstruction were generally freedmen, of which only half of those elected to the House were. Most Black legislators in the House were small businessmen. Robert Elliott, the Representative from South Carolina, had to ask for small loans from his White colleagues to pay for daily expenses (Foner 1996, xxiii). Most black elected officials relied on their office for pay, concludes Foner. A few would die in poverty and obscurity as well. At the end of his political career, Jeremiah Haralson of Alabama moved around from state to state, taking up a number of different jobs, including farming and coal mining, before his death at seventy—reportedly in Denver, although no death certificate exists in that state. The basic pattern was that Blacks returned to their small law practices or businesses in the South. The moderately financially successful ones found administrative posts in government. John A. Hyman of North Carolina had been promised an administrative post after serving in Washington, but that never materialized. He returned to manage his grocery store and farm, but eventually obtained a government job in the Capitol. His biographer writes, "There were brief, condescendingly complimentary obituaries when North Carolina's first Negro congressman died of a paralytic stroke in the nation's capital on September 14, 1891, at the age of fifty-one."

Black officeholding was greatest in South Carolina, where Blacks held a clear majority of the state legislature's lower house and, in 1872, held four of the five posts in the state's congressional delegation (Holt 1977). The biographies of the three Black congressmen and two Whites in the Congressional Directory printed in 1878 read as follows and can be compared, beginning with the black legislators:

Joseph H. Rainey, of Georgetown, was born at Georgetown, South Carolina (where both of his parents were slaves, but by their industry obtained their freedom,) June 21, 1832. Although debarred by law from attending school, he acquired a good education, and further improved his mind by observation and travel. His father was a barber, and he followed that occupation at Charleston till 1862, when, having been forced to work on the fortifications of the Confederates, he escaped to the West Indies, where he remained until the close of the war, when he returned to his native town. He was elected a Delegate to the State Constitutional Convention of 1868, and was a member of the State Senate of South Carolina in 1870, resigning when elected to the Forty-first Congress as a Republican to fill the vacancy caused by the non-reception of B. F. Whittemore; was elected to the Forty-second, Forty-third, and Forty-fourth Congresses; was a Presidential Elector in 1876, and was re-elected to the Forty-fifth Congress as a Republican, receiving 18,180 votes against 16,661 votes for J. S. Richardson, Democrat.

Richard H. Cain, of Charleston, was born in Greenbrier County, Virginia, April 12, 1825; removed to Ohio in 1831, and settled in Gallipolis; received a limited education entered the ministry at an early age; became a student at Wilberforce University, at Xenia, Ohio, in 1860; removed to Brooklyn, N.Y., where he discharged ministerial duties for four years; was sent as a missionary to the freedmen in South Carolina; was chosen a member of the Constitutional Convention of South Carolina; was elected a member of the State Senate and served two years; edited a newspaper from 1868; was elected to the Forty-third Congress as a Republican, receiving 21,385 votes against 16,071 votes for M. P. O'Connor, Democrat.

Robert Smalls, of Beaufort, was born at Beaufort, South Carolina, April 5, 1839; being a slave, was debarred by statute from attending school, but educated himself with such limited advantages as he could secure; removed to Charleston in 1851, worked as a rigger, and led a seafaring life; became connected in 1861 with the "Planter," a steamer plying in Charleston Harbor as a transport, which he took over Charleston Bar in May, 1862, and delivered her and his services to the Commander of the United States Blockading Squadron; was appointed Pilot in the United States Navy, and served in that capacity on the monitor "Keokuk" in the attack on Fort Sumter; served as Pilot in the Quartermaster's Department, and was promoted as Captain for gallant and meritorious conduct December 1, 1863, and placed in command of the "Planter," serving until she was put out of commission in 1866; was elected a member of the State Constitutional Convention of 1868; was elected a member of the State House of Representatives in 1868, and of the Senate Senate, to fill a vacancy, in 1870, and re-elected in 1872; was elected to the Forty-fourth Congress, and re-elected to the Forty-fifth Congress as a Republican, receiving 19,954 votes against 18,516 votes for G. D. Tillman.

Below are the biographies of the two White Democrats in South Carolina's delegation:

D. Wyatt Aiken, of Cokesbury, was born at Winnsboro, Fairfield County, South Carolina, March 1828; received an academic education at Mount Zion Institute, Winnsboro; graduated at the South Carolina College, Columbia, in 1849; taught school two years; settled upon a farm in 1852, and has continued until the present time to profess and practice farming; in 1861 entered the volunteer service of the Southern Confederacy as a private; was appointed Adjutant of the Seventh Regiment of Volunteers; was elected Colonel of the same when re-organized at the expiration of their term of serve; was relieved form service by reason of wounds received on the 17th of September, 1862; at Antietam; was elected to the State Legislature in 1864 and again in 1866; was Master of the State Grange for two years and member of the Executive Committee of the National Grange for six years; was a Delegate to the National Democratic Convention at Saint Louis that nominated Tilden and Hendricks; was elected to the Forty-fifth Congress as a Democrat, receiving 21,479 votes against 15,553 votes for L. Cass Carpenter, Republican. *Re-elected.*

John H. Evins, of Spartanburg, was born in Spartanburg District, (now county,) South Carolina, July 18, 1830; entered South Carolina College in December, 1850, and graduated in 1853; studied law, and was admitted to practice in 1856; was an officer in the Confederate service, serving first as a First Lieutenant in the Fifth South Carolina Regiment, and afterwards as a Captain in the Palmetto Sharpshooters; was wounded, and being disabled from active service n the field was appointed Lieutenant-Colonel, and assigned to duty in his own State; was a member of the Legislature of South Carolina for two terms; and was elected to the Forty-fifty Congress as a Democrat, receiving 21,875 votes against 16,071 votes for A. S. Wallace, Republican. *Re-elected.*

The biographies reveal vast social differences between the men that extend well beyond merely their race. First, there was slavery. Although only Smalls had been born a slave, Rainey pointedly includes the fact that his parents have been plantation slaves who had purchased their freedom. Secondly, while both White representatives had college degrees, none of the Black legislators had degrees. Because he had been raised in the North, Richard Cain had attended college before entering the ministry, while the other two Black legislators point out that as Blacks in the South they had been "debarred by law" from attending school. In terms of occupations, Rainey was a barber, Cain a minister, and Smalls had become a captain because, as explained earlier, of his courageous mutiny from the Confederate army during the war. In contrast, Aiken had worked as a school teacher before purchasing his farm, while Evins practiced law. Last but not least, the two White lawmakers were Democrats who both had been Confederate army officers during the war. In contrast, among the Black Republicans only Smalls could boast of military service during the war, but having served, of course, on the Union side. Rainey had escaped Confederate conscription for the West Indies, while Cain remained safely in the North during the war.

The Black men elected to the House of Representatives during Reconstruction were vastly different from their White colleagues in a number of social dimensions. First and foremost, half of the Blacks serving in Congress during this period had known slavery. This alone separated them socially and experientially from their White colleagues in government. Secondly, although all were literate, few had educations comparable to their White colleagues. None of the Black lawmakers in the Reconstruction House had college degrees, in fact. Moreover, the occupations that they had held prior to entering politics provided at best a modest living for them and their families. A few practiced law, representing the poorest in their community, while several of them were in trades, as barbers or tailors. The most financially secure found government jobs after leaving office. However, even small economic success in a profession or business put these Black lawmakers among the elite of Black America at the time.

In the end, Black members of Congress still appeared closer to their Black constituents than to their White colleagues. These men hardly fit the profile of nineteenth-century Washington politicians who alternated between public service and managing their families' estates and fortunes back home. Had the Reconstruction not ended, these Black men would have likely remained in public office, becoming the earliest type of career politician that we see in Washington today.

THE CIVIL RIGHTS GENERATION OF BLACKS ELECTED TO THE HOUSE

The Civil Rights Era covers 1928 to 1972, which for some scholars represents the end of the Black civil rights movement (McAdam 1982). After George White's election in 1898, no Black would be elected to Congress until 1928 with Oscar De Priest's election in Illinois. De Priest was a Republican as were all Blacks at this time. The Great Depression and Franklin Delano Roosevelt's New Deal agenda would eventually turn Blacks into Roosevelt Republicans — Republicans who voted Democratic. De Priest served as the lone Black in Congress, until his defeat by Black Democrat Arthur Mitchell in 1934. Mitchell was replaced by William L. Dawson in 1942. The lone Black representative Dawson was eventually joined by Adam Clayton Powell of New York in the 79th Congress in 1945. Detroit and Philadelphia sent the third and fourth postwar Blacks to serve in the House of Representatives by 1958. By 1968, the number of Blacks to serve concurrently in the U.S. House increased to six for a total of seven, including Edward William Brooke III, who was elected as a Republican to the U.S. Senate from Massachusetts in 1966 (see table 2.2).

In contrast to the nineteenth-century Black House representatives, none of the Blacks who served during this most recent period were elected in the deep South. Excluding William L. Clay of Missouri, all fifteen came from the North or West, and all represented urban districts. Blacks would not win seats to Congress from the deep South until 1972 at the end of the movement. With the exception of De Priest, and in contrast to the Blacks elected to the U.S. Congress during Reconstruction, all were Democrats.

As the first three Blacks elected to Congress of the twentieth century, De Priest, Mitchell, and Dawson were all native sons of the South. De Priest and Mitchell were from Alabama, while Dawson was born in Georgia.

Six of the fifteen elected during the Civil Rights Era had law degrees and worked in law or in fields related to law. Philadelphia's Robert N. C. Nix was a successful criminal attorney whose father, a former slave, had a Ph.D. in mathematics and was dean of the faculty at South Carolina State College. To ensure that his son had good educational opportunity, Nix's father nevertheless sent hime to New York, where he was raised by relatives. In contrast, the father of John Conyers, Jr. worked in one of the automobile plants in Detroit. After serving in the military during the Korean War, Conyers returned to school to earn his law

Table 2.2
The Civil Rights Generation of Blacks Who Served in the House, 1900–71

State	Black Representative	Years Served	Occupation
California	Augustus F. Hawkins	1963–90	Public servant
	Ronald V. Dellums	1971–98	Public servant
Illinois	Oscar De Priest	1929–35	Businessman
	Arthur W. Mitchell	1935–42	Lawyer
	William L. Dawson	1943–70	Lawyer
	George W. Collins	1970–72	Public servant
	Ralph H. Metcalfe	1971–78	Administrator
Maryland	Parren J. Mitchell	1971–87	Professor/ Administrator
Michigan	Charles C. Diggs, Jr.	1955–80	Businessman
	John Conyers, Jr.	1965–present	Lawyer
Missouri	William L. Clay	1969–2000	Public servant
New York	Adam Clayton Powell	1945–67, 69–70	Minister
	Shirley Chisholm	1969–82	Educator
Ohio	Louis Stokes	1969–98	Lawyer
Pennsylvania	Robert N. C. Nix	1957–79	Lawyer

degree. Louis Stokes of Ohio also served in the army but during World War II and through the G.I. bill obtained his law degree. He practiced law with his brother Carl, who a year earlier, in 1967, had made history by becoming Cleveland's first elected Black mayor.

Four of the civil rights generation of Black elected officials — George Collins, Augustus Hawkins, William Clay, and Ronald Dellums — entered Congress having served in their local and state governments. Although Dellums, Hawkins, and Clay had spent nearly all of their lives in politics, all started out in different occupations before pursuing political careers. Before establishing a real estate firm with his brother, Hawkins had failed in another business venture. In an interview, his wife stated that as a businessman, Hawkins never made that much money — "he made only hundred dollars a month. It took wealthy or very dedicated people [to enter politics], and Gus was never wealthy" (Christopher 1971, 223). Like Hawkins, William Clay entered politics without having a secure financial base. His biographer writes, "After finishing his military hitch, Clay moved restlessly from job to job for several years. He tried aeronautical chart-making, bus driving, real estate, and insurance" (250). After serving in the St. Louis city legislature,

Clay took a job with a union, and from there ran for Congress after a court order forced the state to construct a majority-Black district around St. Louis. Dellums had a Master's degree in social work, but served on the Berkeley City Council.

While the stereotype of the civil rights Black politician is that of the fiery clergyman, only Adam Clayton Powell, Jr. of New York was actually a Baptist minister. Although a few of the Blacks elected to the House of Representatives during Reconstruction were ministers, the stereotype undoubtedly persists because of the vital role Black churches had played in facilitating the elections of Blacks. Powell was born into a financially secure family; his father was the leader of an established, well-known Black church, the Abyssinian Baptist Church. Under the leadership of Powell, Sr., the church had relocated to Harlem and become prosperous. As Powell Jr.'s biographer notes, "The Powells lived well" (Hamilton 1991, 76). In addition to free housing, a car, and extended vacations, the parishioners gave their pastor an annual salary of $5,000, which was five times the average annual income of Blacks in New York at that time. Powell took over leadership of the church after his father retired in 1937. He was among the few to inherit wealth, which he then used to launch and advance his political career (Charles Diggs Jr. is another that comes immediately to mind.) But more than having inherited an economically secure foundation, Powell also gained an independent political base to make his racial justice advocacy possible. Powell's attempts to attach antidiscimination measures to routine legislation making its way out of the House were so well established that they were listed in congressional records as the "Powell Amendments" (Singh 1998, 47). In 1945, Powell demanded an end to the segregation of the dining and rest room facilities in Congress, which the other Black congressmen (De Priest, Mitchell, and Dawson) had quietly accepted.

Oscar De Priest and Charles C. Diggs Jr. of Michigan were both businessmen. De Priest had started out as a house painter, but entered politics in Chicago early, at the same time acquiring real estate property, which, after his defeat by Mitchell, he managed until his death in 1951.

Because of unrestricted educational opportunities in the North for Blacks, the civil rights generation of Black lawmakers were vastly better educated than their Black predecessors. In terms of education, although hardly wealth and occupation, the civil rights generation of Black members of Congress resembled their White counterparts. Most of the first Black Democrats elected to Congress were experienced politicians, having served in their local or state governments before entering Congress.

THE POST–CIVIL RIGHTS GENERATION OF BLACKS ELECTED TO THE HOUSE

The post–civil rights period begins with President Richard Nixon's successful reelection in 1972. Nixon's record on civil rights was moderate. However, in a calculated bid to win the White Southern vote, he appeared to campaign against civil rights in 1968 and 1972. By 1972, the civil rights movement had ended. Dr. Martin Luther King's assassination in 1968 had left the movement leaderless. The major civil rights organizations were in disarray. The Vietnam War and, later, Watergate redirected public attention away from the many civil rights injustices and racial problems that remained after landmark civil rights legislation had passed.

Even with the end of the protest movement, Blacks had successfully put their energies into electoral politics (Tate 1994). The 1965 Voting Rights Act eliminated the barriers that Southern states had erected to prevent Blacks from registering and voting. In this regard, the act was extremely effective. Black voting shot up in the South from 12 percent in 1947 to 62 percent in 1968 (Alt 1994). Court challenges on the basis of the act would also target electoral systems designed to limit the effectiveness of the Black vote. It would take decades of litigation, but ultimately districts that had Black voting majorities would be restored or created, and Blacks would eventually elect members of their own race to Congress.

Adolph L. Reed, Jr. (1986) argues that with the end of the civil rights movement a new type of Black leader emerged. Black leaders, even elected ones, had traditionally come from the Black church. As increasing numbers of Blacks won elective office, he maintains, Black ministers were displaced as the natural source of Black political leadership. Reed's claim that elected Black officials are displacing Black ministers as political spokespersons remains controversial. The Reverend Jesse Jackson remains strongly popular in the black community and is still considered an important spokesperson for the community. However, the NAACP recently asked former Maryland Congressman Kweisi Mfume to head its organization and lead it out of bankruptcy and scandal. The first Blacks elected in the post-Reconstruction South were Barbara Charline Jordan of Texas and Andrew Young of Georgia. This generation of Black House representatives would be uniformly better educated than the previous generations of Black House members. Jordan, for example, graduated from a segregated public high school in Houston, Texas, and earned her B.A. from Texas Southern University in 1956. She then obtained a law degree from Boston University School of Law in 1958 and was admitted to the Massachusetts and Texas bars in 1959. She prac-

TABLE 2.3
The Number of African Americans in the U.S. Congress, 1947–99

Congress	Number	Congress	Number
79th (1945)	2	93rd (1973)	17
80th (1947)	2	94th (1975)	18
81st (1949)	2	95th (1977)	17
82nd (1951)	2	96th (1979)	16
83rd (1953)	2	97th (1981)	18
84th (1955)	3	98th (1983)	21
85th (1957)	4	99th (1985)	21
86th (1959)	4	100th (1987)	23
87th (1961)	4	101st (1989)	24
88th (1963)	5	102nd (1991)	26
89th (1965)	6	103rd (1993)	40
90th (1967)	7	104th (1995)	40
91st (1969)	10	105th (1997)	39
92nd (1971)	14	106th (1999)	38
		107th (2001)	38

Note: Includes District of Columbia's nonvoting delegate. See Appendix A for a discussion on who I counted in each Congress and Appendix B for a list of Black members by each Congress beginning with the 92nd Congress.

ticed law in Texas where she ultimately ran for public office. A number of Blacks during this period would earn their college degrees from historically Black colleges, including Jordan, John Lewis of Georgia (Fisk University), Kweise Mfume of Maryland (Morgan State University), Andrew Young of Georgia (Howard University), Mike Espy of Mississippi (Howard University), and Charles C. Diggs Jr. (Fisk University). Still some other Blacks of this current generation would earn degrees from liberal private colleges such as Grinnell and Antioch and public institutions, specifically the University of California.

Comparing the number of members of Congress in each of seventeen occupational categories from 1969 to 1994 (see table 2.4), one finds that Black members are concentrated in the same occupations as Whites. Most Black members of Congress—like most White members—have law degrees, and many have been lawyers, businesspersons, or public servants. In addition, Black members are as likely as White members to have been war veterans. Overall, it does not appear that Black members of Congress come from different occupations than White members.

Most Black members of Congress had more than one occupation. For example, Rep. Eva Clayton from North Carolina owned a consulting firm and had worked as an executive for a nonprofit firm and as a university official before her election to the House. The most common

TABLE 2.4
Occupations of Members of Congress, 1969–1995: Black Members Compared to the Total

Occupation	Congress													
	91st	92nd	93rd	94th	95th	96th	97th	98th	99th	100th	101st	102nd	103rd	104th
Acting/Entertainment	–	–	–	–	–	–	–	–	–	0/1	0/2	1/2	1/1	1/1
Aeronautics	–	–	–	–	–	–	–	0/3	0/4	0/3	0/3	0/1	0/2	0/1
Agriculture	0/34	0/36	0/38	0/31	0/16	0/19	0/28	0/26	0/29	0/20	0/19	0/20	0/19	0/20
Business/Banking	3/159	3/145	3/155	5/140	4/118	6/127	4/134	5/138	5/147	6/142	7/138	6/157	10/131	10/162
Clergy	1/2	0/2	1/4	1/5	0/6	1/6	1/3	1/2	1/2	2/2	2/2	2/2	1/2	2/2
Congressional Aide	–	–	–	–	0/5	0/10	0/11	2/16	1/16	–	–	–	–	–
Education	1/59	2/61	2/59	2/64	3/70	2/57	4/59	2/43	3/37	3/38	3/42	3/57	7/66	8/75
Engineering	0/6	0/3	0/2	0/3	0/2	0/2	0/5	0/5	0/6	0/4	0/4	0/7	0/5	0/6
Journalism	1/39	0/30	0/23	0/24	0/27	1/11	1/21	1/22	1/20	1/20	1/17	1/25	0/24	0/15
Labor Leader	0/3	1/3	1/3	1/3	1/6	0/4	0/5	0/2	0/2	1/2	1/2	1/3	1/2	0/2
Law	4/242	4/236	6/221	6/221	6/222	4/205	6/194	6/200	5/190	6/184	7/184	7/183	13/181	13/171
Law Enforcement	0/2	0/1	0/2	0/2	0/7	0/5	0/5	0/5	2/8	0/7	0/8	0/5	0/10	0/11
Medicine	0/5	0/6	0/5	0/5	2/2	3/6	2/6	1/6	0/5	1/3	0/4	0/5	0/6	0/10
Military	–	–	–	–	–	–	–	0/1	0/1	0/0	0/0	0/1	0/0	0/0
Professional Sports	–	–	–	–	–	–	–	0/3	0/3	0/5	0/4	0/3	0/1	0/2
Public Service/Politics	–	–	–	–	–	–	–	–	–	5/94	5/94	5/61	9/87	9/102
Veteran	4/320	7/316	7/317	7/307	–	–	–	–	–	–	–	–	–	–

Note: Entries in the table represent the number of Black members of Congress in the occupational category/the total number of members of Congress in the occupational category. Dashed entries indicate categories for which Congressional Quarterly did not code in that particular year.
Source: Congressional Quarterly Almanac.

route for Black members of Congress was to practice law and then pursue a career in politics through local and state government.

The occupational differences between Black and White members of Congress are small. Although there were only four Black clergymen elected to the House from 1969 to 1994, the clergy is an overrepresented occupation for Black members. Furthermore, in contrast to the small but consistent proportion of White members of Congress who were farmers, engineers, or doctors, no Black member in any given Congress emerged from these occupations.

Over time, as the number of Black members of Congress increased, the variety of occupations from which they emerge has grown. In the 1970s, Black members of Congress were generally former aldermen or attorneys, but as more Blacks were elected to the House, the diversity of occupations grew. For example, a newspaper publisher, a mortician, and a radio-talk show host were elected. Although in the 1970s the proportion of Black members who were former lawyers was lower than the proportion of White members, by the 1990s, the proportion of Black attorneys serving in the House grew to match that of Whites.

Closer inspection reveals that Blacks do bring slightly different occupational experiences to their position in Congress. While many Black members fall into the category of "public service/politician," this broad category obscures subtle differences. Rather than a career solely in politics, many Black members have ties to less conventional forms of public service, often rooted in urban problems. Blacks in this category include former civil rights activists, a Head Start official, community coordinators, and social workers. By comparison, some Whites traditionally begin their congressional careers as legislative aides, waiting until their boss retires, then running for office.

African American Women in Congress

A striking difference between White and Black member of Congress is the higher proportion of women found among Black lawmakers relative to the total. In the 106th Congress, 12 of the 38 Black lawmakers are female representing 37.5 percent. In contrast, only 12 percent of all the House representatives are female. The growth in the number of female Black legislators is a relatively recent phenomenon. Women gained the right to vote in federal elections only in 1920, and so, of course, all of the Blacks elected during Reconstruction were men. The first Black woman elected to Congress was Shirley Chisholm of New York. Her election in 1968 came nearly fifty years after the first White woman and nearly 100 years after the first Black man were elected. In 1975, Chisholm would be joined by two more Black women, one the widow of a

Black congressman, whose seat she won in a special election. The numbers of Black women to Black men in the House would remain consistent with the gender ratio in Congress until 1992. Women in general made historic gains in 1992, their numbers in the House increasing from 29 to 47. Black women also achieved record gains that year. Not only did Carol Moseley Braun make history by becoming the first Black woman (and first Black Democrat) to be elected to the U.S. Senate, but the number of Black women in the House would more than double, from four to nine. Among Black House members, women would represent 15 percent in the 102nd and increase to 25 percent in the 103rd. Table 2.5 identifies each Black woman elected to the U.S. House of Representatives by name, state, and terms served.

Shirley Chisholm was part of the new, more race-conscious generation of Black elected officials produced by the 1968 and 1970 elections produced. Chisholm along with the other twelve Black lawmakers in the House then banded together to found the Congressional Black Caucus or CBC. She is perhaps best remembered, however, for running for the 1972 Democratic presidential nomination. She ran to take advantage of the new groups that were gaining power within the Democratic party's rank-and-file and in the "new politics" — not only Blacks, but also feminists and the young (Gill 1997; Chisholm 1973). Well before Jesse Jackson seized on the same initiative to empower Black Democrats through his 1984 and 1988 presidential bids, Chisholm hoped that her candidacy would forever cement, as it were, the party's wavering stance on the Vietnam War (Chisholm was opposed to it) and the party's role as the advocate of the oppressed and weak (the party was still divided, although its Southern wing was slowly liberalizing). Although Chisholm was a founding member of the CBC and a charter member of the National Organization for Women (NOW), neither group endorsed her. A few more progressive CBC members, such as Ron Dellums of California, supported her bid. Most others CBC members were downright hostile to her and her candidacy. While Chisholm and her supporters felt it was sexism that got in the way of her earning support from her male Black colleagues on the Hill, it was apparently more than simple sexism. After all, Jesse Jackson failed to receive endorsements from Black lawmakers in his 1984 bid for the Democratic party's presidential nomination. As in the case of Jackson, many of Chisholm's CBC colleagues felt that the one-term congresswoman from New York had not yet paid her dues. Her confrontational and steamroller working style had alienated them. While Adam Clayton Powell had a similar, even more extreme, manner and ran into trouble with his colleagues on Capitol Hill, Dawson of Chicago, Diggs, and Nix, had no interest in competing with Powell as the lone crusader for racial justice,

TABLE 2.5
List of Black Women Elected to the U.S. House of Representatives by State, Years Served, Degrees Earned, Occupation, Marital Status, and Number of Children

State	Black Representative	Years Served	Degrees Earned	Occupation	Marital Status upon Entering Congress	Number of Children
California	Yvonne Brathwaite Burke	1973–78	A.A., B.A., J.D.	Lawyer	Married	2
	Barbara Lee	1998–present	B.A., M.S.W.	State legislator/legislative aide/mental health	Married	2
	Juanita Millender-McDonald	1996–present	B.S., M.A.	Teacher/state legislator	Married	5
	Maxine Waters	1991–present	B.A.	Social worker	Married	2
	Diane Edith Watson	2001–present	B.A., M.S., Ph.D.	University professor	Single	None
District of Columbia	Eleanor Holmes Norton	1991–present	B.A., M.A., J.D.	Lawyer	Separated	2
Florida	Carrie Pittman Meek	1993–present	B.S., M.S.	College administrator	Divorced	3
	Corrine Brown	1993–present	B.S., M.S.	College Administrator	Single	1
Georgia	Cynthia Ann McKinney	1993–present	A.B, Ph.D. candidate	College Lecturer	Divorced	1

State	Name	Years	Education	Occupation	Marital status	Children
Illinois	Cardiss Robertson Collins	1973–96	None	Auditor	Widowed	1
Indiana	Katie Beatrice Hall	1982–84	B.S., M.S.	Teacher	Married	3
	Julia Carson	1997–present	None	Clothing store owner, administrator	Divorced	2
Michigan	Barbara-Rose Collins	1991–96	None	Purchasing Clerk	Separated/widowed	2
	Carolyn Cheeks Kilpatrick	1997–present	A.A., B.S., M.S.	Teacher/state legislator	Divorced	2
New York	Shirley Chisholm	1969–82	B.A., M.A.	Teacher	Married	None
North Carolina	Eva McPherson Clayton	1993–present	B.S., M.S.	Consultant	Married	4
Ohio	Stephanie Tubbs Jones	1999–present	B.A., J.D.	Judge	Married	1
Texas	Barbara Charline Jordan	1973–78	B.A., LL.B.	Lawyer	Single	None
	Eddie Bernice Johnson	1993–present	B.S., M.P.A.	Nurse	Divorced	1
	Sheila Jackson-Lee	1995–present	B.A., J.D.	Lawyer	Married	2

Source: Gill (1997, 8); and updated by author.

in contrast to Chisholm's colleagues. Missouri congressman William Clay's recollection of his clashes with Chisholm in the 1990 are both vividly clear and direct:

> They [those in Chisholm's camp] alleged that other Caucus members were either "male chauvinists," egotistical bastards, or envious eunuchs. Elected officials are known to have unusually large egos, but the disagreement black members of Congress and hundreds of state and local black elected officials had with Shirley Chisholm was a matter of politics, not ego. The congresswoman was difficult, if not impossible to work with (1992, 198).

Clay then goes on to belittle her legislative record. Sexism still was a part of it, however. Chisholm moved out front, to take a leadership position, at a time when Black women were integral to the struggle for racial justice, but had served behind the scenes. The fact that women were mobilizing and organizing politically for gender equality was criticized by Black civil rights leaders as untimely. If anything, Black male leaders felt that Chisholm's candidacy, rather than providing a forum for Black interests that had been suppressed and slighted within the party, was itself divisive to the Black political cause.

Chisholm's bid would not earn an endorsement from the National Organization for Women, either. NOW leaders gave several reasons for its nonsupport of Chisholm. They claimed that Chisholm, by her own admission, was not a serious presidential candidate. Additionally, they maintained, NOW, founded in 1966, should remain nonpartisan and refrain from endorsing presidential candidates. In 1976, however, the organization endorsed Jimmy Carter's presidential bid, and in 1984 it endorsed Walter Mondale (Mansbridge 1986). Was race a reason why NOW did not see her candidacy as facilitating the push for gender equality? NOW also ignored the candidacy of Jesse Jackson in 1984 and 1988 as well. For a number of reasons, feminist-Black political coalitions, while sometimes successful, as in blocking the confirmation of ultraconservative Robert Bork to the Supreme Court in 1987 and in electing Carol Moseley Braun to the Senate in 1992, are difficult to form and sustain (see Tate 1997). While Chisholm's 1972 presidential campaign was historic and path breaking, history would forget, and remember her mostly as the first Black woman elected to Congress.

Other Black women would not join Chisholm in the House until 1972, when California and Texas elected Yvonne Burke and Barbara Jordan respectively. Like Chisholm, Yvonne Brathwaite Burke (D-CA) would make "firsts." She was the first female chair of the Congressional Black Caucus. She was also the first member of Congress to have a child while serving. Burke's decision to have a child while serving as U.S.

House Representative would garner additional public attention because she was forty. As biographer LaVerne McCain Gill writes, "The reality was that in the 1970s, forty-year-old women were not having babies in large numbers, and certainly not congresswomen. Conventional wisdom and taboos dictated that women avoid middle-aged pregnancies" (1997, 63). One-termer Enid Greene Waldholtz (R-UT) would become the second in 1995, although an FEC investigation of campaign finance abuse overshadowed her pregnancy. In contrast, the pregnancy of New York Congresswoman Susan Molinari (R-NY) who met and married another representative from her state's delegation would garner much more attention, especially since Molinari and her husband were prominent players within the Republican party, and they frequently brought their daughter (Susan Rose) to public events. Burke served only three terms, leaving, in part, to "raise her daughter" (65). (Burke actually ran again in 1980 for the Los Angeles County Board of Supervisors, narrowly losing to her Republican opponent who ran "the most openly racist campaign in the recent history of the Los Angeles County Board of Supervisions" [Kousser 1999, 94]). Waldholtz lost her second bid as a result of her husband's federal indictment. Of the three, Molinari served longest but quit the House in 1997, after serving five terms, to devote more time to her family.

Barbara Charline Jordan (D-TX) was another trailblazer. Elected in 1972, she and Andrew Young of Georgia would be the first Blacks elected in the post-Reconstruction South. Jordan also served only three terms, but was notable because, writes Gill, of the "quality" of those years in elective office (1997, 40). Jordan became known as a political moderate who worked with other legislators privately rather than hashing out their differences in public. Yet her impeccable persona, and her extraordinary and distinctive manner of speech, would make her a leading figure during the Watergate era of the 1970s when President Richard Nixon, caught in a maze of lies and obstruction of justice, resigned.

Cynthia McKinney (D-GA) is the youngest of the Black woman elected to Congress and wears her hair in African-styled braids as does Carolyn Cheeks Kilpatrick (D-MI). African braids remain controversial in the workplace. It is generally unacceptable in corporate America as well as the military. Black professional women normally have their hair straightened as natural Black hairstyles invite public disapproval. (Voting rights law professor Lani Guinier was publicly criticized not only for her "radical" political record but also for having "wild" hair.) McKinney's and Kilpatrick's preference for braids, while clearly personal, has strong political implications.

The occupations of Black women verge in a direction unlike most House members. Although some of the Black women were attorneys, a significant number started out, like Chisholm, as teachers or as college administrators. Maxine Waters of Los Angeles was a social worker. Their education backgrounds are consistent with that of the Black men except that three of the Black women elected to Congress—Julia Carson, Cardiss Collins, and Barbara-Rose Collins—lacked college diplomas. With the exception of Oscar De Priest, all other Black members of Congress of the twentieth century had degrees. The somewhat lower ranking of Black women legislators on education may be the legacy of a number of things. While only Cardiss Collins belongs to the generation of Americans who experienced the Second World War, the G.I. Bill from that war gave men, such as Congressman Louis Stokes (D-OH), unprecedented educational opportunities that the vast majority of women were excluded from. (Cardiss Collins, incidentally, would represent her district for twenty-four years, making her the longest serving Black woman in the U.S. Congress; Collins also "inherited" the district from her late husband.) Whatever the reason, however, this fact makes it plain that Black women legislators came from less privileged backgrounds even in comparison to Black men.

Perhaps the single most striking difference between Black women members and all other members of the House relates to their marital status. Within the U.S. adult population, there are striking differences across race and gender on the social dimension of marital status. Among adults eighteen years and older in the 1998 Current Population Survey, 31 percent of Black women are married and living with their spouse in contrast to 40 percent of Black men, 57 percent of White women, and 61 percent of White men (see also P. N. Cohen 2001). The 31 percent of married Black women matches that for Black women elected to the U.S. House of Representatives. Only one-third of the Black women elected were married when they entered Congress. The remaining two-thirds were either widowed, separated, divorced, or single. To put this statistic in perspective, in the 106th, 86 percent of the members are married, while 7 percent are divorced.[2] Of the married, Shirley Chisholm's husband clearly had facilitated her entrance into New York politics and into the House of Representatives. Her biographer writes that the "unassuming Conrad [Chisholm] was a powerful force behind the soon-to-be dynamic politician" (Gill 1997, 21). They remained married for nearly thirty years, and it was only at the end of her congressional career that they divorced. As the most recent Black woman elected to the House, Diane Edith Watson (D-CA) who won in a special election to fill the late Julian Dixon's seat has never married. Watson's career has been a long one, marked by "firsts." She was the first Black woman elected to L.A. Board of Education in 1975 and the first Black woman elected to the state senate in California in 1978, where she might have remained longer had not term limits ended her career.

Child-raising responsibilities have been identified as a principal reason why so few women choose to run for elective office. Watson and
Chisholm, for example, had no children. Women generally postpone
their pursuit of public office until the children leave the home. And, in
fact, women elected to the U.S. Congress are on average older than their
males counterparts. This probably delayed the entrance of another married Black congresswoman into politics—Eva Clayton of North Carolina. She admits that she dropped out of law school because raising four
children was more than she could handle. "I wasn't super enough to be
a super mom. . . . My husband was supportive, but I felt enormously
guilty. I think I would do it differently now. I think I would know how
to demand more of my husband" (Gill 1997, 209). She won her first
and only elected seat to the county's board of commissioners in 1982 at
the age of forty-eight. Ten years later she ran and won a seat to the U.S.
House of Representatives. Without wishing to exaggerate the point, to
some extent, male role expectations have changed along with women's
so that men do participate more in the raising of children. Sheila Jackson-Lee has frequently commented on the fact that she wouldn't have
been able to run for office if she hadn't had the full cooperation of her
husband. While she works in Washington representing her district, her
husband, a university administrator, is back home in Texas taking care
of their two children—a teenage daughter and preteen son.

It is the large number of Black women legislators who serve as single
mothers, however, that makes this group special. Since the U.S. Census
finds that over half of all Black women head their own homes as single
parents, this fact heightens the descriptive role of Black women representatives. Cynthia McKinney (the youngest Black female legislator)
would return to the Georgia community of her family and pursue a life
in politics in the aftermath of her divorce and with her infant son in
tow. Her father, a state senator, encouraged her to run for Congress and
continues to direct her campaigns. State Senator Billy McKinney has
made headlines for the aggressive manner in which he "protects" his
daughter. One time he chased Black Republican Gary Franks, who had
testified against the creation of the majority-Black district in which his
daughter represented, out of a meeting, threatening him the whole time
with physical violence. For this, he was later fined $500 by a judge—a
fine that he boasted was still very much worth it (Gill 1997, 197). It
must be noted that State Senator McKinney's reportedly anti-Semitic
remarks would also cause his daughter considerable trouble in the district she represents, which contains many Jewish voters.

As the District of Columbia's nonvoting delegate to Congress, Eleanor Holmes Norton's marriage publicly collapsed as she ran for Congress. Denying rumors that she and her husband, both well-known social figures in D.C., had separated after thirty years of marriage, she and

her husband nevertheless divorced shortly after her victory. Norton's marriage, however, ended at a time when her children were grown. Most of the Black Congresswomen, however, had marriages that ended when their children were very young. Carrie Meek, of Florida, endured two divorces that left her responsible for three children to raise alone. Barbara-Rose Collins of Detroit had been separated from her husband after about ten years of marriage when she became his widow. They had two children whom she worked full time to support. Corrine Brown, also of Florida, never married, raising her daughter, whom she had in 1964, alone (Gill 1997).

Even some of the successfully married Black congresswomen experienced life as single parents. California's Maxine Waters, whose second husband, Sidney Williams was the U.S. ambassador to the Bahamas, had married early when she was only nineteen. While the marriage lasted fifteen years, it still ended in divorce. By the end of the marriage, Waters had been in school earning her bachelor's degree. It was only shortly after winning a seat to the California state assembly that she married Williams, a former professional football player and luxury car salesman. While Yvonne Burke had not the experience of solo parenting, her courtship and marriage was very similar to that of Waters. Burke's first marriage at twenty-four ended in divorce after nearly ten years. She bounced back from divorce to serve in the California state legislature. Two days after winning the Democratic primary for the Thirty-seventh Congressional District, she married the campaign aide of the Democratic rival she had beaten! (One wonders if Burke's bested primary opponent had attended the wedding?)

I also compared the single status of Black women to White and other minority women in the House for the 106th Congress. Among the forty-four women legislators — White, Asian or Latina — 27 percent were presently unmarried, either single, divorced or widowed, and, in one case, gay. Like Corinne Brown, one White legislator, Lynn Woosley and her children spent some time on welfare. Regardless of race and ethnicity, almost all (over 90 percent) of the women serving in the House are mothers. A large percentage of women in the House, regardless of race and ethnicity, also come from the teaching profession. The difference between numbers of Black and White and minority women having worked as teachers prior to entering politics is relatively small. The percentage of teachers among White, Latina, and Asian women in the House is 19 percent in comparison to 15 percent for Blacks. When one includes instruction at the college or postgraduate level or work in college administration, the percentage of White and minority women working in education shoots up to 28 percent, while among Black women it increases to 31 percent, because both Carrie Meek and Corrine Brown were college administrators. Constance Morella and Nydia Vélazquez both taught at the university level, while Lois Capps and Zoe Lofgren were part-time college and law school instructors. That one-quarter to nearly one-third of the women worked as teachers or in education prior to winning office to the U.S. House of Representatives is a key difference in the occupational backgrounds of men and women serving in Congress.

Edith Barrett's (1995) analysis of the political priorities of Black women legislators based on a mail survey of 230 legislators found that Black women legislators were no different from Black male counterparts in terms of having a pro-Black legislative agenda. Black women lawmakers were also much like their White female counterparts in having a pro-women's policy agenda as well. Unlike other race and gender groups, Black women shared a strongly unified consensus on which policies should be priorities across the thirty-three states that Barrett targeted.

CONCLUSION

Because half of them had endured slavery, nineteenth-century Black legislators were vastly different from their White colleagues in the House. All the Blacks serving in Congress were literate, but lacked the formal public and private education that many of their White counterparts had received. It was illegal to teach slaves to read and write in slave-owning states, and, thus, the best educated Black members of Congress, those who had at least some high school and college experience, had been educated in the North. Moreover, while some Blacks elected during Reconstruction were wealthy, the majority of those who served in the U.S. House of Representatives were of modest means. Most members survived on the basis of their congressional pay. After Reconstruction, the most prosperous had administrative posts in government. In terms of social status, education, occupation, and wealth, nineteenth-century Black lawmakers contrasted greatly from their White counterparts.

Black lawmakers in the first three-quarters of the twentieth century were typically Southerners who had escaped the degrading and impoverished conditions of the South for a fairer shot at economic prosperity in the North. It is this generation of Black lawmakers who begin to resemble their White colleagues in terms of education and occupation. Like Whites, Black members of Congress come from prestigious occupations. Based on an analysis of their biographies, these Black legislators were less likely to be as wealthy as Whites, however. Their financial insecurity is reflected in the numerous occupations that Black members held before winning public office. Like White members, however, the career choices of Black officeholders favored self-employment. Blacks either were lawyers managing their own practices, or businessmen, or public servants. These were occupations in which they were ultimately accountable only to the people. But their social class, based on their education and their occupations sets them apart from most of their Black constituents. Arguments for the necessity of their presence in Congress as Black legislators would have to be largely based on the race that they have in common with their Black constituents, not their class.

Apart from the slavery experience of the Reconstruction Era Black officeholders, the single-parent experience of Black women is perhaps the most significant social characteristic that sets them apart from White and even Black male members of Congress. Why and how Black women have won more seats proportionately than White women in Congress is an issue I take up in the next chapter. However, it is the single-parent experience that the Black female members of Congress share most directly with their Black female constituents, as single women head over half of all Black families. Black female legislators, therefore, on the basis of their gender as well as their race, make a strong case about being socially "authentic" representatives of their community.

James Button and David Hedge's (1997) mail survey of 170 Black and 162 White state legislators in 1991–92 (achieving a 40 and 34 percent response rate respectively) concurs that while both groups are similarly well educated and have similar political histories, there remain some key differences. First, a higher percentage of black lawmakers were educators prior to entering politics (20 percent versus 9 percent) and female (31 percent versus 21 percent). Button and Hedge's research finds that while the two groups are fairly similar on a social level, there are vast differences in how open they perceive the legislative process to be to their issues, and in the degree to which Blacks have made progress. Although Black lawmakers from majority-White districts expressed less racial pessimism than those from majority-Black districts, the racial makeup of White legislators' districts had no impact on their racial outlook. And indeed, while much can be made of the fact that the backgrounds of Blacks and Whites in Congress are similar, social class has not isolated them from racial discrimination. Button and Hedge asked their legislators if they had ever experienced discrimination, and while 24 percent of the White lawmakers said that they had, a full 62 percent of the Black legislators reported having been discriminated against. While 35 percent of White legislators said that Blacks have achieved considerable progress in jobs over the past ten years, only 8 percent of the Black legislators agreed.

CHAPTER 3

The Elections of Blacks to Congress

Gary Trudeau's Doonesbury cartoon reprinted below makes the point that while Black members of Congress may claim that their race makes them different from their colleagues, the fact of the matter is that they are no different. They may have different backgrounds and claim to have different agendas during the campaign. But once elected, they become just like everybody else. The first agenda on the elected official's mind, his or her highest priority, is to win reelection.

Doonesbury

BY GARRY TRUDEAU

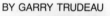

Figure 3.1. DOONESBURY © 1997 G. B. Trudeau. Reprinted with permission of UNIVERSAL PRESS SYNDICATE. All rights reserved.

How HAVE BLACKS WON seats to the U.S. Congress, and has their race been a factor in their elections? In this chapter I show that in the Reconstruction and the Civil Rights and Post-Civil Rights eras, Blacks, with rare exception, have only won office in majority-Black House-districts. There is considerable diversity, however, in the way in which Blacks have won office to the House even among these majority-Black districts.

THE ELECTIONS OF BLACKS TO CONGRESS DURING RECONSTRUCTION

As David Lublin reports, the twenty Blacks elected to the Reconstruction Congress from 1878 to 1900 would win in districts where Blacks commanded the majority. "No African American," he writes, "won election from a district with a clear white majority during the nineteenth century" (1997, 19). Black representation in the House would peak at eight in 1875 during the 43rd Congress. By the 45th Congress, only three Blacks, all from South Carolina, would be members. In the 46th Congress, no Black was seated in Congress. Two from South Carolina returned in the 47th. This was the Congress in which members would turn a blind eye toward the violent repression of Black voting by White Southerners. The violence affected the balloting of the 1876 presidential election between Hayes and Tilden, as Southern states invalidated the returns in violence-torn (largely Black) counties, enough so that Democrats from South Carolina and Louisiana disputed the results. Thus, writes historian Eric Foner, "within two months of taking office, President Hayes ordered federal troops surrounding the South Carolina and Louisiana statehouses to return to their barracks" (1990, 244). While "removing" federal troops from the South became the symbol for the end of Reconstruction, Foner goes on to write that it "was as much a cause of the crisis of 1876–77 as a consequence, for had Republicans been willing to intervene in defense of black [voting] rights, Tilden would never have come close to carrying the entire South" (245).

The suppression of Black voting rights was evident even in the 1876 elections, in which Rainey, Cain, and Smalls were reelected. Rainey and Cains won decisively over their Democratic rivals, but Smalls's victory over Democrat George Tillman (brother of Benjamin R. Tillman, the racist governor of South Carolina from 1890 to 1894) was contested. Smalls was eventually seated in the 45th Congress, but in 1880 the seat was handed over to Tillman. In fact, in 1880 no Black served in Congress as Rainey and Cain were replaced by the two White Democrats whom they had decisively defeated in 1876. Smalls won and served again briefly in 1882–83 and from 1884–87, but through violence, fraud, and redistricting, Whites were winning the war of suppressing Black voting rights in the state. In 1890, an all-White Democratic delegation would "represent" South Carolina. One of these redeemers would include in his biographical statement that he "took active part in the memorable campaign of 1876" when South Carolina was reclaimed from "carpet bag rule." Although the Democrats disputed the election results in 1897, George Washington Murray was the last Black to represent South Carolina until 1992.

North Carolina elected George H. White in 1896, and, serving two terms, he was the last Black sent to Congress until 1928. For about twenty years, the 2nd district of North Carolina had sent a Black to Washington. White segregationists took over the state, although not exclusively through violence, as in the case of South Carolina. In North Carolina, White Republicans also abandoned their Black allies. Even prominent White Republicans in the state began to denounce George White and the principle of Black officeholding as "against common sense." White knew that his last nominations had been contested within his own party—his biography states that he won the nomination in 1894 but withdrew in the interest of "harmony in his party."

Ironically, Robin Tallon's (D-SC) statement as to why he would not seek reelection in 1992 sounded much like White's reason for his retirement from politics—for the "sake of racial harmony." Tallon's South Carolina House district had been reconstituted with a new Black majority during the 1990 round of redistricting. A White Democrat, Tallon had held this seat since 1982, largely thanks to his support in the Black community. However, as the 1992 campaign season approached, criticism mounted that his reelection would impede "minority political empowerment" (Canon 1999, 135).

White Republicans in North Carolina abandoned their Black allies by the late 1800s. At the same time, North Carolina Democrats engaged in voter fraud, but not in exclusively denying the franchise to Blacks. Democrats, in seeking to regain political control of the state, allowed anybody to register, but with the intention of counting as many votes for the Democrats regardless of the actual balloting (Anderson 1981). The Democratic victories accumulated at the expense of the Republicans and Populists. One Republican's complaint about voter fraud was included in his congressional biography; he "was defeated for certificate of election" to the 58th Congress by 183 votes in an election where over 1,200 men who had not paid their poll taxes had voted. Disavowing Black voters and Black officeholding, the Republicans hoped in vain to hold on politically. But after having been reduced to one district in 1896, the Democrats of North Carolina would win back six of the nine congressional districts in 1898.

Using violence and fraud throughout the old confederacy, the Democrats had returned and the period of Black officeholding was over. The end of Black officeholding at the federal level was also cemented through the adoption of vote-dilutive devices as well as racial gerrymandering (Kousser 1974). Southern states enacted plans whereby all congressional districts had White voting-age majorities so that White political domination could be preserved just in case Blacks got the franchise (Parker 1990).

MACHINES AND COURTS IN THE CREATION
OF MAJORITY-BLACK DISTRICTS

Black officeholding resumed in the North in the twentieth century. By 1900, 80 percent of Blacks still lived in the South. Their great migration Northern to urban centers, however, created political jurisdictions where they constituted a voting majority.[1] In fact, the growth in number of Black members of Congress would closely track the growth in the number of majority-Black congressional districts.

The first Blacks elected to Congress in the twentieth century were elected in Northern urban areas experiencing the greatest Black growth. Black officeholding was not automatic but spurred along by Black participation in political machines that were dependent on the Black vote in cities such as Chicago, New York, and Philadelphia. Machine leaders, such as Chicago's legendary Richard Daley rewarded Black voters for their political loyalty with two congressional seats. After decades of satisfaction with this arrangement, a few Black machine leaders, such as Ralph Metcalfe, and the masses eventually revolted against the machine (Grimshaw 1992). Daley would select Bennett Stewart, a ward alderman, to succeed Metcalfe in 1978. Stewart would last only one term, successfully challenged by Black maverick Harold Washington in 1980. Cardiss Collins, who represented her Black district for three decades, owed her seat to the Daley machine through her late husband, a machine-controlled Black alderman. In the late 1980s, she, too, was challenged on the basis of her past relationship with the machine, but running on her record, she retained her seat.

Majority-Black districts in urban areas emerged as a consequence of Black migration from the South, but without machine aid, Blacks had to rely on the courts to preserve their numerical majority. White-dominated state legislatures, not only in the South but in the North as well, racially gerrymandered Blacks out of a voting majority in areas where they could easily constitute a majority in congressional districts. In Cleveland, for example, Louis Stokes would make history becoming Ohio's first Black Congressman in 1968, and yet, his district came about only through a lawsuit that he himself initiated. Representing a Black Republican, Stokes successfully filed a voting rights discrimination lawsuit against the Ohio Legislature charging it with cracking the Black majority in Cleveland and depriving it of the opportunity to elect one of its own to Congress. Stokes' lawsuit won on appeal before the U.S. Supreme Court. The state was forced to create a new district that was 60 percent Black, which prompted its former White Democratic legislator to retire. Stokes's younger brother had been elected as the city's first Black mayor in 1967, and as a result, having great name recognition, Louis Stokes won 41 percent of the vote in the Democratic primary contest among thirteen other candidates. He then won the general election becoming the state's first Black congressman.

The first Blacks elected from the South also won in majority-Black or majority-minority districts ordered by the courts. Both William Clay's and Barbara Jordan's districts, for example, were court-ordered ones. Congressman Andrew Young was the exception, as he was elected in a district where Blacks made up a plurality. He vacated that district to become the first Black secretary to the United Nations, and his district then elected White Democrat Wyche Fowler. In 1982, State Senator Julian Bond pushed the Georgia legislature to redraw the district's boundary to create a firm Black majority. When Fowler decided to run for the U.S. Senate, Bond was the likely successor, but he was defeated in a bitter primary by another Black civil rights activist, John Lewis, in 1986. In 1984 Lewis had failed to unseat Congressman Fowler in a district that now had a Black majority. Thus, in addition to Black electoral mobilization, Black state legislators were critical in pushing for redistricting plans that provided for districts with Black pluralities or majorities.

Redistricting in 1972 also increased the Black population in a Memphis district to 48 percent. This increase permitted Harold Ford, Sr. to successfully challenge the district's Republican representative whose electoral safety had been undermined by his ties to the politically embroiled Nixon. Ford narrowly beat the incumbent by 744 votes. Then, court-ordered redistricting in 1976 gave Ford a Black majority in his district.

On the heels of *Reynolds v. Sims* (1964) affirming the one person, one vote principle, Texas was under attack from voting ligitation because of the malapportionment carried through to its 1960 redistricting plans. Barbara Jordan, who had twice failed to win election to the State House, finally won in 1966 after redistricting that had created two districts in which Blacks and Hispanics constituted the majority (Brischetto et al. 1994). Barbara Jordan's historic election to the U.S. Congress in 1972 was similarly facilitated by the fact that her district was the only one in Texas at the time without a White majority. (Whites were originally only 41 percent of Jordan's House district.) Thus, the electoral history of the growth in Black officeholding in the Post-Reconstruction and Post-Civil Rights eras illustrates quite clearly that Black population growth combined with either Black participation in political machines and/or litigation under the Voting Rights Act led to majority-Black districts in which Blacks won.

The clear exceptions to winning in districts where Blacks represented the majority took place first, and most frequently, in California. Augustus F. Hawkins and Ronald V. Dellums won in districts lacking Black majorities. Hawkins had served in the State Assembly and was greatly supported by in his election by the dominant White liberal power brokers in the state. Although he identified as Black, the quiet-spoken Hawkins was frequently mistaken for White. Hawkins also greatly deemphasized his race when he won election to the U.S. House of Representatives from Los Angeles in 1962. He told one reporter once that "race was just not a factor." His district eventually became majority-Black, and his successor, Representative Maxine Waters, regularly makes race the issue. The other early California House district to send a Black to Congress was originally held by Ronald Dellums. Elected to the Berkeley city council, Dellums in 1970 challenged a six-term Democrat who had been slow to oppose the Vietnam War. Dellums mobilized the already-active base of Blacks in the district and campaigned on the peace issue to decisively defeat the incumbent with 55 percent of the primary vote. Dellum's election differed notably from that of Hawkins as he was a party maverick and independently pursued his seat to the U.S. Congress. Dellum's election was also special because the political makeup of his district, with an extremely liberal base, is unusual. The two Black men who won in nonmajority Black districts in California, however, all illustrated the lesson Rufus Browning, Dale Rogers Marshall, and David H. Tabb (1984) stress in their important book, *Protest is Not Enough*: that Blacks can win only through political mobilization and biracial coalitions.

Another Black member of the House elected in a majority-White district in 1982, Katie Hall of Gary, Indiana, however, served only one term in Congress. In contrast, Alan Wheat of Kansas City, Missouri, also elected initially in 1982, served six terms before abandoning his seat to make an unsuccessful bid for the U.S. Senate. Gary's Black mayor Richard Hatcher chose Katie Hall to fill the remaining term of a White Democrat, Adam Benjamin, Jr., who had died unexpectedly. As the 1st district's party chairman, Hatcher had the legal right to choose Hall, who had been a tireless campaign worker for him and for the Democratic party in Gary. Hall's selection, nevertheless, angered the district's three Democratic county chairmen who had wanted the widow of Adam Benjamin Jr. to fill the seat. They even went to court over the matter and lost. Hall won her first election in 1982 in part because her opponents did not have enough time to challenge her effectively. She would lose the next. While some analysts have suggested that Hall was "too liberal" and too focused on "race" to adequately represent her district, the fact that she did not belong to a broad-based biracial coalition was the key reason why she could not hang onto her seat in 1984.

Alan Wheat in contrast represented a 75-percent White district for six terms before abandoning it to make a poorly timed run for the U.S. Senate. Wheat's district was only 23 percent Black. The 1982 House contest was an open-seat one in that the Democrat who represented the district for seventeen terms had retired. Wheat took 31 percent of the primary vote in a crowded field of eight Democrats and seven Republicans. Yet Wheat's racial cross-over appeal could not get him to the U.S. Senate. In an open-seat contest for a retiring Republican senator,

Wheat's Republican opponent won 60 percent of the total vote and carried all of the state's 114 counties. Only the city of St. Louis gave Wheat the majority share of its vote.

COMPARING THE DISTRICTS AND ELECTIONS OF BLACKS AND WHITES
TO THE 104TH CONGRESS

Table 3.1 presents summaries of the types of districts and election characteristics of the 252 Black Democrats, White Democrats and White Republicans who fell into the NBES sample. On almost every dimension, Black Democrats are significantly different from White Democrats, who are in turn different from White Republicans. First, the average Black population in districts that Black Democrats represent is 58 percent as opposed to 14 percent for White Democrats and 9 percent for White Republicans. At the same time, Black legislators represent districts that are significantly poorer than those represented by Whites, with White Republican members representing on average the wealthiest communities in America.

Blacks spent about $100,000 less on their campaigns in 1994 than White Democrats did, but their margin of victory was significantly higher than that for White Republicans and White Democrats. The average margin of victory for Black Democrats was 56 percent with a standard deviation of 23 percent, indicating that one-third of the Black candidates elected to Congress won with 80 percent of the vote or more. Averages for the margin of victory in the general election can be misleading since Republicans may not even bother to challenge Blacks in majority-Black districts. Because districts having 30 percent or more Blacks in them are safe seats for Democrats, Republicans don't generally run in them (Lublin 1997).

When the margin of victory in the primary races are compared across the three groups, one finds that White Democrats enjoy higher margins of victories than do Black Democrats. Many incumbents face no challengers in their primaries. Table 3.1 presents the percentage of House members who were not challenged in the 1994 primaries. The percentages are roughly comparable across the three groups, with 54 percent of Blacks facing no challengers in their primaries compared to 60 percent of White Democrats. The truth of the matter is that the vast majority of House incumbents who seek reelection are reelected. In 1990, 88 percent of all incumbents seeking reelection won with 60 percent or more of the total vote. In 1996, that percentage fell to a mere 74 percent.

Table 3.2 provides a clearer picture of the turnover in the number of blacks elected to the House. Because there were so few Blacks serving in Congress until the late 1970s, no Black during this period retired until

Table 3.1
Average Districts and Election Characteristics of Black and White Members by Party in the 1996 NBES Data Set (Standard Deviations in Parentheses)

	Black Democrat	White/Other Democrat	White/Other Republican
Median Household Income*	$24,302	$29,493	$33,643
	($6,567)	($7,266)	($8,873)
Per Capita Income*	$11,543	$13,922	$17,013
	($3,068)	($3,790)	($11,769)
%Black in District*	58% (10%)	14% (11%)	9% (7%)
PAC Contributions in 1996	$182,480	$322,366	$299,274
	($120,676)	($213,537)	($204,182)
Individual Contributions in 1996	$162,424	$344,321	$478,332
	($145,160)	($356,596)	($509,358)
Campaign Expenditure in 1994	$391,792	$610,414	$502,259
	($243,520)	($395,476)	($290,866)
%Unchallenged in Primary	54%	60%	50%
Margin of Victory in Primary in 1994	75% (31%)	80% (29%)	67% (37%)
Margin of Victory in General Election in 1994	56% (23%)	26% (20%)	40% (30%)
Years in Office*	10 (9)	12 (8)	8 (7)

Note: These figures are not based on all 435 members of the House, but only on those 252 members that fell into the NBES sample randomly.
*F-statistic prob. value < .01.

1978. After 1978, almost every Congress has had one or two retirements, with the 1990–91 Congress having four retirees, two of whom were elected in the "precivil rights" period. Few blacks who have sought reelection to Congress have been defeated. Notably the few blacks defeated include the two elected in majority-White districts, Katie Hall and Black Republican Gary Franks. The other remaining Blacks who have suffered defeat are concentrated in the Chicago area, where machine-backed Blacks battled with Black mavericks for control of these districts. In 1992, one such maverick, Gus Savage was defeated, along with Charles Hayes. Alton Waldon, Jr., who won a special election to fill a vacancy caused by the death of the incumbent, narrowly beat out Floyd Flake, who two months later would defeat him to represent the district from the 100th through the 105th Congresses. During the 1990s, two Blacks convicted separately for fraud and sexual misconduct resigned from office. Most recently, in 1994 Chaka Fattah (D-PA) defeated incumbent Lucien Blackwell in the Democratic House primaries.

In the end, Black House incumbents represent poorer districts, run

TABLE 3.2
Retirements and Reelection Rates in the U.S. House of Representatives for All Incumbents and Black Incumbents

	Retirements		Percentage Reelected	
Year	All Incumbents	Black Incumbents	All Incumbents	Black Incumbents
1970	6.9	0	94.5%	100%
1972	9.2	0	93.6	100
1974	10.1	0 (1 death)	87.7	100
1976	10.8	0	95.8	100
1978	11.3	18.8 (Nix, Metcalfe, Burke)	93.7	100
1980	7.8	6.3 (Jordan)	90.7	93.8 (Stewart defeated)
1982	9.2	5.5 (Chisholm)	90.1	100
1984	5.3	4.8 (Washington)	95.4	95.2 (Hall defeated)
1986	9.2	0	97.7	(Waldon, Jr. defeated)
1988	5.3	4.3 (Mitchell)	98.3	100
1990	6.2	16.6 (Hawkins, Crockett, Fauntroy, Gray) (1 death)	96.0	100
1992	14.9	0	88.3	92.3 (Savage, Hayes defeated)
1994	9.4	5.1 (Fields; Blackwell)	90.2	100 (resignations by Reynolds and Tucker)
1996	9.6	2.6 (C. Collins)	94.0	94.9 (Franks, B. R. Collins defeated)

Note: These figures do not include members who died or resigned before the end of Congress. I show such numbers for deaths and resignations for black incumbents only.

Source: Based on data in Vital Statistics on Congress, 1997–1998, Table 2-9, and compiled by author.

less expensive campaigns, and almost always are reelected. Representing districts that are typically 60 percent Black, these districts are incredibly safe districts for Democrats to hold and Republicans generally do not challenge them. While reelection rates of black members in general elections are typically 100 percent, the majority of them almost always face competition in their primary races (see Singh 1998). Furthermore this reelection rate of Black members of Congress is not dramatically higher than that of their colleagues, the vast majority of whom are reelected as well. To quote Robert Singh, who has reached similar conclusions as mine, Black members' "electoral environments exaggerate the trends" readily apparent among their White colleagues (130).

Blacks in majority-Black districts are like their White colleagues in their preoccupation with winning reelection. In fact, because both the Senate and White House are pie-in-the-sky goals for them, Black members may be even more invested in keeping their seats than Whites. As Morris Fiorina, a senior scholar of Congress, points out, with a 90 percent reelection rate, "Congress today is occupied by career politicians. Generally speaking the only congressmen who do not intend to spend the rest of their careers in Congress are those senators who hope to move up to the presidency" (1989:7). Congressional scholars have long argued that members of Congress residing in "safe" districts are no less responsive to their constituents because members "run scared" and take nothing for granted (Fiorina 1989; Mann 1978; Jacobson 1987). Swain's (1993) concern that majority-Black districts give Black members greater electoral immunity than White members is baseless.

THE "OVERREPRESENTATION" OF BLACK WOMEN IN CONGRESS?

Chapter 2 demonstrated that social backgrounds and experiences of Black women elected to Congress were significantly different from their White and Black male counterparts. Black women members of Congress deserve a special note in this chapter as well, because within their race, they make up a higher percentage of Congress than women do in the total membership. Figure 3.2 displays the percentage of Black women among Black members against the percentage of women among all members in the House of Representatives. Whereas women today make up 12 percent of Congress, Black women are 34.5 percent of the Black members serving in Congress. Are Black women somehow electorally advantaged relative to Black men and White women? While a substantial literature has emerged attempting to make explicit those factors associated with the high failure rates of Black men and White women in winning statewide, prestigious seats, little has been written about Black women's political chances in this arena (Tate 1997).

There is a substantial literature seeking to explain why women in general are numerically underrepresented proportionally to men in the U.S. Congress. The answer is that first, few women run, and secondly, few women win. In both cases, cultural and structural explanations have been advanced to explain why few women run and few women win. Women are socialized differently than men and that explains why only a handful ever consider running for political office. Write Darcy,

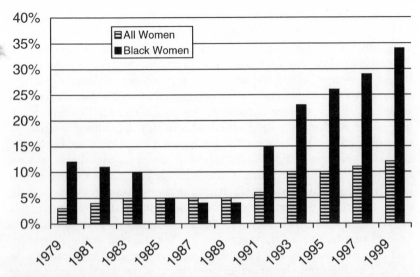

Figure 3.2. Percentage of women in Congress and percentage of women among Black members of Congress, 1979–99. *Source*: Center for the American Women and Politics.

Welch, and Clark, "The traditional role assigned to women makes it difficult for them to enter public office. The role of homemaker and mother as traditionally defined is isolated from and perhaps mutually exclusive of many societal roles, including intensive political activity. Men can be breadwinners and political leaders as well as fathers, but mothering has traditionally been seen as a full-time job" (1994, 106). As they go on to explain, women's life experiences are generally different than men's. Women are burdened with the traditional roles of childcare responsibilities. Women's role as homemaker conflicts with a public, political role. Early research on gender and political officeholding found that women state legislators were more likely to be elected in districts close to the state capital than men, reasoning that closeness to the state capital facilitated female legislative membership since service closer to home was probably less disruptive to family responsibilities than long distances. Another study found that female state legislators tended to be older than male state legislators, suggesting that women defer political careers until after their children become adults.

Rejecting largely the socialization thesis as inadequate, R. Darcy, Susan Welch, and Janet Clark (1994) argue that because politicians tend to come from the economic and social elite, this, too, negatively impacts upon women as political officeseekers. Thus, a substantial part of the underrepresentation of women in public office in the United States is because of their underrepresentation in this eligible pool: the business and professional occupations from which most officials are recruited. This effect is strongest at the national and state levels of government. This structural explanation posits that changing the occupational distribution of women would influence their recruitment to public office.

Another explanation for the underrepresentation on women rests on voter bias against women candidates. Surveys as late as 1984 find that 6 percent of Americans would refuse to vote for a qualified woman of their own party for Congress. Six percent is a small number, but in the world of congressional elections where incumbents are almost always returned to Washington, such a disadvantage represents the proverbial last straw breaking the camel's back for women congressional candidates. And this 6 percent might be an underestimate since some may not be willing to admit their prejudice against women in a poll. Researchers have examined this issue, and most, but not all, still argue that voter bias against women is not a factor. Bias, they argue, is balanced out or negated by the campaign. Furthermore, the congressional campaigns of women candidates are as well financed and supported as those of similar men. Other researchers have reopened this issue, finding that gender bias is a serious problem hampering the elections of women (Kahn 1996). Another form of gender bias comes from party leaders. Like voter bias, the prominent researchers on gender politics have concluded that there is no evidence that women are more likely than men to face politically invulnerable incumbents as candidates in congressional races. However, this early conclusion is, again, being challenged by new research on the different patterns of recruitment for women and men by party leaders (Sanbonmatsu 2002).

Perhaps the chief reason for the numerical underrepresentation of American women in government is the U.S. election system, which confers not only advantages to the economic and social elite but to political incumbents. First-past-the-post plurality systems with single-member districts, used here in the United States, seem to disadvantage women. Women tend to do better under party list systems of proportional representation. Second, party and legislative competition, including the effect of incumbency and turnover are important. Finally, the political culture of a country, whether egalitarian or traditional, plays a role. Most but not all analysts argue that proportional representation (PR) systems elect more women than do single-member district (SMD) systems, nearly twice as many, although there is considerable variation within election systems. Why do more women get elected in PR systems? In single-member districts, parties must nominate one candidate. Women may appear as riskier choices than men do, and lacking comparable resources, women find it difficult to self-nominate. In the United States, women candidates scramble to raise the enormous amounts of money needed to challenge incumbents or to contest the nearly nonexistent open seats in the House. But when voters are presented with a list of candidates for each party, parties have a rational incentive to present a balanced ticket. In party-list/PR countries, women are added to the party list to broaden the general appeal of the ticket and to give them the opportunity to be elected. Affirmative action also caused parties to balance their tickets in PR systems (Caul-Kittelson 2001). Among twenty-five Western democracies, the United States is the fourth lowest in women's representation — only 6.6 percent of the House in 1990.

Given this literature, one would imagine that Black women candidates suffer doubly from the political disadvantages that women and Blacks in general face. Nevertheless, despite the dismal prospects for women and Black candidates, and given the large advantage accorded to incumbents and the negative effect of racially biased voting patterns, Black women candidates may still have special advantages over their White female and Black male counterparts. First, limited evidence suggests that Black women are more inclined to run for political office than are White women. In contrast to White women, Black women have a much longer tradition of simultaneously working and raising families. Thus, sex-role expectations may have a less dampening effect on Black women's political ambitions. Research has found that Black women tend to have higher levels of political ambition than do White women (Darcy and Hadley 1988). Black women delegates at a Democratic party state convention, for example, were more likely than White women delegates to express a desire to hold higher party positions and elected positions. This may be due to African American women's historical experience of participation and activism in the civil rights movement. Researchers have also suggested that resources extant within the African American community help African American women with political ambitions to overcome individual disadvantages such as low earning power and single-parent status. Two such resources are strong religious orientation and family background (Perkins 1986).

Second, although Black votes have been pivotal in the elections of a number of White female Democratic mayors, as in Chicago and Houston, Black women candidates can more likely depend on their base of support coming from African American voters than can White women candidates. Of course, majority-Black support is never automatically handed over to every Black candidate who runs for public office. Black Republicans in particular have only been able to obtain a one-quarter share of the Black vote in most electoral contests. African American voters are more likely to support Black liberals, and turnout among Blacks tends to peak in those elections involving viable Black candidates.

Lastly, Black women candidates may be better able to mobilize women voters as a whole across racial barriers. Notwithstanding, the "women's vote" in contrast to the "Black vote" has historically been far more elusive because women, for a variety of reasons, are less likely than Blacks to vote as a bloc. Indeed, the women's vote is a relatively recent phenomenon, first witnessed in the 1980 presidential election. Prior to 1980, there were only small differences (0–6 percent) in the proportions of women and men voting Democratic. (This gap is also substantially smaller than the racial gap that first emerged full blown in the 1968 presidential election.) The existence of a gender gap in electoral politics owes more to a shift in the voting preferences of men than of women, however. Nevertheless, the issue-based nature of women's support for the Democratic party and its candidates implies that women candidates, even Democratic female candidates, cannot count on a women's vote, since women are supporting Democrats, not necessarily women. At best, liberal female candidates are more likely to obtain reliable support from feminist voters, but feminists represent only a minority of female voters, estimated at from one-tenth to about one-third of the female population. Although feminist organizations have become prominent financial backers of female candidates, their endorsements have not increased female support for their candidates. Contrasting the African American vote to the women's vote, one might sense that Black voters are more receptive than White women voters to the campaigns of African American women candidates. The women's vote is dependent on contextual factors that emphasize substantive, not symbolic, factors related to their vote. Carol Moseley-Braun's historic election the U.S. Senate as its first Black female and first Black Democrat was based on the women's vote and the African American vote (Tate 1997). She captured the overwhelming majority of the Black vote and well as 58 percent of the female vote in Illinois. The gender gap in her Senate race was 9 percentage points, almost twice the 5-point difference between women and men in the 1992 presidential election.

While evidence suggests that Black women are more likely to enter politics at higher rates than White women, and that Black women can benefit from a Black-and-women's-vote coalition, the single most important fact that explains the higher percentage of Black women serving in the U.S. Congress is the new opportunities created by the Voting Rights Act in providing new majority-Black districts from which to run. As explained earlier, a central reason why so few women are elected to Congress in the United States is linked to the single-member plurality system, which favors political incumbents. With rare exception, almost all the Black women who have been elected to the U.S. House of Representatives have been elected in new majority-Black districts. The largest surge in the numbers of women occurred in 1992 when thirteen new

Black lawmakers were added to the House, all because of the new Black districts that had been created. Among the thirteen new Black lawmakers five were women.

A not-so-insignificant number of women have been elected to fill congressional vacancies created by the deaths of their husbands. Freshmen in the 106th Congress, Mary Bono (R-CA) and Lois Capps (D-CA) are two of the most recent examples of wives who successfully won the seats of their deceased husbands. Of the thirty-seven such women who succeeded their husbands in the House, however, only one was Black: Cardiss Collins of Illinois.

Once Shirley Chisholm retired, Collins was the lone Black woman in the House from the 99th to 102nd Congress, when Maxine Waters, Barbara-Rose Collins, and Eleanor Holmes Norton were elected. All three Blacks won in open-seat contests, having prudently waited for the retirement of the Black Congressmen whom they succeeded. Diane Edith Watson (D-CA) would win her seat to the 107th Congress in a special election in 2001 to fill the vacancy caused by Julian Dixon's unexpected death. In fact, with her election, the entire slate of California's Black House-members was now female, as is, presently, that state's delegation to the U.S. Senate. Watson won her election in a race overflowing with Democrats, and thus, it was no easy seat to win. Her victory was made harder by the fact that Congresswoman Maxine Waters endorsed the bid of one of her Democratic rivals. A seasoned campaigner and politician herself, having been the first Black woman elected to California's state senate in 1978 until term limits kicked in, Watson earned even more congressional endorsements than her rival, including those from Millender-McDonald, Rangel, Loretta Sanchez, and Eddie Bernice Johnson, the 107th Congress's chair of the CBC.

Thus a mixture of strong ambition, open seats, and new districts explain why Black women are "overrepresented" in Congress. With the low prospects of additional new Black congressional districts being created today, their rate of entry to the House is expected to slow down considerably, converging to the rate of entry for women generally, which is slow. R. Darcy, Susan Welch, and Janet Clark (1994) argue that the only way to speed up the election of women to Congress is through term limits. If term limits were imposed on members of Congress, Black women would probably achieve numerical parity with Black men in advance of White women reaching parity with White men.

CAN BLACKS WIN IN WHITE-MAJORITY DISTRICTS?

Great emphasis has been placed on the elections of Blacks in White-majority districts, even though they are exceptional. My case studies indicate that most blacks got to Congress in majority-Black districts, and that these districts were created and sustained either through Black participation in political machines or through the courts. Greatly more extensive empirical evidence is provided by Chandler Davidson and Bernard Grofman in *Quiet Revolution* (1994). They show that only one percent of majority-White districts have elected Blacks to Congress over the past twenty years. David Lublin's (1997) analysis of congressional elections from 1972 to 1994 shows that, controlling for all sorts of district-level variables (including region, percent-urban, median income, open-seat), the racial demographics of the district basically predict the race of the candidate who wins. Of the 5,079 elections Lublin analyzed over this twenty-two-year period, whites and other non-blacks won 5,007 elections held in majority-White districts (41).

Black congressional victories in White majority districts are becoming less exceptional because of recent court decisions that have transformed new majority-Black districts into majority-White ones. In Louisiana, the district in 1992 that had first sent Cleo Fields to Congress was substantially redrawn, and like the White incumbents who had declined to seek reelection when their districts became majority-Black, Fields bowed out after serving two terms. His 1995 gubernatorial bid, which most considered ill advised, may have been his strategy of winning White support and building a biracial coalition from which he could return to Washington. It was instead a disaster. His Republican challenger, Mike Foster, referred to the race of his Democratic opponent Fields as much as he could to capitalize on Whites' latent fears of Black leadership. He did this subtly and ingeniously through a television advertisement that stated that the over-sixty-year old, bald, and overweight Foster was "not just another pretty face." He told a *New York Times* reporter that people were attracted to his 1995 gubernatorial campaign because he "look[s] a lot like them and think[s] like a lot of them" (Sacks 1995). His expectation to win votes on the basis of his physical appearance might not have been so strong had not his runoff Democratic opponent been Black.

Still, Fields was remarkably the only casualty of the conservative swing in the Supreme Court on racial redistricting. In 1998, five Blacks, including four incumbents, were elected in congressional districts where Whites were the majority. Cynthia McKinney's district was originally 60 percent Black, but because of court rulings invalidating her district as "racially gerrymandered," it was redrawn to being only 37 percent black (see table 3.3). Districts over 30 percent Black are almost always safe seats for Democrats. As a Democrat, she has not really been at risk of defeat from a Republican challenger, although eventually she could suffer defeat in a primary. As a Black, she credits her ability to retain her seat, despite the radical redistribution of the demographics of her

TABLE 3.3
African-American Representatives in 1999

Name	District	%Black	%Latino	%Minority
Major Owens	NY 11	74.0%	11.5%	88.7%
Elijah Cummings	MD 07	71.0	0.9	73.5
Carolyn Cheeks Kilpatrick	MI 15	70.0	4.3	75.4
Bobby Rush	IL 01	69.7	3.6	74.4
John Conyers	MI 14	69.1	1.1	71.5
Jesse Jackson Jr.	IL 02	68.5	6.6	75.8
Earl Hilliard	AL 07	67.5	0.3	68.1
Danny Davis	IL 07	65.6	4.3	73.2
Robert Scott	VA 03	64.4	1.3	67.1
Bennie Thompson	MS 02	63.0	0.5	63.9
John Lewis	GA 05	62.3	1.8	65.1
James Clyburn	SC 06	62.3	0.5	63.1
Chaka Fattah	PA 02	62.2	1.6	66.3
William Jefferson	LA 02	61.1	3.4	66.5
Ed Towns	NY 10	60.7	19.7	83.1
Donald Payne	NJ 10	60.2	12.3	75.2
Harold Ford Jr.	TN 09	59.2	0.7	60.8
Stephanie Tubbs Jones	OH 11	58.6	1.1	60.9
Albert Wynn	MD 04	58.5	6.4	69.8
Carrie Meek	FL 17	58.4	23.0	82.9
Gregory Meeks	NY 06	56.2	16.9	80.0
William Clay	MO 01	52.3	0.9	54.4
Alcee Hastings	FL 23	51.6	9.4	62.1
Sheila Jackson-Lee	TX 18	50.9	15.3	69.4
Eva Clayton	NC 01	50.3	0.3	51.4
Eddie Bernice Johnson	TX 30	50.0	17.1	69.5
Corrine Brown*	FL 03	47.0	3.4	51.2
Charles Rangel	NY 15	46.9	46.4	96.4
Maxine Waters	CA 35	42.7	43.1	92.2
Julian Dixon	CA 32	40.3	30.2	78.8
Sanford Bishop*	GA 02	39.2	1.7	41.5
Cynthia McKinney*	GA 04	36.6	3.2	43.6
Melvin Watt*	NC 12	35.6	0.4	37.3
Juanita Millender-McDonald	CA 37	33.6	45.1	90.0
Barbara Lee	CA 09	31.8	12.0	60.1
Julia Carson	IN 10	29.8	1.2	31.0
J. C. Watts	OK 04	7.1	3.9	17.2

Note: * originally elected from Black-majority districts. "Percent Minority" is the percentage in the total population who are not non-Hispanic whites. The table does not include the district of Eleanor Norton Holmes, D.C.'s nonvoting delegate to the House.

Sources: Based on *Politics in America 1996* (Washington, D.C.: Congressional Quarterly, 1995); *1990 U.S. Census of Population and Housing: 104th Congress: Congressional Districts of the United States, Summary Tape File Summary Tape File 4D* (CD-Rom). See also Lublin (1997).

district, to her incumbency, which gave her a record to run on and the ability to secure the now-requisite one million dollars for campaigning. Mel Watt of North Carolina won originally in a majority-minority district and won reelection in 1998 in a redrawn district where minority voters constituted slightly more than one-third of the district's population. He credits his victory to his political incumbency, stressing that it was not because White racial fears toward Black candidates have radically changed. As he explained to one *New York Times* reporter, "There are still whites who under no circumstance will vote for a black person. They're never going to touch me, they're never going to be in a room with me. As far as they're concerned, I'm not their congressman" (Sacks 2000). Is the future brighter for Black candidates seeking election in open, majority-White congressional districts? In June 2001, Black Democrat and Virginia State Senator Louise Lucas sought to win the vacant seat created by Democrat Norman Sisisky's death in a special election. This district is 40 percent Black and considered a safe district, therefore, for Democrats. It was an election in which both parties spent millions. The contest was marked by racial overtones, and Lucas lost narrowly to Republican State Senator Randy Forbes by a 4 percent margin.

The other Blacks elected in districts where Whites are the voting majority are Sanford Bishop, Julia Carson, and J. C. Watts. Ronald Dellum's old district, now represented by Barbara Lee, was once a district where Whites made up the majority, but today, minorities are 60 percent of the district's population. In 2000 California became the only state having a Black, Latino, and Asian population majority. As in the case of Lee, other Black representatives are sometimes misreported as representing majority-"White" districts, such as Maxine Waters and Charles Rangel, when in fact Whites are less than 10 percent of their districts.

Litigation forced Texas to redraw its congressional districts for the 1998 elections, and the Black population in both Sheila Jackson-Lee's and Eddie Bernice Johnson's districts was reduced to a bare 50 percent. Although Johnson easily won her reelection with 70 percent of the vote, her district may have a slight White-voting majority. In future reelection bids, Florida's three Black House members are presently open targets for reducing the percentage of Blacks and minorities in their districts. In 1996, 95 percent of the thirty-eight Black members of the House elected won in majority-Black districts or districts where Blacks and Latinos constituted the majority. Only two Blacks served districts with White majorities. It is possible that in the twenty-first century, as a consequence of voting rights litigation, as many as one-third of the Blacks serving in the House will represent districts where Whites are the majority.

The different ways through which Blacks have won office to the U.S. Congress can be simplified as exemplifying essentially two basic approaches: Black independent or biracial/multiracial campaign styles. In their ten-city study of Californian cities, Rufus Browning, Dale Rogers Marshall, and David Tabb (1984) argue that Blacks could more fruitfully win office through a bi- or multiracial approach. David T. Canon (1999) claims that Black candidates have won election to the U.S. Congress both ways. Candidates such as Bennie Thompson (D-MS) and Maxine Waters (D-CA) he labels as "traditional" Black politicians, while those whose campaign styles are equally oriented toward Whites or balanced between Blacks and Whites in the district, such as Sanford Bishop (D-GA) or Cleo Fields, he labels as "new-style." He finds that it is not so much the racial demographics of the district that predict which type of Black candidate would have the best chances of winning, as it is the field of candidates among which they compete. If a pool of Black candidates competes against a White in a solidly-Black majority district, the traditional Black will win if there is a runoff election. In a district where Whites make up at least 30 percent, with multiple Black candidates but no White candidates in the race, the new-type Black will win on the basis of a biracial coalition. Canon finds that these campaign styles feed into their representation of the districts, a matter I explore further in the next chapter.

III. Representing Black Interests

CHAPTER 4

Legislative Styles and Voting Records

> Blacks elected to Congress in the twentieth century, as a
> group, rate in the top percentile on all criteria used for
> measuring effective legislative performance. We are rated
> above the national average in educational attainment,
> intelligence, oratorical skills, and the ability to work amiably
> with colleagues.
>
> — Representative William Clay (D-MO),
> in *Just Permanent Interests*

Do BLACKS REPRESENT their Black constituents differently than do
Whites? Carol Swain (1993) addressed this question empirically, analyzing the legislative votes of Black and White members of the House and
through her field study observations of thirteen Black and White legislators. From this she concludes that Black Democrats were politically represented even when their Democratic representatives were White. In
fact, she asserts that White members of Congress have represented their
Black constituents better than some Black members have (221). Since
Swain's study was first published, however, a number of other analysts
have examined this question (e.g., Canon 1999; Lublin 1997; Whitby
1998), and there is considerable evidence that race does matter. Black
Democrats have legislative records that are quite distinct from the policy records of White Democrats.

In this chapter, I compare Black legislative behavior to that of Whites.
In addition to their summary voting scores, I also examine committee
assignments, bill sponsorship, and individual votes on major legislation.

THE LEGISLATIVE ACTIVITIES OF BLACK AND WHITE HOUSE MEMBERS

In her investigation of women members of state houses, Sue Thomas
(1994) asks whether women bring to government a different style based
on their distinctive life experiences? Politics is after all the premier
power game, but do women, having been socialized as the "gentler
sex," eschew the harsher "zero-sum" aspects of politics, whereby every-
one is either a winner or a loser, and work in a more conciliatory fashion? Her answer is not really: while women legislators were critical of

the ways in which business was conducted in state government, they adapted to, as opposed to challenged, the dominant legislative norms and procedures. She quotes one female member of the Washington House of Representatives, who stated, "I don't like the process, but in order to make a change, you have to get power, and in order to get power you have to play the system" (122). Another earlier published study of personal interviews with women in statehouses found that women frequently stressed the importance of being "tough" to be effective legislators (Blair and Stanley 1991).

In an interview published in the The New York Times (July 15, 2000), Representative Maxine Waters (D-CA) said that some of her White male colleagues in the House find her "too aggressive." She encounters such labels, she believes, because of her race and gender. Her male colleagues think that being female and a minority, Waters ought to behave more deferentially in striving to represent her constituents in Washington. The life experiences of Blacks are clearly expected to impact upon their policy agendas, but not necessarily their working styles in Washington. Like women, Black members of Congress may have distinctive goals, but function no differently from White members in the ways in which they advance such goals.

Table 4.1 displays the average number of years, committee and subcommittee assignments, and staff size by the race and political party of the 252 House legislators whose districts fell randomly into the 1996 NBES sample (the list of these legislators can be found in Appendix A). While Republican members had less seniority than Democrats, essentially no differences emerged on the basis of race across these measures. House members are allocated a fixed allowance to hire staff, and while White Democrats on average employed one additional staff person over Black Democrats and Republicans, this difference was not dramatic. Notably as well, the same percentages of Black House members were serving in party leadership positions as were White Democrats in the 103rd Congress—approximately one-third of those whose districts fell in the sample. Republicans in the sample, however, were less likely to hold leadership positions in their party and in Congress.

Race and Committee Assignments. A closer examination of the committee assignments of Black and White House-members reveals, however, a key difference among members based on their race. Most of the legislative work in Congress is done through committees. While members may submit legislation directly to the floor, in general it must first pass through a committee before it can be voted on the floor. Committees draft the actual language of bills and resolutions, and report on the legislation to the floor. They also collect information through hear-

TABLE 4.1
Average Number of Committee, Subcommittee, Staff Size, and Party
Leadership by Race and Party of House Members in the 104th Congress in
NBES Sample

	Black Democrat	White Democrat	White Republican
Average Number of Years in House	10.2	12.3	7.6
Average Number of Committee Assignments	1.8	1.6	1.9
Average Number of Subcommittee Assignments	2.7	2.5	3.3
Average Total Staff Size	14.8	15.4	14.7
Average Total Staff Size at Home	7.7	7.5	6.5
Percentage Party Leaders	27%	39%	21.5%

ings and hold investigations, but the policymaking process flows through committees. Many more bills are introduced than Congress has time to consider, and most die while in committee or subcommittee, and never make it to the floor. The pivotal role of committees in the policymaking process makes committee assignments important to the attainment of members' political objectives (Shepsle 1978; Hall 1996; Deering and Smith 1997).

Most new members of Congress arrive knowing which committees they want to serve on since there is great competition for serving on important ones. House rules limit members to no more than two major committee assignments. Assignment to subcommittees, however, is less constrained by rules (Hall 1996, 114). Returning members almost always retain their old assignments, while newly elected members must rank their preferences for committee assignments and hope that they get their top choice. Kenneth Shepsle (1978) has referred to committee assignment procedures as the "giant jigsaw puzzle" as members' preferences much be matched to overlapping and competing factors such as the needs of their parties, partisan and geographical forces, rules and procedures, as well as the member's expertise, reputation, and ability. Deering and Smith (1997) retell the story of Carrie Meek (D-FL), one of the new Black faces in Congress sent from a newly created majority-Black district. Shortly after winning her primary, she traveled to Washington to meet with House Democratic party leaders — including the Democratic House Speaker — and indicated her interest in serving on the House Appropriations Committee — one of the most powerful committees in Congress. In her interview with the CQ reporter, she said that she "never asked for a commitment" from the many people she met in

Washington, but sent thank you notes reminding them of her interest in Appropriations (105). Although freshmen usually never get a seat on Appropriations, Meeks did in large measure because she actively campaigned for it.

The most prestigious committees in the House are those seen as the most influential or powerful. These committees include the Rules, Appropriations, Budget, and Ways and Means Committee. Appropriations is appropriately viewed as powerful because it initially determines who gets how much. As former Rep. Silvio Conte (R-MA) used to say, "If you're in the butcher shop when the hog gets slaughtered, you get to take home the best bacon." Deering and Smith (1997) classify policy-oriented committees, such as Commerce, Education and the Workforce, and International Relations, as those that can address key policy domains. Constituency committees are those that can directly address the specific needs and concerns of a member's district, such as Agriculture, Public Works, and Armed Services. The committees that members generally don't want include the Post Office and Civil Service Committee, Standards of Official Conduct, and the District of Columbia Committee.

While no racial differences were found in the number of committee assignments, table 4.2 displays the percentages of Black and White legislators grouped by party serving on prestigious, constituency, policy, and undesirable committees. While a large plurality of White Democrats have assignments to prestigious committees (39 percent), only 18 percent of Blacks' committee assignments can be considered prestigious. The majority of committees that Blacks serve on are policy or constituency focused — a pattern that they actually share with White Republicans. Another difference is that while about 10 percent of the committees that White Democrats and White Republicans serve on are "undesirable," about one-fifth of the committees that Blacks belong to are low-prestige committees.

The higher percentage of Blacks having undesirable assignments can be readily explained by the fact that two out of the five committees have jurisdictions covering the Post Office and Civil Service and District of Columbia. Blacks have long been well employed in the ranks of the federal civil service and postal systems and make up the majority of residents in the District of Columbia. Black members may consider these two committees as "Black constituency" committees, as desirable to them as the "constituency" committees that Deering and Smith (1997) identify. The finding that significantly fewer committees that Blacks serve on are as prestigious as those served on by their White counterparts in the House is tougher to account for. Do Blacks lack the ambition to serve on powerful and influence committees? The story of Carrie Meek of Florida discredits this as a possibility. Are Blacks over-

Table 4.2

Types of Committee Assignments by Race and Party of House Member in NBES Sample (Weighted Percentages)

	Black Democrat	White Democrat	White Republican
Prestigious*	18%	39%	32%
Constituency	59	50.5	51
Policy*	59	40	53
Undesirable	21	10	12

Note: Committee types based on typology developed by Deering and Smith (1997). Includes only the 252 House members whose districts fell into the 1996 NBES sample, including 34 of the 39 Black members of the 104th Congress.
*p < .10.

looked or discriminated against in the allocation of seats to such committees by party leaders? The last explanation seems odd given that Blacks are proportionately represented in party leadership positions. During Reconstruction, however, no Black legislator was assigned to an important committee (Singh 1998). The Speaker of the House controlled the appointment process and presumably chose not to appoint Blacks. Republicans were split, after all, over the issue of Black officeholding, which was too radical for many to support. Placing a Black man on an important committee would give Blacks a measure of power over their White colleagues in Congress, which, at that time, was unimaginable.

Another scholar using a different measure for committee prestige finds no race difference in the committee assignments of Black and White members (Friedman 1996). This measure of prestige, however, is problematic as it does not rank the District of Columbia Committee assignment, and assumes a neat linear and equal drop in committees' levels of prestige from 1 to 19. In fact, bracketing the scale, Friedman reports that since the 1980s Blacks and women were as likely as White males to get the top committee assignments. It could be that the new generation of Black elected officials, those elected to the 103rd Congress notably, including Carrie Meek, have been more openly ambitious in seeking top committee assignments. Dividing the Black members into those elected before 1992 and those elected in 1992 and 1994, I compared the percentages of Blacks serving on prestigious committees. The results are shown in table 4.3.

The percentages reveal that Meek's appointment to Appropriations was an anomaly. Newly elected members generally lack the political clout to win appointments to highly coveted committees. While the 6.6

TABLE 4.3

Prestigious Committee Assignments by Race, Party, and Year Elected:
(Percentage of Appointees within Their Respective Affiliations)

Appointees to Prestigious Committees	Elected Prior to 103rd Congress	Elected to 103rd/104th Congresses
Black Democrat	29%	6%
White Democrat	43	21
White Republican	35	30

percent of Blacks having seats on prestigious committees is still lower than the 21 percent of White Democratic House members, the 15 percent gap between the two groups is somewhat smaller than the 21 percent racial gap that exists in the proportion of prestigious committee assignments as shown in table 4.2. Republicans, in contrast, appointed as many recently elected members (the freshmen of the 104th Congress who collectively shifted the balance of power in the House to the Republican party) to prestigious committees as more senior members. A large gap between more senior White and Black Democrats reappears in table 4.3, however. While 29 percent of Black members elected before 1992 serve on committees that are considered prestigious, 43 percent of White Democrats elected before 1992 serve on prestigious committees. Either Blacks did not want to serve on these committees or they were discriminated against by party leaders. In the latter case, Robert Singh (1998) reports that early committee assignments for Black members did spark controversy. Ron Dellum's (D-CA) desire to serve on the Armed Services Committee in 1974 was objected to by the Democratic Speaker. CBC members protested, and Dellums ultimately received his assignment. Shirley Chisholm tells the story that she was originally assigned to Agriculture, but after protesting that there were "no trees in Brooklyn" was reassigned to the Veterans Affairs Committee (Singh 1998, 79–80). The Democratic Caucus also refused the requests of Harold Washington (D-IL) and Julian Dixon (D-CA) to serve on the Budget Committee. Thus, the absence of Blacks on prestigious committees in the past could be a measure of discrimination by party leaders.

At the same time, in striving to service the needs of Black Americans, Black members may have initially been less interested in participating on powerhouse committees than serving on committees that enhance their chances of winning passage on specific policy areas or pro-Black legislation. Since preferences must be rank-ordered, and given the history of racial discrimination against Black members by party leaders in committee assignments, Black members may have found that requests for seats on less sought-after committees were a more "realizable" ambition.

Race, Bill Sponsorship, and Legislation. While committee work is understood to be the way members can enhance their influence in the policymaking process, bill sponsorship is the most obvious and direct means for members to fulfill Congress's chief lawmaking function. Legislation introduced in Congress can be of two types: bills or resolutions. Resolutions can be policy statements without the force of the law or a matter of public law. Bills generally have many multiple sponsors and greatly outnumber resolutions. During the 105th Congress (1997–98), 7,529 bills and 200 joint resolutions were introduced in both Houses. Of that total, 4,874 bills and 140 joint resolutions originated in the House of Representatives. These bills were no longer read out loud as was customary, but published and referred to committee, where most then die. In the 105th, about 5 percent of the sponsored bills were passed into law.

The literature suggests that Blacks are less successful at lawmaking than Whites. Drawing upon a set of personal interviews with Black House members, Canon suggests that they are less interested in sponsoring winning legislation if it does not directly represent their constituents' interests. Another set of interviews with state lawmakers found that Black legislators think that they have a harder time representing Blacks in the legislative process (Button and Hedge 1997). It is possible that as a consequence Black lawmakers don't sponsor as many bills as White legislators do. Finally, a recent study by Bratton and Haynie (1999) found that compared to their White colleagues, Black state legislators have been less successful in getting their legislation passed.

The data from the 104th Congress strongly contradicts the view that Black legislators are less successful than their White counterparts in winning passage of their legislation. As table 4.4 shows, while Black Democrats sponsored slightly fewer bills and resolutions than their White counterparts, the difference is not striking. Typically Blacks sponsored about seven pieces of legislation in the 104th Congress, while White Democrats sponsored ten and Republicans about thirteen. Because Republicans had a greater chance of winning passage of their legislation in the Republican-controlled 104th Congress, it is not surprising that Republican members sponsored more legislation than Democratic members did. Republican members whose districts fell into the 1996 NBES sample on average got one piece of legislation, bill or resolution, passed in the 104th Congress. Democratic members met with much, much less success, although the Black Democrats success rate for bill sponsorship, one third of that for Republicans, was still somewhat higher than the success rate for White Democrats. Bill success rate data from the 103rd Congress show that Black Democrats were as successful as White Democrats in getting their legislation through Congress. Thirteen percent of all bills sponsored or cosponsored by Black Democratic legislators won

TABLE 4.4

Bill Sponsorship and Voting Summaries by Race and Party of House Member in the NBES Sample (Standard Deviations in Parentheses)

	Black Democrat	White Democrat	White Republican
Average Number of Bills Sponsored in 104th	7.2 (8.6)	9.8 (9.6)	13.0 (11.2)
Average Number of Bills that Became Law in 104th	.24 (.59)	.16 (.45)	.94 (2.00)
CQ's Presidential Support Index 1993	79	69	32
CQ's Presidential Opposition Index 1993	16	29	74
CQ's Presidential Support Index 1992	79	78	40
CQ's Presidential Opposition Index 1992	12	20	60
ADA Rating 1994	90	69.5	12
ADA Rating 1993	90	73	14
AFL-CIO Rating 1994	89	75	19
AFL-CIO Rating 1993	95.5	88	18
CCUS Rating 1993	12	27	87
ACU Rating 1994	8	21	85.5
ACU Rating 1993	3.5	20	87
Poole-Rosenthal Index 1	− .698	− .336	.644
Poole-Rosenthal Index 2	− .014	.041	− .014

Note: The four interest group ratings are from Americans for Democratic Action (ADA), American Federation of Labor Congress of Industrial Organization (AFL-CIO), Chamber of Commerce of the United States (CCUS), and American Conservative Union (ACU).

Source: Summaries were those reported in Congressional Quarterly and taken from Poole-Rosenthal's web site.

passage compared to 12 percent of the bills sponsored by White legislators. In the 103rd Congress, which had a Democratic House majority, Republican members fared significantly less well, winning passage for only 5 percent of the bills that they sponsored.[1]

The large standard deviations reveal that these averages cover up a great deal of intragroup variation on bill sponsorship. For example, five of the 37 NBES Black legislators failed to sponsor any legislation in the 104th Congress. The 13.5 percent of Black legislators, who did not submit any legislation in the 104th, is much higher than the percentages of White Republicans and Democrats who also failed to sponsor any legislation — less than 1 percent and 5 percent respectively. Two of the Black

Democrats who didn't sponsor any legislation, Tucker and Reynolds, resigned after their convictions. Other Black members who didn't sponsor any legislation, Watt (D-NC) and Bishop (D-GA), were dealing with litigation over their districts' boundaries. Representative Cummings (D-MD) won his seat to the 104th in a special election. Still, Ford, Jr., albeit a freshman who "inherited" his father's district, failed to sponsor any of his own legislation in the 104th.

The Black women House legislators, in contrast, were especially active in initiating legislation. Although the average number of bills sponsored is seven for Black Democrats, Maxine Waters (D-CA) sponsored twenty-six pieces of legislation, none of which passed in the 104th Congress. D.C.'s nonvoting delegate, Eleanor Holmes Norton, and House veteran Cardiss Collins surpassed Waters by sponsoring thirty-one and thirty-eight bills respectively. Both women were successful; Holmes won passage of three bills, while Collins won passage of one. These women were still surpassed in productivity by several Republican and Democrat members. The highest number of bills passed for an individual member in the 1996 NBES sample in the 104th Congress was fifty-seven (sponsored by a Republican). Albert Wynn (D-MA) sponsored four pieces of successful legislation. The highest number of bills passed for an individual member in the House was seventeen for House Republican Robert Livingston of Louisiana. Livingston just happened to be the chairman of the Committee on Appropriations for the 104th and 105th congresses. In the end, while 56 percent of the House Republicans failed to win passage for any of the legislation that they sponsored, 87, 78, and 80 percent of the White, Black, and Latino Democrats failed to sponsor any legislation that was signed into law by the president.

What types of bills sponsored by Black Democrats made it out of the Republican-dominated Congress? Mostly symbolic legislation that neither distributed nor redistributed tangible public goods but conferred special recognition on persons or groups. For example, Cardiss Collins of Illinois got the Congress and president to approve naming one of Chicago's post offices on the South side the "Charles A. Hayes Post Office Building." Charles Hayes had represented this district until his defeat by Bobby Rush in the 1994 Democratic primary. The bill naming the post office after Hayes had eighteen other cosponsors, including Representative Rush. Although Norton can't vote, she sponsored three successful pieces of legislation in the 104th Congress, two of which might be labeled "pork" spending projects. One bill transferred title of a D.C. park in order to build a new family and culturally oriented park. Another raised federal revenues spent on certain transportation projects in the District. The third bill won new federal dollars for a second convention center to be built in the District. Norton's success might be partly due to the fact that Congress has a special responsibility for D.C. Still, Norton is a very prolific legislator, having initiated thirty-one bills and resolutions in the 104th Congress.

While most members fail to win passage of legislation that they sponsor, most manage to win passage of legislation that they cosponsor. For example, Corrine Brown (D-FL) was one of 78 cosponsors of a bill designating a U.S. courthouse in Florida the "Sam M. Gibbons" U.S. Courthouse. And while Earl Hilliard of Alabama failed to win passage of any of his bills or resolutions, including one to recognize and celebrate the 40th anniversary of the Montgomery Bus Boycott (H. Res. 285) and one that would increase the income tax deduction for health insurance costs of self-employed persons, he can be credited as a successful cosponsor of ten bills that became law in 1996. Of these ten bills, the majority were bipartisan having more 100 cosponsors and in some cases well over 300.

The bottom line is that in terms of sponsoring and passing legislation, the race differences that the previous literature alleges do not exist in the House. Black Democrats, in fact, were somewhat more likely than White Democrats to get their bills passed in the U.S. Congress. At the same time, a higher percentage (13.5 percent) of Black legislators than Whites failed to introduce any bills or resolutions of their own during the 104th Congress. This could be due to the litigation in which several members who failed to initiate bills were embroiled. Cosponsoring is frequently done in the U.S. Congress, and while I did not have data on cosponsoring by the race of the legislator, Black members appeared to be as likely as White members to successfully sign on and cosponsor legislation likely to pass the House and Senate, and be signed into law. The evidence presented here suggests that the legislative styles of Black members are essentially no different from their White colleagues, except in the types of committees that they serve on. Even on this dimension, however, race differences may be fading as more Blacks win more appointments to the powerhouse committees in Congress (and, ironically, since two of the least-prestigious committees — Post Office and Civil Service and District of Columbia — in which Blacks were clearly overrepresented, were abolished in the 104th Congress).

REVIEW OF THE ROLL-CALL VOTING LITERATURE

In her book, Carol M. Swain's (1993) regression analysis of summaries of House members' floor votes in the 100th Congress were unaffected by the percentage of the Blacks in their districts or by the representatives' race, once the political party of the legislator was included in the model. Political party, as opposed to race, predicted the voting behavior of legislators, she concluded, and therefore Blacks could be effectively represented by Democrat legislators, regardless of their race.

In *The Paradox of Representation* (1997), David Lublin analyzes summaries of members' floor votes on legislation over a twenty-year period (1972 to 1992). He finds that the racial composition of the district is an important predictor of the legislator's roll-call voting pattern even when a host of other controls, including political party, are included in the model. Legislators, Democrats as well as Republicans, are generally unresponsive to Blacks in their district when Blacks form less than 40 percent of that district. Thus, Blacks can expect to be substantively represented only when they constitute 40 percent of the district.

Districts less than 50 percent Black, however, have until recently failed to elect Black candidates. In the end, Lublin (1997) breaks with Swain, in arguing that Blacks are substantively better represented by members of their own race. Yet descriptive representation, he concludes, is only politically beneficial to Blacks when it does not reduce the number of Democrats elected in the state's congressional delegation. He advocates some balance between districts no greater than 55 percent Black and districts less than that to facilitate their representation through the Democratic party.

In *The Color of Representation* (1998), Kenny J. Whitby first examines the responsiveness of legislators to the Black population in their districts on voting rights and civil rights legislation. He finds that legislators were not responsive to Black constituents on voting rights bills but significantly so for fair housing legislation. More than the racial demographics of the district, the legislators' political party, region, and the proportion of the district that is urban had important effects on their voting behavior. In contrast to Swain, Whitby finds that the race of the legislator had an important impact on the roll-call votes on civil rights legislation in many of the congresses he analyzed from 1973 to 1992. The effect of the members' race on their votes is "periodic," he concludes, depending upon the content of the legislation.

David T. Canon (1999) has taken up this issue in *Race, Redistricting and Representation*. His analysis is significantly more comprehensive than the previous studies I just reviewed. While he analyzes the Leadership Conference on Civil Rights (LCCR) scores as did the others, he also examines the bills that members sponsored in the 103rd Congress, their floor speeches, and committee assignments. Representation is defined and analyzed more broadly than previous studies in that the analysis of speeches and bills provides information on how members seek to advance their constituents' interests. Another significant finding from Canon's work is that there are also differences between Black members of Congress in their voting records based on their representational styles.

Blacks elected in 1992 who won by appealing to biracial support were somewhat less supportive (about six points less) of the LCCR agenda in the 103rd as opposed to traditional Black members whose campaigns were crafted chiefly to appeal to Blacks. Most recently, Kerry L. Haynie's (2001) analysis of Blacks in state legislators corroborates Canon's research. Haynie reports that while Black state legislators are more likely to prioritize race-related policies, they also include other issues that are not racial and address broader constituency concerns as part of their overall legislative agendas.

Table 4.4 presents the presidential support measures as tabulated by *Congressional Quarterly*, as well as standard interest group ratings and Poole-Rosenthal indices for the 104th Congress by the race and political party of House members. The presidential support measures indicate the degree to which the legislator's voting record is in accordance with the president's announced position on the bill at the time of the vote, even though the president's position may have changed from an earlier one taken. Legislation that was extensively amended or on which the president's position cannot be ascertained is excluded. Presidential opposition indicates the degree to which a legislator opposes the president on pending legislation. The statistics establish that in the 103rd Congress Black Democrats supported President Clinton in their votes to the same degree that White and other minority Democratic legislators did. The same is true with respect to presidential opposition.

The four interest group ratings shown in table 4.4 are Americans for Democratic Action (ADA), a liberal Democrat organization; the American Federation of Labor-Congress of Industrial Organization (AFL-CIO), the lobbying arm of labor unions; the Chamber of Commerce of the United States (CCUS), which represents local and state business interests; and the American Conservative Union (ACU), a group organized to further the cause of "conservatism." Because interest groups ratings are known to be biased, based on the selection of votes, Poole-Rosenthal indices are reported as well. In their study of roll-call voting behavior among House members, Keith Poole and Howard Rosenthal (1991) created two measures that can account for 80 percent or more of the legislator's roll-call votes — a stunning achievement. The first index captures partisanship, scaled such that the higher the score, the more loyal the Republican member is to the ideological conservatism of the Republican party. The second measure boosts the explanatory power of the first by capturing the residual differences in the members' voting behavior, largely rooted in the intraparty conflict over civil rights during the 1950s, 1960s, and 1970s. Since the realignment of the Democratic party as the party of Blacks (Carmines and Stimson 1989), the second dimension has become increasingly less predictive of legislative votes in the 1990s. Poole (1999) finds that the voting behavior of members is extremely stable. Once elected, members vote in a consistent fashion.

In contrast to the presidential support and opposition scores, large intraparty differences based on race exist across all the summaries of roll-call voting behavior. Whether the interest group is pro-Democrat, pro-labor, or pro-business, Black Democrats are strikingly more liberal or less conservative than White Democrats. Blacks Democrats' voting behavior as measured by Poole and Rosenthal is significantly more consistent with the liberal Democratic party agenda than that of White and other minority Democratic legislators. Differences were slight on Poole and Rosenthal's second dimension, which captures votes on issues that are not clearly partisan. But even here, Black Democrats were to the Left of their White Democratic and Republican counterparts. The data shown in table 4.4 establish conclusively that Black Democratic legislators are distinctively more liberal in their voting behavior in the House, even while they are no less active in pursuing their own legislative agenda and no less successful in winning passage of it.

COMPARING VOTES ON MAJOR LEGISLATION IN THE 103RD AND 104TH CONGRESSES

The data shown in table 4.4 indicates that while Black Democrats generally cast more liberal votes on policy matters than their White Democratic colleagues, as Democrats, both groups are equally loyal to the president, voting most of the time in a manner consistent with the president's public policy agenda. The nature of the American two-party system is characterized by weak party discipline. While Democrats voted mostly in line with the president, they did so only three-quarters of the time. In parliamentary systems, legislators' roll-call votes are well over 90 percent in accordance with their party's position.

In tables 4.5 and 4.6, I identify the percentage of votes on major legislation in two Congresses by the party and race of the House members. The two Congresses are compared because the 103rd had a Democratic House majority while the 104th had a Republican majority. The majority generally controls the flow of legislation onto the House floor. The tables reveal two important facts. First, they show how unified Black members are in their votes on important policy matters, and how unified White members are based on party. Secondly, they reveal the degree to which Blacks defect or are in line with their Democrat counterparts on these issues.

While the interest group ratings give the strong impression that Black members vote alike, the figures presented in tables 4.5 and 4.6 show that on a subset of issues, Black members themselves were divided.

Table 4.5
Votes on Key Legislation in 103rd Congress by Race and Party of House
Member (Percent in Support)

| | | Democrats | | |
| | | White/ | Intraparty | |
103rd Congress Legislation	Black	Other	Voting Gap	Republicans
HR 2518: Appropriations Vote on Hyde-Anti-Abortion Amendment	0%	43.5%	−43.5%	89%
HR 3355: Omnibus Crime Bill (House conference vote)	28	74	−46	26
HR 3540: NAFTA Implementation	24	42	−18	75
HR 5110: Trade Bill	53	67	−14	68
HR 2520: Grazing Fees	92	87	5	28
HR 2: Motor Voter	100	93	7	11
HR 1: Family Leave	97	87	10	23
HR 4296: Assault Weapons Ban	97	81	+16	22
HR 2264: 1994 Budget Reconciliation	100	82.5	17.5	0
HR 1025: Brady Handgun Bill	92	69	+23	31
S 636: Abortion Clinic Access	100	74	+26	22

Source: Calculated by author as reported in the Library of Congress's legislative web site, Thomas (http://thomas.loc.gov/).

They were divided ideologically over the matter of free trade and crime control, both policies pushed through the 103rd Congress by the president with critical support from the Republican party. The omnibus crime bill won favor with only one-fourth of the Black Democratic members of the House, but with three-quarters of that among White members. Black defection from the crime bill that was signed into law by the president was especially bitter. Blacks along with Hispanic Democratic legislators had preserved an amendment in the House to allow defendants in capital cases to use statistical evidence to argue that the death penalty was being imposed in a racially discriminatory fashion. Different members of Congress had been trying to get a racial justice law passed since 1988. The Senate rejected it that year, again in 1989, and again in 1990. Attempts in 1991 also failed, but by then a clear majority in favor of such legislation had coalesced in the House. The House floor vote had been 212 to 217 against striking the provision, a

TABLE 4.6
"Yea" Votes on Key Legislation in 104th Congress by Race and Party of
House Member

104th Congress Legislation	Democrat			Republicans
	Black	White/Other	Intraparty Voting Gap	
HR 3734: Budget and Welfare Reform	3	59	−56	98
HR 2202: Illegal Immigration Deterrence	8	64	−56	97
HJ Res 1: Balanced Budget Amendment	5.5	42	−36.5	99
HR 125: Repeal Assault Weapons Ban	5.5	34	−29	78
HR 1833: Partial Birth Abortion Ban	5.5	34	−28.5	92
HR 961: Clean Water	5.5	26	−20.5	85
HR 2099: HUD appropriations	0	16	−16	87
HR 2425: Cut Medicare	0	2	−2	97
HR 2491: GOP Budget	0	2	−2	96
HR 3610: Defense Freeze	47	44	+3	81
HR 2854: Farm Bill	31	28	+3	92
HR 1227 (amendment): Increase Min. Wage	100	94	+6	40

Source: Calculated by author as reported in the Library of Congress's legislative web
site, Thomas (http://thomas.loc.gov/).

victory that had not been possible three years earlier. Republicans along
with a sizeable minority of Democrats opposed the provision claiming
that it would lead to "racial quotas" in sentencing. Responding to the
threat to tie up the legislation through filibuster if the bill retained its
racial justice provision in the Senate, President Clinton dropped his support of it. Thus, the final bill emerged shorn of the "Racial Justice Act."
Eleven members of the thirty-eight Black Democrats voted against it.
The other twenty-seven caucus members decided that the crime bill's
promise of more police, more prisons and more money for crime prevention was too important to jeopardize by holding out for the racial-justice provision.

Free trade legislation in the 103rd Congress also divided Blacks, but
in this case Democrats more generally. Sixty-seven percent of fellow
Democrats would vote for HR 5110 — a trade bill that passed in the

103rd — but only 53 percent of Black Democrats did. Black opposition to free trade legislation is not tied to issues of race, but stems from broader concerns about protecting U.S. workers from unfair economic competition abroad. Most recently, 7 of the 36 Black Democrats in the 106th Congress voted against a free trade provision for Africa and the Caribbean basin.

On other bills in the Democrat-controlled 103rd Congress, Black Democrats voted solidly in favor of their party's legislation that had been blocked under the previous set of Republican presidents, including Motor-Voter, the Brady Bill imposing a waiting period for gun purchases, and family leave. Two Blacks, however, have indicated their opposition to gun control legislation: Earl Hilliard of Alabama and Sanford Bishop of Georgia. Hilliard and Bishop voted against the Brady Bill in the 103rd, while Hilliard voted against the assault weapons ban and to repeal the assault weapons ban in the 104th that failed in the Senate. While Black Democrats have consistently favored abortion rights, two Black Democrats (Flake of NY and Jefferson of LA) have voted with Republicans and a substantial minority of Democrats to ban so-called partial-birth abortions. This anti-abortion measure failed to win enough votes to bypass President Clinton's veto. The crime control spending bill was an aberration, while trade policy, defense spending, and farm bill legislation (the latter two passed in the 104th Congress) represented general splits within the Democratic party based on ideology and region.

Black members' steadfast loyalty to their party's policy agenda (seen in the roll-call voting behavior of the House's two Black Republicans as well) would be tested more severely in the 104th as President Clinton in his "triangulation" strategy would support certain bills that already had strong Republican backing. Indeed, some would accuse Clinton in 1996 of having stolen the Republican party's play book. The 104th Congress, as explained in chapter 1, has a special place in history in that it was the first with a Republican majority in the lower chamber in forty years. On key components of the Republicans' "Contract with America," Black Democrats lined up solidly against it with only one or two defections, notably Bishop of Georgia. These bills included not only the partial birth abortion ban, but the balanced budget amendment as well. Party defection was more rampant among White and other minority Democratic legislators, 42 percent of whom voted for the balanced budget amendment, and 34 percent for the partial-birth abortion ban and for repealing the assault weapons ban. And while Republicans were able to win passage of NAFTA over the objections of the House's Democratic majority, Democrats in the 104th were able to raise the minimum wage through strict party discipline and defections of many House Republicans (40 percent).

In the 104th, two bills that won passage and that most severely tested Democrats were welfare reform and immigration control. Twice before, President Clinton had vetoed welfare reform bills that ended the sixty-year guarantee of government support for poor families with children on the grounds that they were considered too draconian. While they imposed the five-year limit that Clinton approved of, they didn't provide much financial support to states to help welfare recipients find jobs. However, the third welfare reform bill that cleared Congress was not much different from the first two. It turned over the responsibility for welfare to the fifty states; it limited individuals to five years of support over their lifetime and required half of the state's welfare recipients to be working or training for a job by 2002. Furthermore, food stamps aid was cut. Clinton had originally sought to increase federal spending on welfare programs by 9.3 billion dollars. The welfare bill Clinton signed cut $56 billion from federal welfare funds. Moreover, legal immigrants who had worked less than ten years in the country were barred from Medicaid. (Later legislation would restore the eligibility of those legal immigrants currently receiving Medicaid, but still bar noncitizens from Medicaid.) Single jobless adults would be able to collect food stamps only for three months each year over a three-year period.

Only Sanford Bishop of Georgia would vote to end "welfare as we know it;" all other Black Democrats would vote against it. Nevertheless, welfare reform would receive majority support among White and other minority Democratic legislators—a full 60 percent. That along with 98 percent of the Republican vote, and along with the president's promise not to veto this version, enabled it to become national law on August 22, 1996. While prominent White Democrats, notably in the Senate, would denounce the president's move to eliminate the "safety net," the Black members of Congress, including Senator Carol Moseley Braun, were notably muted in their opposition. One reason for this is that the CBC had also been hit organizationally. Once the Republicans won control of the House, the CBC found itself defunded. Black members of Congress were also mindful that this was an election year. Not only did they not want to endanger the reelection of President Clinton, but their dependence on the power of the White House had increased sharply. Black House legislators were also running for reelection themselves, and they found that blacks were divided with most in favor of welfare reform. Thus, they voted with their conscience but kept quiet.

Jesse Jackson also opposed the bill, but lined up with all the other Democratic leaders to support Bill Clinton's reelection bid. The reasons for Jackson's support as well as that from Black Democrats in general are straightforward enough. Republican control of Congress, in fact, increased their dependence on the goodwill of the president. Moreover, especially at the 1996 National Convention, Democrats were quick to point out that Republican Newt Gingrich's leadership in the House was more dangerous than an ideologically moderate Democrat as president.

Increasing immigration is seen as harmful to the interests of Blacks because their rates of unemployment are higher than the national average, and immigrants compete with citizens in the job market. That said, the vast majority of Black members voted unlike their White Democratic counterparts to oppose H.R. 2002, which was an amendment aimed at deterring illegal immigration by barring the children of illegal immigrations from the public school system. It was similar to Proposition 187, a 1994 controversial law adopted in California pushed by the Republican party, but won majority support among White Democrats. Senate majority leader and Republican presidential nominee Bob Dole backed HR 2002, but could not muster enough support in the Senate.

While 97 percent of the House Republicans voted for the illegal immigration-deterrence measure, a full 64 percent of White Democrats also did. In contrast, only three of the thirty-six Black Democrats supported the measure. Part of the problem was that Democrats were divided over the measure of denying education to children of undocumented workers, although most would support measures making it harder for immigrants to enter the country illegally. When the majority in the House voted in favor of this bill, President Clinton did not claim that he would veto the bill, since it would increase the number of Border Patrol officers, for example. He did, however, state his opposition to the provision denying education to the children of illegal immigrants. The bill died in the Senate in part because Presidential contender Bob Dole's campaign advisers insisted that the amendment be retained and the bill not pass so that Clinton could not take credit for passing anti-illegal immigration legislation in the campaign. The provision was also a popular campaign issue for Dole in states like California.

The votes on key legislation show greater diversity in the voting patterns of Black legislators that the interest group ratings obscure. Several Black members elected in the South have cast votes like moderate Democrats. Ford, Jr. (D-TN) and Bishop (D-GA), in fact, belong to the "Blue Dogs" House coalition, a group of twenty-nine Democrats who consider themselves economic conservatives and who endorse bipartisan cooperation with the Republican party. Some past members of the Blue Dogs coalition have favored Republican legislation so much that they later switched parties. The group gets its name from the paintings depicting a blue dog by a well-known Louisiana painter. The Blue Dog coalition of conservative Democrats is considered to be influential, especially in congresses having Republican majorities. Ford's and Bishop's membership in this coalition defies the pattern documented here of

Black Democrats' unswerving loyalty to the Democratic party's legislative agenda. Their district compositions, however, are quite different, as Ford Jr.'s district has a solid Black majority, while Bishop's does not. Nonetheless, both are Southerners, and, having been elected in the 1990s when majority-Black districts were being attacked, they may participate in the Blue Dog coalition for strategic as well as ideological grounds.

POLICY CONGRUENCY AND BLACK PUBLIC OPINION

The statistics presented in tables 4.5 and 4.6 establish that Black Democrats are generally unified on economic and racial issues, but divided somewhat, as are all Democrats generally, over trade policy, the environment, farm legislation, and defense. Black Democrats have been significantly more pro-Democratic in their votes than fellow Democrats, except in the 104th Congress, on welfare reform, crime and immigration legislation. How well do these votes represent Black policy interests?

The 1996 NBES found Blacks to have somewhat more conservative opinions on social policy matters when compared to Black opinion in the 1984 NBES (Jackson 1993). When asked whether federal spending on crime, food stamps, and Medicare should be increased, decreased, or kept about the same, more Blacks in 1996 said spending should be decreased, except in the area of crime. One of the most striking pieces of evidence that Blacks have become more conservative is reflected in their attitudes toward welfare. In 1984, nearly half of the Blacks (49 percent) polled felt that spending on food stamps should be increased, while only 11 percent thought it should be decreased. Twelve years later, however, that near-majority was cut down by 28 percent, while one in five in the Black community thought spending on food stamps should be cut. There was a less dramatic but still significant drop in the proportion of Blacks who felt that federal spending on Medicare should be increased. Whereas 79 percent of Blacks thought more federal dollars should go to Medicare in 1984, only 69 percent did in 1996. As in the case of food stamps, most in the Black community today feel that the spending levels for Medicare should remain at their present levels. Only on the matter of a federal program guaranteeing a job and a minimum standard of living for Americans did Black opinion not move in a conservative direction. Here, the percentage of Blacks favoring such a program increased by about 7 percent over the twelve-year period, such that a majority (52 percent) now favors it.

Blacks' attitudes on welfare reform match their views on spending levels for welfare programs. A solid majority (67 percent) in the Black community favors the new law limiting welfare recipients to five years

TABLE 4.7
Black Opinion on Public Policies in 1984 and 1996

	1984	1996
Guaranteed Jobs		
Support	45%	52%
Oppose	32	32
	N = 580	N = 919
Minority Aid		
Support	59	51
Oppose	28	35
	N = 915	N = 927
Affirmative Action		
Support	61	58
Oppose	39	42
	N = 831	N = 817
School Busing		
Support	50	57
Oppose	50	43
	N = 832	N = 826
Most Important Problem		
Crime	17	41
Discrimination	20	25
Unemployment	63	35
	N = 851	N = 848
Crime Spending		
Increase	60	64
No Change	31	31
Decrease	9	6
	N = 838	N = 844
Food Stamps Spending		
Increase	49	21
No Change	40	59
Decrease	11	19.5
	N = 837	N = 838
Medicare Spending		
Increase	79	69
No Change	19	29
Decrease	2	3
	N = 847	N = 844

Note: Due to rounding error, cell entries may not sum to 100%. "Guaranteed Jobs" and "Minority Aid" are each measured on 7-point scales. For these policy areas, "support" includes values 1 through 3; "oppose" includes values 5 through 7.

Source: 1984 and 1996 NBES.

of benefits over the course of their lives; only 30 percent oppose it. Blacks are divided, however, on the family cap policy, which, under waivers from the Clinton administration, states enacted. Under this new policy, welfare payments are not increased for welfare recipients who have additional children while on welfare. About half (48 percent) favor such a policy, while 46 percent oppose it.

Support for racial programs, including affirmative action, although remaining quite high, also slipped slighly in the Black community over the past decade. Whereas 59 percent favored the idea of federal aid to minorities in 1984, only 51 percent did in 1996. Opposition to minority aid increased by 7 percent during this period. Black support for affirmative action slipped as well, falling by three percentage points. On crime, 64 percent said spending should be increased in 1996, in contrast to 60 percent in 1984. The growth in the proportion of Blacks favoring an expansion of federal efforts on crime corresponds with other attitudinal shifts in the Black community. More today than in 1984 view crime as the single-most important problem in the Black community relative to unemployment or discrimination. In 1996, a large plurality (41 percent) of Blacks ranked crime first and unemployment and discrimination as second and third. In 1984, only 17 percent had placed crime above the other two problems; crime, in fact, came in third for half of the sample. However, in 1996 discrimination fell to third place while unemployment dropped to second.

While Black legislators voted overwhelmingly against welfare reform, legislation aimed at curbing illegal immigration, and stricter crime control measures, Black opinion was far more divided on these issues. The majority of Blacks (66 percent) favored the five-year life-time limit for welfare benefits for poor families. The vast majority (76 percent) also felt that welfare benefits should not be provided to immigrants immediately, but rather, immigrants should wait a year or more to receive them. In the 1996 survey, Blacks were asked where they stood on crime control on a scale from 1 to 7, where 1 was criminals should be apprehended and locked up, and seven was the government should do more to prevent crime. Blacks were roughly split between the two extremes, with 45 percent favoring the tougher method of locking criminals up.

The public opinion poll data suggest two things. First and most immediately, Blacks are very divided in opinion on most social and economic policy matters, more so than Black legislators. Secondly, Black opinion has become somewhat more conservative over time. This makes the distinctively liberal policy representation of Blacks less representative of their real policy interests. In fact, when one compares where Blacks stand on welfare reform and the actual votes by the 252 House legislators in the 1996 NBES, only 49.5 percent of Blacks were repre-

TABLE 4.8
Percentage of Black Respondents Whose Legislator's Vote on Welfare Reform
Matched Their Position (Number of Respondents in Parentheses)

	Representative: *Black* *Democrats*	*Representative:* *White/Other* *Democrats*	*Representative:* *White/Other* *Republicans*
Black Constituents			
No Congruency	66%	61.5%	30%
Policy Congruency	34	38.5	70
	100	100	100
N	(260)	(205)	(303)

Source: 1996 NBES and as compiled by author from the Library of Congress's Thomas
web site.

sented by legislators who voted according to their position on welfare
reform. When one examines further the congruency between Black public opinion and legislative votes on welfare reform, one finds that Republicans more than Black Democrats, or even White Democrats, represented more accurately Black opinion on this issue (see table 4.8).

Research on the matter of the policy representation of citizens in the
U.S. Congress has found congruency to be fairly low (e.g., Miller and
Stokes 1963). John Kingdon (1981) contends that perfect policy congruency is difficult to obtain, because of the many constituencies to
whom elected representatives are accountable, and because of the many
complicated facets involved in the decision-making process. The decades of scholarship on the voting behavior of members of Congress
suggests that members seek to avoid "risky" or unpopular votes. While
the participation of Sanford Bishop (D-GA) in the conservative Blue
Dog coalition may not present a big electoral risk since his district is
majority-White, it ultimately may be a problem for Harold Ford, Jr.,
whose conservative votes on budgetary matters could become the basis
for a challenge. Members must explain their votes on policies that do
not correspond with their constituents' opinions. Can Black members
justify their votes against welfare reform to their Black constituents?
Probably yes.

While the idealized form of political representation in the United
States is that elected leaders should follow and not lead, recent scholarship in public opinion has shown that elite opinion has a strong impact on mass public opinion (Page and Shapiro 1992; Zaller 1992).
That leaders influence public opinion has been incorporated in a model
of political representation developed by James H. Kuklinski and Gary
M. Segura (1995). They argue that as much as citizens direct the actions

of representatives they also represent an audience in the policy-making process. As much as members of Congress try to emulate and respond to their constituents' interests, they direct them in a more liberal or more conservative direction. Representation is a dynamic process, therefore. Clearly, Black leaders attempt to direct Blacks in a more liberal direction by their votes. Yet as more of them have won office, some are also pushing Black interests in a more conservative direction, notably on gun control legislation. The type of data I would need to empirically test the Kuklinski-Segura model of dynamic policy representation do not presently exist, however.

The policy-making process remains at the heart of representational government. Still, it may not be the process most valued by constituents. In fact, as Hibbing and Theiss-Morse's (1995) work shows, it is the endless debating, bickering, mudslinging, confusion, and bargaining that the public sees involved in legislative work that explain the public's lack of confidence in Congress. And it may be that the ongoing efforts by individual members of Congress to connect to their constituents, as established in Fenno's seminal (1978) work, account for the generally quite high public evaluations members of Congress receive. In their effort to build trust, loyalty, and support in their districts, symbolic acts may go further than substantive accomplishments.

CHAPTER 5

Symbols and Substance

> To point to congressional symbolism is not, of course, to
> denounce it. The Constitution does not require, nor does
> political theory decisively insist, that legislative processes
> enshrine high standards of instrumental rationality. By some
> defensible criteria it is perfectly proper to put laws on the
> books and then not to enforce them. Among other things
> doing so may offer a murky way of maximizing governmental
> satisfaction of popular preferences; Prohibition is a case in
> point.
> —David R. Mayhew, in *Congress: The Electoral Connection*

WHILE THE PERCEPTION of Black legislators is that they are not very successful in winning passage of the bills that they sponsor, I establish in chapter 4 that the opposite it true. Black members of Congress are just as successful in bill attainment as White members of Congress are. This stereotype of Black lawmakers in Congress being less successful at bill attainment exists because of their liberal policy agendas. Because public policy-making is a process of coalitions and compromises, Black members are seen as too ideologically extreme to be successful at it. Part of the reputation is based on studies of the Congressional Black Caucus (CBC). Early studies have characterized the CBC as cohesive but ineffectual. As Robert Singh writes in his important work on the CBC, "As an interest group for blacks, the CBC's impact on public policy has been—and remains—marginal" (1998, xvii). Singh attributes its lack of policy success not only to the institutional features of the American legislative system, but also to the growing diversification of Black members' interests (1998; Barnett 1982). Other studies challenge the negative depiction of the CBC (Bositis 1994; Canon 1995). Still, the larger question is whether Black representation in the House can deliver anything of substance to Black constituents, or whether at most Black legislators represent symbols that do nothing to improve the lives of African American constituents. The crowning achievement of the CBC in Singh's analysis was the imposition of sanctions against South Africa and the commemoration of Dr. Martin Luther King, Jr.'s birthday as a national holiday, while its "Alternative Budget" legislation faced ignominious defeat after defeat.

To typecast Black legislators as "symbolic" legislators lacks perspective. Much of the legislation initiated in Congress can be labeled symbolic, as the quote from political scientist David Mayhew indicates (see also Arnold 1991). Black legislators provide Black constituents with the greatest amount of "symbolic" representation, but also initiate and participate in providing their Black constituents with policies of substance, namely those that distribute or redistribute tangible public goods. Legislative success needs to be evaluated on a broader plane than how previous scholars have defined it. Whether one considers symbolic legislation important or not, members of Congress in general spend a great deal of energy providing it to constituents. In the end, if Blacks are to win their fair share of symbolic representation, Black faces need to be a visible part of the U.S. Congress.

SYMBOLIC LEGISLATION

Few bills make it out of Congress and become public law. Individual members are beating large odds then if one of their bills, among the thousands, becomes law. What types of bills become laws? While the public might imagine that in the competition of bills and resolutions only the most pressing and important public policies become a matter of national law, a review of the 466 laws enacted during the 103rd Congress reveals a different story. The first fifty laws were House resolutions. Below are ten examples of such resolutions:

1. H. J. Resolution 75: A joint resolution designating January 16, 1994, as "National Good Teen Day."
2. H. J. Resolution 78: A joint resolution designating the weeks beginning May 23, 1993, and May 15, 1994, as "Emergency Medical Services Week."
3. H. J. Resolution 79: A joint resolution to authorize the president to issue a proclamation designating the week beginning on November 21, 1993, and November 20, 1994, as "National Family Week."
4. H. J. Resolution 131: A joint resolution designating December 7 of each year as "National Pearl Harbor Remembrance Day."
5. H. J. Resolution 220: A joint resolution to designate the month of August as "National Scleroderma Awareness Month."
6. H. J. Resolution 175: A joint resolution designating October 1993 and October 1994 as "Italian American Heritage and Culture Month."

7. H. J. Resolution 127: A joint resolution to authorize the president to proclaim the last Friday of April 1993 as "National Arbor Day."
8. S. J. Resolution 22: A joint resolution designating March 25, 1993, as "Greek Independence Day: A National Day of Celebration of Greek and American Democracy."
9. S. J. Resolution 21: A joint resolution to designate the week beginning September 19, 1993, as "National Historically Black Colleges and Universities Week."
10. S. J. Resolution 19: A joint resolution to acknowledge the 100th anniversary of the January 17, 1898, overthrow of the Kingdom of Hawaii, and to offer an apology to Native Hawaiians on behalf of the United States for the overthrow of the Kingdom of Hawaii.

Joint resolutions are essentially bills by another name, having a slightly different written format. Like bills that are introduced, these joint resolutions require the president's review and likely signature to become law. In contrast, simple and concurrent resolutions must pass one or both chambers of Congress to be enacted, but do not go to the president. Concurrent and simple resolutions pertain generally to the operations of Congress, but are additionally used to give an opinion of the Congress, but without the force of law (the so-called "sense of Congress" language). Upon adoption, simple resolutions are published in the Congressional Record, a document undoubtedly that a rare few in the public consults.

Symbolic policies, however, are still public policies, but of a different sort. In general, public policies are classified according to the kinds of objectives or results they seek. Scholars generally agree that public policies with domestic (as opposed to foreign) policy objectives seek either to regulate the behavior of individuals and corporations; protect consumers; foster competition in the corporate marketplace; or redistribute wealth, property, legally prescribed advantages, or civil rights among classes of people or ethnic groups. Symbolic policies are those that do not distribute or redistribute any public good or regulate in the standard sense, but reflect their constituents' interests and concerns. Valeria Sinclair Chapman (2002) defines symbolic legislation as "legislation sponsored with the objective of giving psychological reassurance to constituents that representatives are working in their interests and are responsive to their needs." Most concretely, symbolic legislation can:

1. provide political cover — to conceal a voting record that otherwise could be interpreted as contrary to the objectives of the symbolic bill,

2. initiate or augment a larger political objective or agenda,
3. persuade fellow members on core principles before specific bills
   are introduced,
4. cultivate support in the White House,
5. speak to and address the concerns of groups and constituents that
   otherwise would not get addressed.

It is somewhat problematic to question the political motives of members of Congress, but Senator Strom Thurmond's resolution designating a week in September 1993 as "National Historically Black Colleges and University Week" smacks of political cover. After all, Thurmond was initially a strict segregationist, having been elected governor of South Carolina from 1947 to 1951. As a delegate to the Democratic party's 1948 national convention, he participated in the Dixiecrat revolt of Southern members who walked out to express their displeasure at President Truman's moderate civil rights stands. In 1948, he ran for president as the States' Rights Democratic candidate, winning four states in the South. Because of his strong opposition to the Democratic party's liberalizing racial policy views, he switched to the Republican party in 1964. Resolutions like this one by Thurmond can provide cover against criticism that his opposition to affirmative action and public policies that benefit African Americans is motivated by racial antipathy toward Blacks.

While some resolutions may indeed offer politicians "political cover," others appear to be focused on policy and constituents. "Family Awareness Week," for example, may be a way that the member can claim kinship and support for American families.

The three standard types of policy—distributive, regulatory, and redistributive—engage different types of politics (Morrow 2000). Symbolic resolutions are debated and legislated differently as well. Distributive policies, for example, are generally very popular because they distribute public goods, like price supports for farmers and contracts for defense suppliers, to a vast array of groups. In fact, "pork barrel" politics refers to distributive public policies. Pork barrel politics gets its name from the practice of slave owners who would hand out rations of salt pork packed in wooden barrels to their slaves. Of course, distributive policies become more controversial in times of fiscal stress. Because regulatory policies are technical and normally apply to a small set of individuals or groups, they are less public, although the politics surrounding them can be as fierce as that surrounding redistributive policies. In contrast, symbolic resolutions and bills that confer symbolic recognition on groups (designating post offices after community leaders and known ethnic or racial leaders) are very often passed through a suspension of the rules. Noncontroversial bills, those "narrow in impact or minor in importance," are generally considered under a suspension of rules (Sinclair 1997, 20). While there is generally a floor vote, debate is generally limited to forty minutes, and the vote is sometimes taken by voice only. Furthermore, no amendments are allowed, and a two-thirds vote is required for passage. These rules are designed to speed up the process, prevent obstructionism, and save time. In this way, symbolic resolution is exceptionally easy to pass—passage that is often hidden from full view of the media and the American public.

The American political system is known to have a distributive policy bias. Policies that distribute small goods across a wide array of groups and interests are more likely to be passed than those redistributing assets or those regulating a business. In this way, symbolic resolutions are like distributive public policies. Recognizing the contributions of Italian Americans does not mean that the contributions of Greek Americans will never win recognition in Congress as well. In contrast to "pork," symbolic policies do not cost taxpayers much, if anything. Thus, symbolic policies are a cheap way to distribute some nonmaterial public goods to constituents.

Symbolic Public Policies in the 103rd Congress

In the 103rd, Representative John Lewis sponsored a bill (HR 1933) that became public law that provided for the establishment of a Martin Luther King Jr. Federal Holiday Commission and a National Service Day to promote community service. Rep. Bennie Thompson successfully sponsored a bill designating a post office in Jackson the "Medgar Wiley Evers Post Office." He also got through a bill (HR 4452) designating another office in Ruleville, Mississippi, the "Fannie Lou Hamer United States Post Office." The rules were suspended, chiefly limiting debate, and the House passed the legislation without controversy. In addition to Thompson, Barbara-Rose Collins and Eleanor Holmes Norton rose up to speak in favor of this bill. Three White colleagues, including Barney Frank of Massachusetts, made statements endorsing this measure. James Clyburn and William Clay also had introduced legislation (HR 4543 and 4551) designating post offices after a Black federal judge and Black woman civil rights advocate and educator. Considered uncontroversial, such bills, as explained earlier, pass easily through the House.

Some Black legislators have introduced legislation recognizing White citizens in the 103rd as well. Missouri Representative Alan Wheat, for example, introduced legislation designating a post office after a White congressman, while Representative Barbara-Rose Collins of Michigan got a federal courthouse named after a White federal judge. Robert

Scott, a freshman elected in Virginia, had a federal courthouse after former Supreme Court Associate Justice Lewis F. Powell, Jr. White legislators, however, did not succeed in the 103rd in symbolically recognizing Blacks. Representative Eliot Engel of New York asked for new courthouse under construction in White Plains, to be named after Thurgood Marshall; it died in a Senate committee. The point is that in the flood of legislation passed giving symbolic recognition to groups and interest organizations, Black legislators chiefly have worked toward the recognition of Blacks.

SUBSTANTIVE LEGISLATION IN THE 103RD CONGRESS

While the majority of legislation Blacks won in the 103rd was generally symbolic, some substantive bills that they sponsored won passage. Notably, two bills sponsored by Black chairs were pertinent to Black interests. Subcommittee Chairman Louis Stokes sponsored legislation increasing federal funding for HUD funding, VA, and other independent agencies, including the National Science Foundation. William Clay, chairman of the Post Office and Civil Service Committee, successfully advanced the "Federal Employees Political Activities Act of 1993" in the 103rd Congress. This bill repealed the Hatch Act of 1939, which prohibited federal employees from running for public office in partisan elections, holding an office in a political party, or actively campaigning for a candidate in partisan activities. Rep. Clay had initially introduced the Hatch Act reform legislation in 1974. Republicans opposed repealing the Act because they felt that federal employees, whom they recognized generally to be Democrats, would be pressured to engage in campaign activities. Common Cause also opposed repealing the Hatch Act. But despite the controversial nature of this bill, it sailed through the House and Senate and was signed into law.

Other, minor bills, less centrally tied to Black interests, but of a substantive nature, included one sponsored by veteran House member Cardiss Collins (D-IL) that imposed tougher toy safety standards on toy manufacturers (HR 965). Representative Alan Wheat (D-MO) would get a bill passed that expanded the Harry S. Truman National Historic Site in Missouri (HR 486), by authorizing the Secretary of the Interior to acquire the Truman Farm Home and add it to the National Site. Wheat asked for an uncontroversial measure (rules suspended) to create a special district of five counties across two states to work cooperatively on cultural issues (HR 4896). Congressman John Conyers's (D-MI) service on Government Operations led him to petition for the extension of funding for the Kennedy Assassination Records Collection Act of 1992.

In contrast, the one bill passed that directly pertained to minorities, the Minority Health Improvement Act of 1994, was sponsored by Senator Ted Kennedy. Senators Carol Moseley Braun and Orren Hatch were its cosponsors. It passed the House without difficulty. The District of Columbia's nonvoting delegate to the House, Eleanor Holmes Norton, bears special mention because of her high degree of bill attainment, many of which were substantive. Norton has a clear advantage, however, over other Black members; Congress bears an institutional mission to oversee her district.

THE LEGISLATIVE OBJECTIVES OF BLACK MEMBERS: SYMBOLIC, SUBSTANTIVE, OR BOTH?

While the volume of symbolic legislation in bill attainment by Black members is larger than the substantive policy bills, Black members clearly are focused on substantive legislation. Eva Clayton of North Carolina is one such legislator, although her bill attainment record is low. In the 105th, she sponsored seven bills and amendments, all substantive, pertaining to credit to farmers, assistance for low-income working families, and a registration reform whereby voter registration applications would be automatically sent to students during enrollment week. In the 103rd Congress, she sponsored five bills, of which only one, a proposal that a week in March be designed as "Small Family Farm Week" was symbolic. Eva Clayton's web link on legislative activities showcases two bills related to farming that she sponsored in the 105th. The first proposes giving relief to farmers faced with the lack of access to credit because of the 1996 Farm Bill, and the second lifts the statute of limitations, allowing farmers to sue for allegations of past discrimination. Clayton emphasizes how her legislative agenda is designed to benefit residents of her state.

Others, like Rep. Chaka Fattah (D-PA), propose a mix of substantive and symbolic legislation. Fattah's legislative initiatives in the 106th included a resolution recognizing African American music, one that would require states to equalize funding for public education, and one that would require states to provide a minimum level of health-care access as a requirement for participation in federal health-care programs. Chaka's legislative agenda reflects his concern for urban development and equal opportunities in public education.

Finally while Black members introduce a great deal of symbolic legislation, they nevertheless stress mostly their substantive policy agendas in their newsletters to constituents, in press releases, and on congressional web pages. For example, Corrine Brown (D-FL), elected to the 103rd, describes her legislative agenda on her congressional web page as including transportation policy, Medicaid and hospitals, and human rights in Latin America. These agendas are presented in a way that somewhat deemphasizes their liberal ideological dimension, while stressing their importance to the residents of her state. Yet here is the complete list of bills that Rep. Brown sponsored in the 105th:

1. H.CON.RES.129: A concurrent resolution expressing the sense of the Congress that a postage stamp should be issued to honor Zora Neale Hurston.
2. H.CON.RES.298: A concurrent resolution expressing deepest condolences to the State and people of Florida for the losses suffered as a result of the wild land fires occuring in June and July 1998, expressing support to the State and people of Florida as they overcome the effects of the fires, and commending the heroic efforts of firefighters from across the Nation in battling the fires.
3. H.RES.173: A resolution honoring the inaugural season of the United States women's professional basketball leagues.
4. H.AMDT.159: An amendment to express the sense of Congress concerning the rights of prisoners in Andean countries.

Another Black member whose legislative initiatives are generally symbolic is Alcee Hastings, also of Florida. But Congressman Hastings's web site showcases only his substantive interests. The site boosts that the Congressman "has helped secure funds for road construction and highway repairs in his district, authored legislation to protect Port Everglades, and amended the Foreign Aid Authorization Bill urging the Arab League to repeal the economic boycott against Israel. He strongly supports environmental protection, but gives careful consideration to legislation that may disproportionately impact the jobs of his constituents. He recently introduced legislation to help protect jobs and employee rights and legislation that would prohibit visiting foreign nationals from purchasing or possessing firearms." Considering the legislative agendas of Black members of Congress, it is difficult to classify them as either symbolic legislators, substantive legislators, or hybrids.

Why is so much of the legislation that Congress passes symbolic? Richard Hall (1996) argues that legislative work in Washington is both "selective and purposive." Members obviously derive clear electoral benefits from passing symbolic legislation. At the same time, symbolic legislation is rooted in the American electoral system. Having single-member districts and a weak party system creates incentives for members to engage legislative activities that confer benefits to groups. The volume of symbolic legislation is due to the ease of passing such bills, in contrast to concrete public policies, and because bill passage is what is expected of legislators in the district-form system of political representation.

The amount of substantive legislation initiated by Black members of Congress is about equal to or more than that of symbolic legislation. Still, all individual members of Congress are sponsors of symbolic legislation, not only Black members. There are bills recognizing Italian Americans, surgeons, the classical music industry, and all manners of groups. But without Black members in Congress, it is doubtful that Blacks would obtain their fair share of symbolic legislation.

THE CONGRESSIONAL BLACK CAUCUS

As one of its founding members, Representative William Clay (D-MO) offers a richly informative account of the birth of the Congressional Black Caucus in *Just Permanent Interests* (1992). In 1969, thirteen Blacks were serving in the House during a period of rising Black militancy. President Nixon, writes Clay, perceiving his reelection mandate "to repeal all of the Johnson Great Society programs" (1992, 126), had the effect of waving a red flag in front of an impatient and ideologically charged bull. As a means of launching their counteroffensive, the thirteen Black House-members first formed the "Democratic Select Committee," but in 1971 it was renamed Congressional Black Caucus (CBC). The founding members had considered many names, and some others wanted to open the door to other minority legislators, notably Chicanos, Puerto Ricans, and Jewish members. But as Clay writes, these proposals were rejected, as ultimately "it was unanimously agreed that the Caucus be composed of only black members and that the word 'black' remain in the name" (121). Its thirteen founding members were: Representatives Shirley Chisholm, William Clay, George Collins, John Conyers, Ronald Dellums, Charles Diggs, Augustus Hawkins, Ralph Metcalfe, Parren Mitchell, Robert Nix, Charles Rangel, Louis Stokes, and the D.C. delegate, Walter Fauntroy. Organized to maximize their collective influence in Congress, the CBC's mission was to represent the concerns of African Americans.

Early on, the CBC's organizational style was characterized as combative. Rebuffed by President Nixon in their efforts to set up a meeting for over one year, members of the CBC boycotted Nixon's January 1971 State of the Union address. The only African American legislator to attend was Senator Ed Brooke of Massachusetts, then the only Black Republican member of the U.S. Congress. The standoff continued through the second year of President Nixon's second administration. Finally, in March 1971, a meeting was granted, during which the CBC presented the president with sixty policy recommendations. Nixon's response to this list was mixed, but polite.

While the CBC was described as a "concrete manifestation of black political power" (Barnett 1982) within a short period of time, many Black legislators, including some of the CBC's original founders became critical of the organization. By Clay's account, the disagreements and points of disunity were real enough but frequently petty. In a chapter entitled, "The CBC Almost Self-Destructs," he recounts how one member would resign in high drama because the CBC failed to reserve enough tables at a legislative weekend for his campaign contributors, only to rejoin "unceremoniously" four months later. Others would express their grave concerns that a contribution to the organization was accepted from the Coors Company, whose founder was a well-known political conservative. Then there was the presidential bid of one of the CBC's founding members, Shirley Chisholm (D-NY), which as noted in chapter 3, provoked disunity among CBC members.

Beneath all of these issues was obviously a larger conflict between the organization's interests in representing Black interests and members' own political goals. Much feuding took place during President Carter's administration. As members rose in seniority, their loyalty to the organization was stretched and tested by other members who wanted unrelenting and uncompromising resistance to public policies that were perceived as harmful to or dilutive of Black interests — resistance that could jeopardize senior members' own standing in the House. Bill Gray (D-PA)'s service on the Budget Committee and his elevation to Chair in 1985 illustrated this tension well. Chairman Gray clearly became an advocate for the Democratic leadership's budget and a target for CBC's criticism. The conflict was rooted in the organization style that the CBC would adopt. Was the CBC a party within a party, or an organization outside of the Democratic party?

It is instructive that the motto of the CBC is "Black people have no permanent friends, no permanent enemies . . . just permanent interests." Charles Diggs (D-MI), one of its founding members, would claim that the "issues and concerns of this caucus are not partisan ones" (quoted in Champagne and Rieselbach 1995), implying that the CBC is a party outside of the Democratic organization, willing to align itself with any interest within Congress that will promote the interests of Blacks. Thus, the CBC could conceivably vote across party lines with Republicans in whatever issue was in the interest of African Americans. Political disunity within the Democratic party was injurious to members who wanted to advance within the party ranks. While seniority is a factor in committee assignments, so is party unity. Thus, as Blacks rose in seniority and began to covet positions of power on key committees, the type of strategy exemplified by the CBC's motto was professionally dangerous.

The CBC's political approach, however, was not premised on a "balance of power" equation whereby Black members would position themselves in between the two major parties and vote depending on which group's legislation promised the most by way of benefits for Blacks. This, in fact, is the approach often taken by the Blue Dogs, a group of conservative Democrats. Instead, the CBC's strategy of Black political independence is not unlike that described by Ronald Walters (1988) in his analysis of Jesse Jackson's presidential bids. The CBC would organize Black members' votes as a bloc, which could be used to bargain with the larger Democratic party to ensure that its policy agenda moved closer to that of Blacks. Furthermore, the CBC would issue policy statements that could become part of the Democratic party's legislative agenda. By running inside of the Democratic party, Jackson could help mobilize a core segment of Black voters who could be used as bargaining chips with the national Democratic party organization (Walters 1988; Tate 1994). In addition, Jackson's candidacy could put Black issues on the national political agenda and on the party's policy platform. (The problem is that as a bargaining vehicle for Black Democratic voters, Jackson's two presidential bids were not especially successful [Tate 1994].) Like Jackson's bids, the CBC's strategy was entirely intraparty, as they sought to negotiate with the larger Democratic party, and not organize anew from outside of it.

Still, in these negotiations with the Democratic party, how far should the CBC be prepared to go? This was the dilemma that dogged members during the Carter presidency. Writes Clay, "Although Congresswoman Chisholm's 1972 bid for the presidency posted a more serious threat to the continued existence of the Congressional Black Caucus than any previous bone of contention, the storm she aroused was minuscule in relation to what happened during President Jimmy Carter's 1980 campaign for reelection" (1992, 302). President Carter's presidency was a disappointment on almost all fronts. He had snubbed many members of Congress. In 1979 he would abruptly remove Andrew Young, the former Black House member from Georgia, from his post as the U.S. Ambassador to the United Nations, for secretly meeting with representatives of the Palestine Liberation Organization (PLO) — a move that would anger members of the CBC. Black members of the House, however, were especially irritated by the fiscal conservatism he practiced as president. While Nixon had begun to dismantle key Johnson-era programs, Carter continued their dismantling especially in programs that benefited large urban areas, which also happened to be the areas that sent Blacks to Congress. Black members were also incensed by President Carter's weak support of the Humphrey-Hawkins bill (H.R. 20), legislation that was intended to commit the federal government to full employment. In the bill, government was to be the employer of "last resort," creating public service jobs like those that had been created during the Great Depression. Augustus F. Hawkins (D-CA) was its House sponsor, with Hubert H. Humphrey sponsoring it in the Senate. The subsequently revised and gutted legislation that President Carter signed into law in 1978 had eliminated the original provision that provided for government jobs.

The reaction to the Carter administration among Black House members was sharply divided. According to Clay, at a May 1979 CBC regional event, "Congressman John Conyers announced on opening night that he was organizing a 'dump President Jimmy Carter campaign.' He told a local reporter, 'The facts are that President Carter has not lived up to his promise. He double-crossed us.' Congressman Diggs characterized Conyers' remarks as 'premature,' and Congressman Harold Ford announced, 'I'm emphatically against such a move. Furthermore, I'm a supporter of the president'" (1992, 303–4). Conyers would be joined by Congresswoman Cardiss Collins in denouncing the President for his harsh cutbacks in federal social programs for young and senior citizens. Republican Ronald Reagan would defeat President Carter in 1980. What is interesting is that the Clinton presidency and his reelection bid did not invite the same kind of polarized perspectives as did the Carter presidency. Yet Clinton's first-term policies could be characterized as more conservative than Carter's. One dramatic change that occurred in the intervening period between the two presidencies was the sharp increase in discipline that the major parties had achieved through reform (Rohde 1991).

The CBC's own alternative budget, which it had developed as the liberal alternative to the Democratic leadership's budget, also exemplifies this inherent conflict as it clearly was a product from "outside" of the party. As one set of scholars put it, the strategy of presenting this alternative budget to the floor for vote "directly challenged the authority of the Budget Committee"' and was a "clear affront to the committee system" (Champagne and Rieselbach 1995, 146). As it turns out, the powerful Budget Committee was the least likely one to encounter budgetary proposals that had reached the floor without its approval, thus making the CBC's tactic especially striking. Alternatively, Singh argues that the "CBC budget was rarely seen as an affront to either a particular committee or the system but was viewed by Democratic leaders as politically essential to submit for floor consideration." In the end, CBC members were "too important a part of the Democratic coalition to ignore," he writes (1998, 150). Thus, this alternative budget was still a strategy within the party.

The CBC's legislative strategy is one that was closely followed by Jesse Jackson in his 1984 and 1988 presidential bids. As I note in my analysis of these bids, Jackson "presented himself as both an insider and an outsider. . . . As an insider, he ran as a Democratic and chose not to become a political independent. As an outsider, he challenged party rules and disregarded party norms" (Tate 1994, 145). After having been its most vocal critic, Jackson in 1996 would fall in line with all the other party leaders, giving his most ringing endorsement ever to Clinton for reelection as president (Barker, Jones, and Tate 1998).

As the membership ranks of CBC grew and as members achieved greater seniority, their allegiances transferred increasingly to that of the party. In Singh's (1998) analysis of strategic budgetary battles between Democratic leaders and CBC members, those rising fastest in the party's ranks and who were chairs of their own committees and subcommittees were the most likely to vote for the Democratic budget in 1986. Their allegiances were not only divided between their party and the CBC, but also between their positions as chairs of committees and their own re-election and constituency interests. As Singh notes, even Conyers (D-MI), whose positions most consistently corresponded to those of the CBC, voted in 1988 to impeach Alcee Hastings, the first Black federal judge in Florida—even as the CBC refused to adopt a position condemning Hastings, who would later win election in 1992 to the House. The transfer of allegiance to a more solid position within the Democratic party did not come about only because of the growing self-interest of Black members, but as the Democratic party leadership wisely began to appoint Blacks to important committees. Early Black members were put on unimportant committees, deliberately or thoughtlessly, as was the case of Chisholm. But if the function of party leaders is to "keep the peace" by providing members meaningful opportunities to influence the legislative process (Sinclair 1983), party leaders wised up and began to integrate Blacks better. Appointing Gray chair of the Budget Committee in the 99th Congress in 1985, and then as the party's majority whip (the third-ranking party leadership position), was a brilliant way to win votes for the leadership's budget initiatives with, perhaps, less wheeling and dealing on the part of party officials. While Gray attempted to bring fellow CBC members quickly into the party fold, his stronger loyalty to the party was affirmed by voting "present" or abstaining on the CBC alternative budget floor vote. While some may interpret Gray's preference for the party's agenda over that of the CBC as a reflection of an ideological shift, the reason behind his choice, again, probably lay in the incentive and disincentive devices that the party leadership had at its disposal. In their efforts to ensure party discipline, committee chairs were made accountable to the party through a regular secret ballot at the beginning of each Congress (Rohde 1991). Thus, party chairs could be dumped if the leadership felt they were not sufficiently supportive. Thus, unity is challenged not on the basis of ideology but as individual members rise in the ranks and strive to win greater policy influence over the legislative process on their own (Champagne and Rieselbach 1995; Singh 1998).

While some scholars have suggested that the increasing numbers of Blacks to the House would undermine the political solidarity of Blacks as they brought into Congress diverse views and perspectives, the apparent division is less the manifestation of growing ideological disunity than cross-cutting allegiances and a matter of political strategy. The confrontational approach that characterized the early CBC is no longer supported by the majority of Black House members. The additions of Black members from the South add not ideological dissension but different constituency concerns, diluting the overarching urban interests of the previous Caucus members. The confrontational strategy would similarly lose its appeal among the House Republicans who, during the holiday period over 1995 to 1996, had advocated shutting down the government to pressure the president to support their provisions. The hard-line House Republicans were notably freshmen, wishing to retain their ideological purity over the twin institutional imperatives of compromises and coalitions. Once the public began to blame the Republicans in Congress for the three shutdowns, they changed strategies, yielding finally to institutional imperatives. As Richard Fenno put it, "You can't possibly run a revolution through the budget process" (1997, 39). Fifteen "determined" Republicans, nevertheless, voted against the compromise budget legislation in defiance (Sinclair 1997, 212). Black members would become ardent proponents of institutional rules, notably the seniority system (Bositis 1994). Under it, as David Bositis explains, even non-centrists can advance to chairmanship, as did Ron Dellums (D-CA) in the case of Armed Services. If the Democrats regain control of the House in 2004 or closely thereafter, Charles Rangel (D-NY) is in line to assume the chairmanship of the powerful Ways and Means Committee.

Policies that appealed to CBC members during the Clinton administration would lose while more conservative and bipartisan measures would be adopted. While such a turn had ignited a strong outcry among Black members during the Carter administration, there was no open talk among Black members about mounting a campaign to "dump Clinton" as the 1996 National Democratic Convention approached. There are many reasons for this, including Clinton's persistently strong showing among Black voters. Republicans winning control of the House in 1994 added more pressure on Blacks to stick together. Because Black members lost their committee and subcommittee chairmanships under Republican control, Black Democrats' dependence on the president in the legislative process increased (Walton 1997, 323–36). But as important as these two political forces were, the institutional pressures that came to bear on Black members had their greatest impact in moderating the political style of the CBC. In this regard, Caucus solidarity on the floor may prove more elusive, as members are cross-pressured to vote with party leaders or committee members.

Accepting Robert Singh's ultimate conclusion that the CBC, institutionally weak, has amassed at best a "modest record" in delivering public policies of substance to the Black community, I challenge the implications of its increasing irrelevance to the interests of African Americans. Singh's conclusions, after all, are predicated on the assumption that political representation is exclusively substantive, policy representation. Representation as I have defined it, however, is far more encompassing and includes symbolic representation as well. The CBC's primary aim is to give voice and recognition to the interests of Blacks and poor Americans. In the marketplace of ideas and ideologies, this voice and recognition has vital currency. Social groups compete for the positioning of their groups' interests and ultimately of their group's rank with other interests and social groups. Some traces of the old-style protest behavior of the CBC still remain. In the 104th, after Republicans replaced the portrait of the late Democratic chairman of the Rules Committee with the painting of an ardent segregationist, Howard Smith of Virginia, Black members staged a "successful sit-in, demanding the portrait be removed" (Payne 1997, xxix).

Conclusion

While Representative Fattah's (D-PA) bill in the 106th Congress to recognize African American music and its contribution to American society may seem inconsequential, it must be understood as one symbol competing with other symbols in this larger marketplace. It is legislation that is literally in competition with other bills, including those recognizing "classical music." Without Black members taking part in the legislative process, the symbolic interests such as the congressional medals to Rosa Parks, would not be there. Martin Luther King's birthday becoming a national holiday symbolized the role he played in transforming the country into a true democracy. As a national holiday, it becomes difficult to diminish his place in history and the role of African Americans generally in America. Their absence would contribute further to the symbolic marginalization of Blacks' place in American society and in history.

IV. The View from Black Constituents

CHAPTER 6

Blacks' Evaluations of House Members: Does Race Matter?

WHAT DO BLACKS THINK of their elected representatives in Washington? What do they expect from them? In this chapter I turn to the very questions that the 1996 NBES survey was designed to address. A total of 252 House districts fell into the sample, including the districts of 34 of 39 Black members of the 104th Congress. In all, these Black legislators represented 33 percent of the Black respondents. In this chapter, I examine the performance ratings of these legislators to determine what impact, whether any, their race has on their constituent evaluations. Next, I determine if being descriptively represented in Washington positively impacts on what Blacks think of their elected representatives in Congress more generally or not. Finally, I look at what focus — national, constituency service, or local — Blacks think that representatives ought to concentrate on in Congress and why.

How Are Representatives Evaluated? A Review of the Literature

Elected representatives should be judged on how well they represent their constituents. But, then, what is representation? In chapter 1, I argued that political representation constitutes everything that the legislator does in his or her formal capacity as an elected representative. House members generally are engaged in three principal activities: (1) constituency service, (2) policymaking, and (3) reelection. Everything means everything, including acts that do not materially benefit the constituents but are "symbolic." Representation also can be constitutive and empowering; this is an issue that I take up in the next chapter. This definition of representation, however, presents a problem. How much of "everything" that members of Congress do actually filters down to the constituent? How much and which parts of it do constituents consider when evaluating the performance of their representatives?

Empirical work in congressional studies has generally focused on elections, not representation. Elections are the principal mechanism to ensure political representation. The two, voting and feeling represented in government, are not the same, however. While voters who don't feel adequately represented in Washington are motivated to vote against incumbents, they may also still support incumbents out of partisan loyalty. Constituents who don't feel represented may not even vote. And indeed, in terms of how legislators view their districts, they rationally write off some communities in their focus on maintaining support in the segments that reelect them (Fenno 1978). Votes in the aggregate in congressional elections have largely been characterized as revolving around the economy and presidential popularity. Voters in congressional elections, in fact, pay little attention to the legislator's performance in office and to local concerns. This view is contested, with some survey research scholars emphasizing the importance of the congressional candidate's political party, ideology, and personal characteristics as critical determinants of the congressional vote (Niemi and Weisberg 1984, 199–209). I base the empirical model of members' evaluations presented in this chapter on this latter literature.

Early survey work established that Americans know very little about their representatives in Washington. Much was made of the 1958 survey that revealed that only about half of the electorate knew the name of their representative in the House. In this study, Miller and Stokes (1966) concluded that being known among voters carries a "positive valence" for candidates. When asked to rate candidates running for Congress, voters would rate higher those candidates they knew by name. Given that so many Americans were unable to identify their elected representatives in Washington, Miller and Stokes concluded that voters generally evaluated members of Congress on the basis of their partisanship. Political participation in midterm congressional elections was also a partisan affair, as only strong partisans generally turned out and voted. For sure, political party remains an important element in evaluating one's elected representative and in congressional elections (Mann and Wolfinger 1980; Erikson and Wright 2001). In low-information congressional elections, party presents a clear choice. All things being equal, constituents judge members of Congress belonging to a rival party more harshly than those belonging to their own political party.

Thomas Mann's (1978) revisionist work established that the public knew the names of many more members of Congress and congressional candidates than the Miller and Stokes' (1963) study implied. First, while many could not spontaneously recall the name of their elected representatives in Washington, most, in fact, 90 percent or more, could recognize their names. Secondly, the public's ratings of their representatives were not always positive, but meaningfully based on their personal image, ideology, and issue stances. Issue-based voting in congressional elections is problematic, since members of Congress may strategically avoid taking clear stands on issues (Page 1981). Since the congruency studies could not establish a direct link between the legislator's voting behavior and the constituent's policy preferences (Miller and Stokes 1963), Thomas Mann argued that policy issues may not be direct determinants of the congressional vote, but are mediated through other factors such as presidential popularity.

Some revisionist work established the importance of ideology and issues in congressional elections. Alan Abramowitz's analysis (1984) shows that ideology was a force in the 1980 and 1982 House races. The more liberal the voter was, the more likely the voter was to vote Democratic. Erikson and Wright (2001) also show that the member's ideological records (as measured by roll-call votes) are consistently linked to the vote decision in House elections. Binder, Maltzman, and Sigelman (1998) also show that ideological congruence impacts on the approval ratings of U.S. Senators. Candidates whose ideological stands are too extreme for their district generally are punished at the polls. Scholars now contend that in the end, while generally uninformed, citizens can meaningfully judge incumbent members of Congress and candidates on the basis of their party, personality, and ideology. Public opinion and legislative responsiveness happens in the aggregate, according to Erikson and Wright (2001; see also Page and Shapiro 1992). While individual voters with little information may mistakenly vote for or against incumbents, incumbents who stray too far from the majority's preferences on policies are risking their reelection. For John Kingdon (1981) and Douglas Arnold (1993), legislators' voting decisions are influenced by public opinion because legislators monitor the state of public opinion in their districts and vote accordingly. Rather than relying on "instructions" from their constituents, legislators are "controlled agents" who anticipate constituent opinions in their districts.

Further work by Thomas Mann and Raymond Wolfinger (1980) on the 1978 National Election Study would downplay the role of issues, ideology, and even party in congressional elections to stress candidate image and reputation. "Voters," they write, "appear to judge candidates and incumbents in particular on the basis of their perceived character, experience, and ties to the local community." Candidate factors are considered to be important generally in the voting decision, especially in light of the waning influence of the political parties (Wattenberg 1996). Voters judge the competence of candidates, in addition to their political party, and their stands on the issues. Samuel Popkin (1991) argues competency, defined as a measure of ability to handle the job, is crucial to voters for several reasons, including that it indicates the probability of the candidate "getting things done" once elected. Bill sponsorship and bill attainment are two ways that members of Congress establish their record of accomplishment.

Popkin argues that demographic facts about the candidate, such as gender, race, and personal history, are other important cues that voters use in their voting decision. Voters look to these demographic facts to ascertain not only competency but also the representativeness of candidate. How likely is the candidate going to represent my side on the issues? How much is the candidate like me, in other words? Campaigns are structured to emphasize the personal history of a candidate to the exclusion of issues, in fact, stressing things such as the length of their marriage, their war service, and their ties to the community. Emphasizing personal qualities, such as "I am trustworthy, hardworking, successful," is the manner in which many members of Congress present themselves back home to their constituents. While members also stressed their stands on the issues in meetings in their districts to their constituents, more stressed their personal qualities (Fenno 1978).

The race of the legislator, therefore, provides information to constituents. Black legislators will likely stress their race in contacts with and in campaign efforts before Black constituents, with the belief that belonging to the same race will be viewed positively by their Black constituents. While Popkin points out how candidates seek to use their personal attributes to their electoral benefit in presidential campaigns, estimating its electoral impact has previously not been done. In this chapter, I develop a model that estimates the effect of one's race on the performance ratings for incumbent House legislators.

A MODEL OF EVALUATING REPRESENTATIVES IN WASHINGTON

The literature on congressional elections suggests that the following three factors are used in the vote decision: party, ideology, and candidate qualities. All three are relevant in how representatives are evaluated. But unlike candidates who may lack previous officeholding experience, House incumbents can be evaluated for competency in a variety of ways.

The legislator's political party is important in how constituents make evaluations. All things being equal, constituents of the same party are going to rate representatives of the same party higher than members belonging to the rival party. In U.S. legislative politics, party membership is not a perfect predictor of the legislator's voting record. Ideology is therefore important. Roll-call votes are the primary basis on which one can determine the legislator's political ideology.

Competency is established in many ways by legislators, through bill sponsorship, seniority, party chairmanships, and staff. Although few bills make it out of committee and actually become policy or law, voters may still value policy activism or the aggressive pursuit or at least articulation of tangible policy goals. Voters may also favor lawmakers who have been successful in the pursuit of their policy goals. However, in addition to determining how many bills in a given Congress are sponsored by the member, I also consider the proportion of bills that become law as additional measures of competency.

The legislator's seniority and party leadership posts can enhance his or her influence in Congress. My study identifies members of Congress as leaders in the 104th Congress if they held a party leadership post. Seniority is measured as the number of years the member has served in the House since first elected. Committee work is another way legislators attempt to represent their district. First, there are chairmanships that clearly amplify legislative influence in Congress. None of the Democrats in this Republican-dominated Congress held chairs. In terms of the numbers of committees that members served on, most members served on two, although a few served on one or three. The type of committee that the member serves on may affect the type of policies he or she can claim credit for, and hence, may influence his or her standing in the district. Christopher Deering and Steven Smith (1997) have identified congressional committees that were either (1) policy oriented, (2) constituency service oriented, (3) prestigious, and/or (4) undesirable. The type of committee a member belonged to was examined to see if it affected his or her rating. Four sets of dummy variables were created on the basis of the Deering-Smith classification and were analyzed.

Staff allowances are the same for all members in the U.S. House of Representatives, and typically, House members employ about twenty people on their personal staffs. Because casework is time consuming, the member's personal staff size might be a useful indicator of constituency service. Of the two measures of legislative staff that were examined here, the number of staff employed within the district, as opposed to the number working at the Capitol, was employed in the analysis.

In addition to legislative and committee work and constituency service, members of Congress devote considerable time to reelection activities. Highly rated members of Congress might be the most effective campaigners, especially since name recognition and approval ratings are strongly correlated. Campaign activity can include campaign expenditures and margin of victory, in this case the 1994 election. Those who win by high margins might be better known and better liked than those who win narrowly. Similarly, incumbents who spent the most on their last campaigns might also be better known, although it is not clear that they are also the best liked. I collapsed campaign expenditures into three categories: low, moderate, and high. High scores constituted expenditures over $600,000 in 1994.

Black attitudes toward their representatives are likely to be affected by the legislator's:

1. political party,
2. race,
3. legislative record, specifically roll-call votes and bill sponsorship,
4. committee work, including the number of committees, chairmanship, or type of committee service,
5. legislative position, such as seniority and party leadership,
6. staff size,
7. campaign activity, such as margin of victory and campaign expenditures.

As noted earlier, 252 districts fell into the 1996 NBES sample. The complete details concerning how the sample was drawn and the response rate are presented in appendix A. Of the thirty-four African American House-members whose districts were represented in the sample, all were Democrats and none were Republican. The 1996 NBES contained a significant number of questions about the Black respondents' elected representatives in Congress. The first measure was one of recognition, whether the respondents knew the name, party, and race of the legislator representing them in the U.S. House of Representatives. These items are analyzed in the next chapter. Following recognition, they were asked to rate their representative on a feeling scale than runs from zero to one hundred. Only respondents who recognized their representatives' names rated them. After a number of other questions, they were then asked whether they approved or disapproved of the representative, making reference to the legislator by name, once again. Respondents, a full 45 percent, who expressed a lack of knowledge and familiarity with their representative in Washington were skipped from a followup battery of evaluative items pertaining to their House legislator. The other 55 percent of respondents were asked the remaining questions about their representatives, such as how many years had their representative been in the House, how often had he or she supported President Clinton's legislative proposals, and whether they had ever contacted their legislator or anyone in his or her office? This approach accounts for the small number of cases for the battery of items regarding the legislator's perceived qualities and accomplishments, such as helpfulness and having done something special for the respondent's district.

Preliminary results shown in table 6.1 reveal a statistically significant link between the representative's race and his or her ratings by Black constituents. Even controlling for party membership, Black legislators

Table 6.1

Blacks' Evaluations of Their Representatives by the Legislator's Race and Political Party

Race and Party of Their Representative	Black Democrat	White Democrat	White/Other Republican
Approve/disapprove of representative's job?*			
Strongly approve	60%	36%	25%
Not strongly approve	24	37	27
Not strongly disapprove	9	14	19
Strongly disapprove	7	12	29
Would representative be helpful?*			
Very	46	24.5	17
Somewhat	42.5	52	54
Not very	8	21	25
Depends	3	2	4
Rep. done anything special for district?*			
Yes	36	20	11
No	64	80	89
How good a job does rep. do in keeping in touch?*			
Very good	41	23	15
Fairly good	44	41	40
Fairly poor	8	16	23
Poor	8	20	23
Is rep. a problem-solver/prestige-seeker?*			
Problem solver	70	48.5	28
Both	4	5	3
Prestige seeker	26	46	68.5

Note: Weighted data.
*Chi-square sig. level (two-tailed) < .01.
Source: 1996 NBES.

received significantly higher ratings on average than their White counterparts. A full 60 percent strongly approved of their legislator's performance when that legislator was a Black Democrat as opposed to only 36 percent when the legislator was a White Democrat. In contrast still, only one-quarter of the respondents represented by White Republicans strongly approved of their performance, while nearly 30 percent strongly disapproved. Blacks represented by Black Democrats were also significantly more likely than Blacks represented by Whites to consider their representatives helpful, in touch, and more likely to solve problems. When asked if they had a problem that their representative could do something about, how helpful would that representative be, the vast majority (88.5 percent) of those represented by Black Democrats felt that their legislator would be somewhat to very helpful. Only 11 percent felt that their Black Democratic representative in Washington would not be very helpful or that their help would "depend." At the same time, 76.5 to 71% of those respondents believed that their White legislator, either Republican or Democrat, would be very or somewhat helpful. The Black constituents of Black Democrats, however, were strikingly more likely to believe that their representative had done something "special" for the district in contrast to those represented by Whites. Finally, a solid majority (70 percent) of the Black constituents of Black Democrats believed their representative to be a "problem solver" as opposed to a "prestige seeker." Fewer Blacks, 48.5 percent, represented by White Democrats characterized their representative as a problem solver. A full 68.5 percent of respondents represented by White Republicans denounced them as mainly preoccupied with winning prestige.

Although results shown in table 6.1 suggest that Blacks in districts that have Black representatives are significantly more satisfied with their representative, it is not clear that the reason is entirely due to the race of representative. It could also be that other political characteristics of House members beyond race and political affiliation explain these preliminary results. It is important to consider different characteristics of House members beyond their race and to control for them in the statistical analysis.

Data corresponding to these eight factors for the legislators whose districts fell into the 1996 NBES sample were collected by the author and appended to the data set. Because the dependent measures are attitudinally and behaviorally linked to key social characteristics of the respondent, such as age, gender, and educational attainment, additional variables were included as controls. These variables were the number of years the respondent had lived in his or her community, age, education, and gender.

Table 6.2 presents the results of a regression analysis of five dependent measures: (1) the representative's approval rating, (2) how helpful the representative is perceived to be, (3) whether the representative has done anything special for the district, (4) how good a job the representative does in keeping in touch, and (5) whether the representative is perceived to be a problem-solver or prestige-seeker.

In terms of the relative weight of race and party affiliation on Black attitudes toward their representatives, political party appeared to over-

TABLE 6.2
The Effect of Descriptive Representation on the Member's Ratings by Blacks (OLS Estimates)

Independent variable	Member's Approval Rating (1-5)		Member's Rating on Helpfulness and Problem Solving		Member's Rating on Keeping in Touch		Member's Rating on Anything Special for District		Member's Rating as Problem Solver v. Prestige Seeker	
	b	SE	b	SE	b	SE	b	SE	b	SE
Intercept	2.624**	.374	-2.138**	.301	-3.892**	.399	-5.632**	.457	-5.000	.555
Member's Race (Black)	.431**	.136	.374**	.112	.761**	.147	.679**	.170	.819**	.208
Party Match	.724**	.140	.206*	.114	.390*	.152	.317	.175	.898**	.211
Party Leader	-.160	.128	-.178	.105	-.423**	.141	-.335*	.159	-.270	.195
Committee Chair	.001	.216	.099	.178	.333	.236	.184	.267	.188	.323
Years of Seniority	-.001	.007	-.006	.005	.005	.007	-.002	.008	-.002	.010
# of Home Staff	.037	.024	-.005	.019	.002	.026	-.007	.029	-.008	.036
# of Bills Law	.037	.045	-.018	.036	-.096	.056	-.062	.055	.034	.072
Campaign Spending	-.097	.085	.010	.068	-.078	.090	-.018	.103	-.081	.124
R's Residency	.000	.002	-.001	.001	.002	.002	.002	.002	.000	.003
R's Age	.005	.004	.001	.003	.017**	.004	.010*	.005	.020**	.006
R's Education	.059	.034	.000	.029	.048	.038	.147**	.043	.164**	.053
R's Gender (male)	-.187	.113	-.069	.093	-.024	.123	.060	.142	-.197	.170
N	663		538		512		564		486	
R-squared	.14		.06		.18		.10		.19	

Note: *statistically significant at .05.
**statistically significant at .01.
Source: 1996 NBES.

shadow race in the overall evaluation of the legislator's approval, but race mattered more when members were rated on specific aspects of their service and representation. As shown in table 6.2, Blacks who had Blacks representing them in Congress were somewhat more approving of their performance than Blacks represented by Whites. All things being equal, Blacks represented by Blacks in Congress gave them approval ratings about one-half point higher on average than Blacks represented by Whites. The political party of the legislator had an even larger impact on the legislator's approval rating, however. Constituents represented by their members of the political party that they identified with (legislators whose party "matched" their constituent's, in other words), got ratings nearly one point higher than those legislators whose party didn't match the respondent's.

This was not the case, however, for the other four evaluation measures. In every other instance, the effect of the legislator's race was greater than that of the legislator's political party. Blacks represented by Blacks in Washington gave them significantly higher marks when it came to helping constituents with problems, keeping in touch, doing things for the district, and caring more about working on behalf of their constituents than accruing prestige in Washington.

Only one of the legislator characteristics impacted upon Black evaluations of their representatives. Party leaders got especially low ratings for keeping in touch with their constituents. Committee chairmanships, seniority, district staff size, bill attainment, and campaign spending were unrelated to the approval ratings of legislators.

Except for age and, to a lesser extent, education, respondent characteristics introduced in the regression models were generally unrelated to Black attitudes toward their representatives. Older Blacks tended to give their representatives higher ratings than younger Blacks, for reasons that are not immediately clear. College-educated Blacks, like the elderly, gave their representatives higher marks on achieving things for the district and solving problems.

In sum, descriptive representation turns out to be very important to Blacks, as Blacks were generally more approving of their legislator when that representative was Black. Political party also mattered when it came to judging the legislator's performance among the 1996 Black respondents, but race mattered a great deal more.

The failure to find that the ideology of legislators, their legislative records, seniority, and service related to Blacks' evaluations of their performance are perhaps statistically rooted. These factors may be indirectly tied to Black evaluations, and a nonrecursive, simultaneous structural equation model might better establish their impact. This could be an intractable methodological problem with survey research methodology; Fiorina and Rivers (1989) go so far as to suggest that it requires a controlled experiment whereby legislative votes and service are manipulated to ascertain their effects.

At the same time, it could be that these factors don't matter much once the legislator obtains a reputation in the district for being "liberal," or "hard working," etc. (see Fiorina and Rivers 1989). My analysis shows that certain factors do matter, namely race and party. Voters rely heavily on political party and certain demographic factors, such as race, to make inferences about the legislator's performance. Only in the long run would deviations from casting liberal votes—such as accusations by challengers that the incumbent is too "old" and "out of touch"—matter decisively in competitive races.

DESCRIPTIVE REPRESENTATION AND ITS IMPACT ON BLACK CONSTITUENTS' EVALUATIONS

More than two decades ago, Richard Fenno (1978) pointed out that while most Americans loath Congress, they still like and respect their individual representatives in this legislative body. That people like their representative in Washington but loath Congress is a persistent finding in the field of congressional scholarship (Hibbing and Theiss-Morse 1995). Blacks are no exception to this pattern. Simply comparing Blacks' attitudes toward their representatives in Congress to those of Whites in 1994, one finds that Blacks are neither more or less satisfied with their own representatives in Congress than Whites. In the 1994 survey, about 87 percent of Blacks as opposed to 81 percent of Whites approved of their House legislator's performance in office (the 6-percentage point difference is not statistically significant). Trend data from as far back as 1980 support this pattern; Black approval ratings of their incumbent House legislators were consistently high and closely tracked that of Whites. In addition, data from the 1978 to 1990 National Election Study show that Blacks are no less likely than Whites to say that they would ask their representative in Washington to help them with a personal problem.

Included in the 1996 survey were a battery of questions about members of Congress, whether they work to serve the people or generally serve themselves. As expected, most Blacks viewed the members of Congress favorably. A majority thought that members of Congress are important community leaders. About half felt that they keep in close contact with their constituents and did a good job representing the diverse interests within the United States. In contrast, only a minority felt that members of Congress were not preoccupied with their reelection and campaign money. Most felt that once elected, members of Congress

TABLE 6.3

Cross-tabulation of the Character of Members of Congress by the Race and Party of Black Respondent's Representative

	Black Democrat	White Democrat	White/Other Republican	N
Race and Party Respondent's Representative				
"Members of Congress are only interested in reelection." (Percent who disagreed.)	28.5%	30%	28%	(1,147)
"Members of Congress keep in close touch with people in their district."	49	44	41	(1,125)
"Members of Congress are important leaders in their community."	72	68	75	(1,144)
"Members of Congress do a good job representing the diverse interests of Americans."	49	54	48	(1,133)
"Members of Congress are only interested in raising campaign money from big corporations and interest groups." (Percent who disagreed.)	39	35.5	33	(1,116)

Note: Weighted data.
*Chi-square sig. level (two-tailed) < .05.
**Chi-square sig. level (two-tailed) < .01.
Source: 1996 NBES.

spent an inordinate amount of time and energy on their next reelection bid and special interests campaign donors. Because House members are elected every two years, this perception that they are preoccupied with campaigning is not misplaced.

Do Blacks represented by Blacks express more positive evaluations about members of Congress in general than those represented by Whites? Table 6.3 displays a cross-tabulation of these items by the race and party of the respondent's representative. In short, the answer is no; having a Black representative has no bearing on the attitudes Blacks express about members of Congress in general.

The multivariate results (not shown here) indicate that the race of one's representative has no effect on the opinions one has about members of Congress in general. Blacks represented by Blacks were no more positive in their evaluations about members of Congress's behavior than those not represented by Blacks. At the same time, judgments concerning members of Congress were significantly related to age, gender, and the respondent's feelings about the responsiveness of government or external political efficacy. Older Blacks and women were more positive than younger Blacks and men in their attitudes about how members of Congress generally behave. As one might expect, those who generally thought government to be responsive to people like themselves were also more positive in their evaluations. These evaluations, however, were unrelated to the respondent's level of education, political interest, or party affiliation.

While Blacks express greater satisfaction when represented by Blacks as opposed to Whites, this representation does not affect their attitudes about members of Congress more generally. Because Blacks represented by Blacks do not think more highly of members of Congress than those represented by Whites, the higher ratings that Black legislators receive from their Black constituents over White legislators may reflect their actual performance in office. Whether the race of the representative, then, still affects the attitudes Blacks have about Congress as an institution and their level of trust in government are questions I explore in chapter 8.

The Burkean Dilemma and the Representative's Focus

The Burkean dilemma refers to an idea proposed by the eighteenth-century politician Edmund Burke: elected representatives should act as a trustee for their district, deciding what policies best serve that district, rather than behave as delegates, voting only according to the majority's preferences. Burke's point of view has its supporters and detractors. Democratic theory, however, favors a delegate role for legislators, but some scholars, such as James Fishkin, still advocate a trustee relationship between legislators and constituents. The impeachment vote on President Bill Clinton's behavior in the Monica Lewinsky affair was a modern-day reflection of the Burkean dilemma. Public opinion polls showed that the majority of Americans were against impeachment even after Special Prosecutor Kenneth Starr released his damaging report about the president. Nevertheless, some Republican members of Congress voted to recommend impeachment of the president by the Senate against the majority wishes of their district, arguing that their vote was a "vote of conscience."

Burke's philosophy mixes the problem of style with focus. Style refers to the question of who should the legislator follow — the majority within the district or him or herself? Focus, however, has to do with whether the legislator responds to local or national pressures. Roger H. Davidson's research found that half of the legislators saw themselves as either pure delegates or pure trustees, with about half expressing a mix of both. In terms of focus, Davidson found that most members of Congress were parochial at heart. They generally cast votes and acted on behalf of the good of their district. Nearly 30 percent, however, claimed that their votes reflected what was best for the country. Democratic theory, once again, favors a local approach. The aggregation of the local good would then work best for the country as a whole.

The question of style and focus is one that Black legislators have addressed as well. Who are their constituents, and whom do they represent in Congress? When Adam Clayton Powell of New York was one of two Blacks serving in Washington, he dealt with problems from Blacks all over the country, and not just those of who had elected him, his Harlem constituents (Hamilton 1991). Powell's twenty-year record in Congress was known for its uncompromising advocacy of racial justice, and not for its service to his district. Not every Black sent to Washington saw their responsibilities as national. Schooled in politics by the Daley machine of Chicago and having been an integral part of it, the other Black Congressman of that era, Representative William Dawson (1943–72), saw his legislative responsibility as fundamentally local. Dawson maintained a complete silence on the national problem of race discrimination.

Carol Swain's research would reveal similar differences among recent Black members of Congress. George Crockett of Michigan, who served in Congress from 1981 to 1990, took radical-liberal, highly controversial stands on foreign policy. Crockett, in fact, became chairman of a subcommittee of the House's Foreign Affairs Committee. Mike Espy, who became Mississippi's first post-Reconstruction Black Congressman when he was elected in 1986, saw his responsibility as local. His campaign literature stressed service to his district. Swain writes, "In these letters he has claimed credit for millions of dollars that have come to the district. He was responsible for the creation of a National Catfish Day, which aids the catfish farmers in his district, and for legislation exploring ways to develop the Mississippi River. During trips around the country, he has personally signed up deals for orders of catfish, soybeans, and cotton worth thousands of dollars" (1993, 84). Espy resigned in 1992 to head the Department of Agriculture in the Clinton Administration.

The Congressional Black Caucus would declare its mission as national with a primary focus on the needs and interests of Black Americans. One of its founding members, Congressman William L. Clay of Mississippi explains that the organization's purpose was logically defined as protecting the interests of Blacks, because "we understand that the destiny of each of us is inextricably bound to the destiny of 32 million other black brothers and sisters, and that their struggle and our struggle are irrevocably tied one to the other" (1992, 353). Political reality was such that the CBC found it difficult to maintain Black unity on all of the issues. But even still, whether Black or White, what for Black constituents is the proper role of the elected representative?

The American National Election Study would include in its survey a question about the proper role of the representative, one that was replicated in the 1996 National Black Election Study. Black respondents in the 1996 survey were given the following instructions: "Here is a list of some activities that occupy Representatives as part of their job. We want to know which of the following three activities you think is the most important: (1) helping people in the district who have personal problems with the government; (2) working in Congress on bills concerning national issues; or (3) making sure the state/district gets its fair share of government money and project." Most Blacks, nearly half (47 percent), felt that legislators should be bringing the money back home to the district or state. Only 20 percent felt that legislators should have a national focus. The remaining 33 percent felt that legislators should be engaged in constituent service. When asked which of the remaining two activities is the next most important part of the representative's job, relatively few chose working on national bills. Three-quarters of the respondents felt the two local responsibilities, helping the district or the constituent, was second-most important.

The survey findings stand at odds with the stated mission of the CBC. Johnson and Secret (1996) interviewed twelve African American Housemembers and found that while they expressed a strong commitment to their districts, they also reported having a commitment to represent Blacks nationwide.

Further multivariate analysis reveals important social divisions in the Black community over the preferred focus of the elected representative. Table 6.4 displays these findings. First, the race of the respondent's representative did not affect Blacks' response to this question. Nor did the race consciousness of the respondent have any impact. In other words, being represented by Blacks or having racial solidarity with Black representatives did not make Blacks more likely to support a national focus over a district or constituency focus. Second, only those having some college experience or college degrees felt that representatives should primary work on bills that concerned the nation. In fact, this same group—

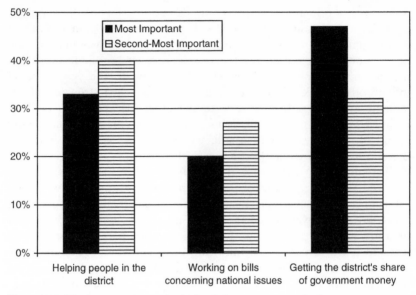

Figure 6.1. Black perceptions of which of three activities of representatives most and second-most important. (Total number of responses: 1,154.) *Source*: 1996 NBES.

the college educated—felt more strongly that representatives should not be overly preoccupied with pork barrel legislation or with procuring federal dollars for the district and state.

Third, the respondent's family income also affected Black responses to this item in a predictable way. The Black poor were more likely to favor legislators working on solving the problems of their constituents than the Black affluent. At the same time, the high-income Blacks were more likely than their low-income counterparts to favor legislators working on bringing home federal dollars. Each group presumably sees these contrasting activities as more being beneficial to their economic condition. The affluent might benefit from the projects and dollars that legislators can bring to the district and state. In the Mike Espy case, they might be the owners of the catfish farm that Espy personally helped in expanding its market share. The poor might need aid in securing government benefits or other such programs designed to assist them or help on legal matters. Swain found a great deal of variation in how the casework of members of Congress in her study was performed, reporting that "[s]ome black members (and a few whites) run their offices like social welfare agencies. Some become actively involved in legal matters and will even write to parole boards; others steer clear of such

TABLE 6.4

Multivariate Analysis of Representative's Most Important Activity —
Constituency Service, National Bills, or Money for District

	Constituent Service		National Bills		Money for District	
	b	SE	b	SE	b	SE
Constant	.516**	.086	.133	.075	.351**	.092
Education	−.001	.011	.023*	.009	−.016	.011
Age	−.003*	.001	−.001	.001	.004**	.001
Sex	.016	.032	−.007	.028	−.009	.034
Rep.'s Race	−.039	.032	−.016	.027	.056	.033
Party ID	.001	.011	−.003	.009	.002	.012
Race ID	.006	.014	.008	.012	−.015	.015
Income	−.013*	.006	.003	.006	.009	.007
N	956		956		956	
R-squared	.02		.01		.02	

Source: 1996 NBES.
*Statistically significant at .05.
**Statistically significant at .01.

matters" (1993, 219). This became a basis of complaint for some of the Black representatives and their staffs, Swain found. Some complained directly to her as her quotes make clear: " 'Black constituents are difficult to help because they wait until the eleventh hour. They appear at the office shortly before an eviction or job loss.' 'Black constituents are so demanding. They want us to turn over the world in a minute, and then they wonder what took us so long' " (1993, 219).

Lastly, the impact of age mirrored that of income. Like the affluent, the elderly felt that serving constituents was less vital than bringing money back home to the district. Older Blacks presumably wanted their representatives in Washington to focus on the economic conditions in the community, and less on their personal needs.

CONCLUSION

The question of whether race matters to Blacks in terms of their political representation in Washington turns critically on how political representation is defined. Political scientist V. O. Key Jr. famously once described public opinion as the invisible, third person (or phantom) in the Christian Trinity, the Holy Ghost. If public opinion can be likened to the Holy Ghost, then political representation is the Holy Grail, the famous and fabled chalice used by Christ at the Last Supper and hotly sought after in the medieval period and since. Representation, as the book makes plain, is as elusive as the concept of power. The definition I provide covers representation most broadly as everything that the elected representatives do in their formal capacity to address the needs and concerns of their constituents. Citizens are represented when their needs and concerns are being addressed and met. The problem is that how do voters keep track of "everything"? Washington is a maze of events and issues that no single person could ever credibly follow. Which of the many things that legislators do are most pertinent to constituents? What do constituents grab on to?

Previous scholarship has shown that with respect to the congressional vote, party matters to the voters. Voters as a rule support candidates belonging to their own party. The lawmaker's political ideology affects the vote but empirically this has been shown mostly in the aggregate. Ideologically extreme candidates, apart from party, are punished at the polls (Erikson and Wright 2001). Constituency service and legislative activity, such as bill sponsorship, however, do not directly affect the vote. This presents a puzzle since members devote so much time and many resources on such activities. If voters don't reward their representatives for service, why work so hard on these things? Discussing this problem, Morris Fiorina and Doug Rivers (1989) think that the empirical work on the impact of service and legislative work is flawed, that the legislator's service and lawmaking efforts work through the voters' perceptions of their representatives. Thus, they argue, direct efforts of service on the congressional vote are hard to establish because incumbents rely on their reputation for service, which may be presently strong or weak. "Those who are weakest," they write, "devote the most effort to it; those who already have established a reputation for constituency service can afford to allocate their resources and efforts in other areas" (1991, 43).

Americans don't know that much about their representatives in Washington, and yet a large majority of Americans express satisfaction with the person who represents them in the House of Representatives. Blacks are no exception here; most Blacks approve of their representative's performance in office. Of the many factors that explain Blacks' satisfaction with their representative's job is race. Blacks were more likely to give high marks to House members when that member was Black than White. Political party, as one might expect, was important as well. Blacks expressed greater satisfaction when represented by someone from their own party. The effect of descriptive representation, however, was equal and most times greater than the impact of political party for these evaluation measures. Ideology and competency measured by seniority, chairmanship, and such, were not statistically related to evaluation measures. This is not to conclude that the legislator's ideology or voting behavior doesn't matter. No doubt it does, but its impact may be indirect, mediated through party and race, perhaps. While chairmanships do enhance the legislator's ability to get things done in a system that works slowly and incrementally, constituents do not find that this benefits them directly.

Why are Blacks more satisfied with their political representation in Washington when their representatives are Black? Members of Congress are elected to represent the 600,000 or so people in their districts, districts that are diverse and complex. Blacks are simply delighted when their representative turns out to be Black, because they feel Black representatives are going to be more representative of their interests. This could be a mistake. A liberal Black in J. C. Watts's district in Oklahoma would not be well represented on policy matters by this conservative Black Republican. In the end, although I've defined representation broadly as everything the legislator does in Washington, it may be that representation from the vantage point of the voter is simply "being like me" on two salient dimensions: race and party. For voters, trying to determine if the legislator is "like them" on other dimensions, and judging the legislator's competency, is too difficult. Also, trying to determine their competency is not as emotionally satisfying as figuring out how much the legislator and constituent are alike.

Being descriptively represented in Washington on the basis of race does not have any impact on what Blacks think of members more generally. In chapter 8, I determine whether descriptive representation is related to the attitudes Blacks have about Congress and about term limits.

Most Blacks think that members of Congress should be working for the district, not the constituent and not the nation more broadly. This view stands at odds with the CBC's mission to represent Blacks nationally. College-educated Blacks were most likely to endorse the CBC mission in this study. The view that members of Congress should be working on behalf of their districts fits with the rationale behind having geographically based single-member districts as opposed to a proportional-representation system. While it seems that the pro-district view might be stronger in racially homogeneous districts that have elected Blacks, it was not.

Race in the end embodies value and importance to Blacks because Black members, as chapters 4 and 5 establish, are racially distinctive in how they represent their constituents. But race may also be valued by Black constituents in part because of the way in which the electoral system works. Single-member geographically based districts encourage the symbolic promotion of groups both within and outside of these districts, as shown in chapter 5. Pure policy representation could be achieved under a proportional-representation, parliamentary system that encourages strict party discipline and eliminates localism. That race could very well be less relevant in the political representation of citizens under a different political system is a matter I discuss at length in the book's conclusion.

CHAPTER 7

Descriptive Representation and Black Political Empowerment

IN PAST CONGRESSIONAL STUDIES literature, political representation is generally understood as instrumental. Political theorist Nancy Schwartz (1988) strongly criticizes this view of representation because, among other things, it ignores the "transformative" role of politics. Citizens are transformed, that is, knitted into the polity as they take part in democratic politics. Schwartz formally defines representation as "the standing and acting for an objective entity—a constituency of citizens—which is constantly in the process of becoming itself" (143). The goal of the elected representative is not simply to convey the majority sentiment, but also to help bring constituents into the process and to unite them into a coherent political whole. Ultimately she sides with Edmund Burke, who felt quite passionately that representatives should lead their constituents and not always act in favor of the district's interests but those of the entire country. A self-described political communitarian, Schwartz's definition of representation is also rooted in a republican view, in which Americans are not simply ruthless individualists, as liberal theorists depict them, but an organic whole, a community who in the ideal form are collectively engaged in the pursuit of the common good (Monroe 1990).

Republicanism presents a problem to African Americans since their race precluded them from membership in the community as it was founded. This nation, after all, was so very long believed to be as Rogers Smith writes, "a white nation, a Protestant nation, a nation in which true Americans were native-born men with Anglo-Saxon ancestors" (1997, 3). Blacks were formally excluded from membership in the republic, and, once brought in as citizens, most were denied the right to participation in civic republicanism until 1965. Blacks since have become incorporated into the political process (Browning, Marshall, and Tabb 1984; R. C. Smith 1981; Tate 1994). Their incorporation—or empowerment as some have called it—has led some voting behavior scholars to see if Blacks have become more politically involved as a result. Larry Bobo and Frank Gilliam (1990), in a seminal article, wrote, "Blacks in high empowerment areas should feel more trusting of government, express higher levels of efficacy, and become more knowledgeable about politics than Blacks in low empowerment areas." They contend that Black citizens, perhaps believing the system to be more responsive to their needs and interests when Blacks hold positions of power in government, become more politically active when represented by Blacks. Black elected officials represent a potent symbol of Blacks' inclusion in the polity, inspiring more Blacks to take part in it.

It may also be that Black officeholders are more than symbols that draw Blacks in. Rather, Black elected officials change the political environment in concrete ways that in turn lead Blacks to participate more. Blacks are brought into politics by these elected officials, who consider them their "primary constituency," to use Richard Fenno's (1978) words, representing their strongest supporters. Candidates, along with parties and interest groups, work to motivate their supporters to go to the polls. Their role in promoting political participation, as Rosenstone and Hansen (1993) show, significantly outweighs the impact of trust as a mobilizing agent. Recent work by Claudine Gay (2001) also establishes that Black voter participation increases in some (but not all) House districts represented by Blacks. In general, the race of the congressional incumbent has no large and consistent effect on Black voter turnout. At the same time, Gay found that in districts represented by Blacks, White voter participation universally decreases. It may be that Whites are not less politically efficacious as much as they are less central to the re-election activities of the Black House incumbent in majority-minority districts.

This chapter explores the behavioral impact of descriptive representation. Does being represented in Washington by a Black member empower Blacks — that is, make them more knowledgeable, deepen their political interest, and encourage them to become more politically active?

POLITICAL KNOWLEDGE, CAMPAIGN INTEREST,
AND POLITICAL PARTICIPATION

As ample scholarship has shown, political knowledge among the American public is extremely low. Blacks are no exception in this regard. As shown in table 7.1 only 14 percent knew the name of their representative in the House, although 73 percent recognized their representative's name and could evaluate him or her. Nearly half or 42 percent correctly identified the political party of their representative, and nearly two-thirds of the Black sample knew their representative's race. Blacks actually know more about their representative in the House than their representatives in the Senate. Table 7.2 indicates that while approximately the same percentage of the sample could name their senators (11 percent), only 28 percent correctly identified one or both of their parties.

TABLE 7.1
Blacks' Knowledge about House Member (Weighted percentages)

Percent in sample who could correctly:	Total Sample	Black Democrat	White Democrat	White Republican
Recall Member's Name	14%	23%	10%	8%**
Recognize Member's Name	73	84	68	66.5**
Identify Member's Party	42	57	37	33
Identify Member's Race	67	79	65	57**
Claimed to Remember Names of House Candidates who Ran in 1996 Elections	37	41	30	38

Note: N = 1,119.
**The differences in the groups' percentages are statistically significant (p < .01).
Source: 1996 NBES.

This number contrasts with the 42 percent of the Black respondents who knew the party of their House legislator.

Political knowledge goes up considerably when one takes into account the race of the House legislator. As shown in table 7.1, while only 14 percent of the sample could spontaneously name their representative in the House, nearly one quarter of the respondents in districts represented by Blacks could correctly recall their names. In contrast, only 10 percent of those represented by White legislators, and only 8 percent of those in districts held by White Republicans, knew their names. The same pattern holds for name recognition, and identification of the member's political party and race. Black House members have significantly higher name recognition among their Black constituents than do White members. Whereas 68 percent of those represented by White Democratic legislators recognized their name when presented with it, 84 percent of the respondents represented by Black legislators recognized their legislator's name. In the case of political party, the political party of the Black legislators was correctly identified by 57 percent of their constituents in contrast to one-third of the sample represented by White Republicans. About 80 percent of the sample knew the race of their Black legislators as opposed to 65 percent in the case of White Democrats. Being descriptively represented in Congress did not increase one's knowledge about House candidates running in the 1996 elections. Whereas Blacks represented by Blacks were somewhat more likely than Blacks represented by Whites to say that they knew the names of House candidates in the 1996 elections, this difference was not statistically significant.

While descriptively represented Blacks appear to be more familiar with the House members that represent them than nondescriptively rep-

TABLE 7.2

Blacks' Knowledge about U.S. Senators (Weighted Percentages)

Percent in sample who could correctly:	Total Sample	Black Democrat	White Democrat	White Republican
Recall Both Senators' Names	11%	12%	11%	9%
Recall One Senator's Name	13	13	11	14
Identify Both Senators' Party	8	8	9	8
Identify One Senator's Party	20	26	15.5	19*

Note: N = 1,119.

*The differences in the groups' percentages are statistically significant (p < .05).

Source: 1996 NBES.

resented Blacks, this does not translate into more knowledge about the elected officials who represent them in the U.S. Senate. Blacks in House districts represented by Blacks were no more likely than Blacks in districts held by Whites to know the political parties of their senators, for example, as shown in table 7.2. The single exception to this was in the case of correctly identifying at least one of the senators' political party. Twenty-six percent of Blacks in Black-led districts correctly identified one of their senator's political parties as opposed to 19 percent of Blacks in districts led by White Republicans.

Blacks expressed a great deal of interest in the 1996 election, and especially so in the presidential race. Although Clinton led his Republican opponent, Bob Dole, by a comfortable margin in the months leading up to the election, the vast majority of Blacks (79 percent) said that they were very much or somewhat interested in the 1996 campaigns (see table 7.3). Eighty-four percent said that they cared a "good deal" about who won the presidential election. Two questions asked in the postelection follow-up survey asked respondents how much of the news did they pay attention to during the campaign for president and the campaigns for election to Congress. Vastly more Blacks expressed interest in news pertaining to the presidential campaign than congressional races. Whereas only 22 percent said that they paid very little or no attention to the news about the campaign for president, almost half, or 45 percent, expressed little to no interest in the news about the House campaigns.

In three of the four interest measures, the race of the House legislator of the respondent had a significant impact. Blacks represented by Black Democrats in the sample were significantly more likely to express great interest in the 1996 campaigns and the news coverage in the presidential race. They were also more likely to care a great deal about who won the presidency. Ironically, while descriptive representation signifi-

TABLE 7.3
Political Interest Measures among Blacks

	Total Sample	Black Democrat	White Democrat	White Republican
"Would you say that you are very much interested, somewhat interested, or not much interested in the political campaigns this year?"				
Very much interested	30%	37%	29%	25%**
Somewhat interested	49	43	41.5	49
Not at all interested	25	21	30	26
"Would you say that you personally care a good deal about who wins the presidential election this fall, or that you don't care very much who wins?"				
Care a good deal	84	90	81	81**
Don't care very much	16	10	19	19
"How much attention did you pay to the national news shows about the campaign for president?"				
A great deal	23	28	17.5	21*
Quite a bit	37.5	39	37	37
Very little	37	30	44	38
None	3	2.5	2	4
"How much attention did you pay to the news about the campaigns for elections to Congress—that is the House of Representatives?"				
A great deal	45	39	49	49
Quite a bit	30	32	29.5	28
Very little	12	13	12	12
None	13	17	9	12

Note: The differences between groups' percentages are statistically different (**p < .01; *p < .05).
Source: 1996 NBES.

TABLE 7.4
Self-Reported Voting Participation among Blacks in the 1994 and 1996 House Elections

	Sample	Black Democrat	White Democrat	White Republican
*Voted for a House Candidate in 1996	60%	65%	52.5%	60%*
Remembered Voting in the Election for the U.S. House of Representatives in 1994	45	52	40	43*

Note: Experimental question wording was used in 1996 post-election survey. Half of the sample was read the names of candidates and asked if they had voted for one of them following the standard ANES version; the other half was asked simply if they had voted for a candidate for Congress. The latter version yielded a lower estimate of voter participation in House elections.
*p < .01, chi-square test.
Source: 1996 NBES.

cantly boosted interest among Blacks in the 1996 election and the presidential race, it did not increase their interest in the campaigns for election to the U.S. House of Representatives. Here, where 25 percent of Blacks represented by Black Democrats reported in the aftermath of the 1996 elections of having had very little to no interest in the news coverage of the House campaigns, 24 percent of Blacks represented by White Republicans expressed this view as well.

In the preelection survey, Blacks were asked if they had voted in the 1994 midterm House elections, and 45 percent of the sample reported voting. In the postelection reinterview, respondents were asked if they had voted in the 1996 national elections, and specifically in the House election. Sixty percent reported voting for a candidate for Congress. These figures, shown in table 7.4, are exceptionally high. About half of the American public turned out to vote in the 1996 presidential election. Black participation was slightly less than that. Political participation in midterm elections was lower, with about 40 percent of the eligible electorate casting votes.

There is a strong correlation between descriptive representation and turnout in congressional elections. Blacks represented by Blacks were about 10 percentage points more likely to report having voted in contrast to Blacks represented by Whites in Congress (see table 7.4). The preliminary results lend considerable support to the Black empowerment thesis developed by Bobo and Gilliam (1990). Blacks represented by Blacks in Congress are considerably more knowledgeable, more interested, and more active than Blacks represented by Whites.

Regression Analysis of Knowledge, Political Interest, Efficacy, and Voting

Scales of the knowledge, interest, and voter participation measures were created and analyzed as dependent measures in regression models. Because descriptive representation competes with the impact of political party, in addition to the member's race, the political party of the House legislator was matched to the respondent's and included in the analysis. It is presumed that being presented in Congress by one's own political party is as transformative and affirming as being descriptively represented on the dimension of race.

Beyond the member's political party and race, two other variables pertaining to the House member were incorporated into some of the models. Because constituents may be more familiar with senior members of Congress as opposed to newcomers, seniority was included in the regression analysis of respondents' knowledge about House members. In addition, because competitive races have been shown to increase name recognition, political interest, and higher levels of voter participation (Patterson and Caldeira 1983; E. Smith 1989), margin of victory was considered as well in two of the regression models.

A number of key demographic variables were introduced in the regression analysis as controls. Previous research has established that education is importantly connected to both political knowledge (E. Smith 1989) and to political participation (Verba and Nie 1972; Wolfinger and Rosenstone 1980; Rosenstone and Hansen 1993; Verba, Schlozman, and Brady 1995). Education increases one's appetite in politics as well as one's ability to manage the abstract concepts involved in following politics. Family income is included in the analysis as well. As Verba, Schlozman, and Brady establish in their important work, political participation is costly in terms of both time and money. Affluent Americans have more time and money to invest in politics. Eric Smith (1989) hypothesizes that like education, affluence expands one's opportunity to be socialized to express greater interest in politics. Age and gender are also related to political participation. Except for the very old and infirm, older Americans are more likely than the young to vote and take part in politics. Recent analysis found gender not to be strongly tied to political participation, yet it was included in this analysis. Length of residency in the community will increase one's familiarity with members of Congress, the vast majority of whom, after all, are reelected every two and six years. Residency may boost one's interest in politics as well.

TABLE 7.5

The Effect of Descriptive Representation on Respondents' Knowledge, Interest, and Voting Participation (OLS Estimates)

Independent variable	R's Knowledge about House Member		R's Knowledge about U.S. Senators	
	b	Sig. Level	b	Sig. Level
Constant	.011	.955	−1.54	.000
Member's Race (Black)	.534	.000	.134	.146
Party Match	.253	.003	−.004	.963
Member's Seniority	.003	.470	N/A	N/A
Member's Margin of Victory	−.411	.005	N/A	N/A
R's Gender (Male)	.139	.071	.485	.000
R's Education	.139	.000	.249	.000
R's Age	.015	.000	.019	.000
R's Residency	.006	.000	.002	.092
R's Race Identification	−.015	.658	.073	.047
R's Family Income	.064	.000	.047	.005
R's Region (South)	−.142	.066	−.163	.045
N	946		966	
Adjusted R-squared	.194		.193	

Source: 1996 NBES.

There may also be regional differences in Black political participation, interest, and knowledge. Finally, race identification, which has been shown to increase Blacks' rates of political participation (Tate 1994) was included in the analysis. Strong race identifiers may also express more interest in the campaign as Gurin, Hatchett, and Jackson (1989) found. Given its role in Black political participation, it is possible that race identification might increase one's ability to recognize or recall names of members of Congress.

The results of the regression analysis are shown in tables 7.5 and 7.6. The columns present the unstandardized regression coefficients (b) and the probability levels attached to the t-statistics for each coefficient. Black empowerment in the district was shown only to increase voter knowledge about the House member. It was not significantly related to knowledge about the respondent's U.S. Senators. It had no impact on campaign interest, the respondent's level of political efficacy, or their rate of participation in the past two congressional elections. In contrast, political party had a wider impact on Black political attitudes and behavior. Blacks represented in Congress by members of their own party

TABLE 7.6
The Impact of Descriptive Representation on Respondents' Campaign Interest,
Political Efficacy, and Voting Participation (OLS Estimates)

	R's Campaign Interest (2–10)		R's Political Efficacy (1–5)		R's Voting Participation (0– 2)	
	b	Sig. Level	b	Sig. Level	b	Sig. Level
Independent variable						
Constant	3.975	.000	2.641	.000	−.712	.000
Member's Race (Black)	−.087	.637	.096	.386	.065	.326
Party Match	.745	.000	.077	.487	.113	.078
Member's Margin of Victory	.849	.004	N/A		.051	.626
R's Gender (Male)	.111	.484	.013	.900	−.041	.479
R's Education	.192	.000	.017	.599	.132	.000
R's Age	.035	.000	−.005	.131	.017	.000
R's Residency	−.002	.446	−.001	.416	.003	.000
R's Race Identification	.177	.012	.082	.071	.078	.003
R's Family Income	.049	.129	.050	.015	.027	.020
R's Region (South)	.150	.335	.168	.088	.138	.015
N	946		692		697	
Adjusted R-squared	.096		.017		.213	

Note: The low and high values of the dependent variables are shown in parentheses.
Source: 1996 NBES.

were more likely to know who their representatives were, and they were more likely to express more interest in the campaign. The coefficient for descriptive representation in the case of knowledge about the House member was still twice that of the coefficient for the party match variable, nevertheless.

As one might expect, education, age, and residency turned out to be the most important determinants of Blacks' level of knowledge about their legislators, voter participation, and to a lesser extent, political interest. Predictably, better-educated Blacks were the most knowledgeable. College-educated Blacks were also more likely than those having only a high school education to express strong interest in the 1996 political campaigns and to vote. Family income was also found to correspond to these measures in a similar fashion. Affluent Blacks knew more about their representatives in Washington than poor Blacks. High-income Blacks were more likely to report feeling politically effective and to have voted in the 1994 and 1996 elections.

Older Blacks, having witnessed politics for a longer period of time, were more likely to know who their representatives were in Washington, express strong interest in the campaign, and vote. Age, however, was unrelated to political efficacy. The longer one lived in the community, the more one knew about one's representative in Congress and the more likely one was to have voted. Length of residency in the community was statistically unrelated to political interest and to political efficacy.

As shown in previous work (Gurin, Hatchett, and Jackson 1989; Tate 1994), race identification was significantly related to Black political interest and to voter participation in congressional elections. Race identification, however, was unrelated to political knowledge and to political efficacy. Being strongly race-committed does not increase Blacks' awareness of who is representing them in Washington; nor does it promote a sense of political effectiveness. Finally, Black Southerners were generally less knowledgeable than Blacks residing in other parts of the country. Black Southerners were also less likely to report feeling efficacious in the political process and less likely to report having voted in the past two elections.

The findings overall establish that except for political knowledge, there is no empowerment effect associated with being represented by a person of one's own race in the U.S. House of Representatives.

Conclusion

While Blacks descriptively represented in Congress knew significantly more about their representatives in Washington than Blacks represented by Whites, Asians, or Latinos, descriptive representation was not found to be politically empowering. Blacks represented by Blacks were not significantly more interested in political campaigns, efficacious, or more likely to vote than Blacks represented by Whites or other racial groups. The fact that being represented by one's own political party was empowering for Blacks is a new finding that underscores the failure of Black officeholding, at least at the congressional level, to empower Blacks. There are two compelling reasons why my study failed to find an empowering effect for descriptive representation.

First, it is possible that the behavioral effect of Black empowerment is greatest at the local level of government. Blacks represented in local governments, in towns and cities having Black mayors, may feel more efficacious and be more participatory than Blacks in communities lacking strong levels of Black officeholding. Related to this is the possibility that Black leadership in executive offices may be more empowering than leadership in legislative offices (Gay 2001). Jesse Jackson's presidential bids did inspire Blacks to mobilize and turn out to vote, at least in the 1984 presidential election (Tate 1994).

Second, the behavioral impact of descriptive representation as an empowering agent may be temporary and wear off once the Black officeholder secures his or her electoral base. In a longitudinal analysis of election data from twenty-six major American cities, David Lublin and Katherine Tate (1995) found that Black office-seeking generally mobilizes urban voters. Urban voters turn out at significantly higher rates when Black candidates compete for the mayor's seat. Contrary to conventional wisdom, turnout for first-time Black office seekers was not significantly higher than turnout in elections involving Black candidates generally. Turnout, however, was about 4 percent less in races involving incumbent Black mayoral office seekers. Since the vast majority of incumbent House legislators that seek reelection win, congressional candidates' reelection campaigns may no longer inspire voters to participate.

CHAPTER 8

Descriptive Representation and Trust in Government

CHAPTER 6 ESTABLISHES that Blacks' evaluations of their representatives in Washington are generally high, but this is not the case with respect to their opinion of the U.S. Congress as a whole. In the 1996 NBES, a full 70 percent disapproved of the way that Congress was handling its job. Blacks are no exception here, but quintessentially American in loving individual members of Congress and hating Congress in general. And like most Americans, a large Black majority (72 percent) also favors imposing term limits on Washington legislators. Those advancing the cause of the descriptive representation of Blacks in government have frequently claimed that the absence of Blacks in government undermines Blacks' trust in government and faith in political system. However, the fact that a majority of Blacks continues to distrust government even as the numbers of Blacks elected to Congress have increased dramatically over the past three decades stands at odds with such claims. In this chapter, I determine whether there is a direct link between the descriptive representation of Blacks in Washington and their attitudes toward government, and notably, Congress.

RACIAL DIFFERENCES IN ATTITUDES TOWARD CONGRESS AND LEVELS OF POLITICAL TRUST

Over-time data from the American National Election Studies (ANES) reveal that racial differences in citizens' approval ratings of Congress are mixed, with Blacks and Whites alternating across some of the years as the group expressing the highest levels of approval or disapproval. The question, "Do you approve or disapprove of the way the U.S. Congress has been handling its job?" appeared in the 1980 ANES and has been asked since. Still, on the whole, Blacks tended to give Congress slightly higher ratings than Whites and other groups over the sixteen-year period, as shown in figure 8.1. In 1980 and again in 1994, Black approval ratings of Congress were significantly higher than that of other racial groups by margins of 15 and 26 percent. Only in two surveys, 1982 and 1984, were Blacks more disapproving of Congress than were Whites and other groups by margins approximating 10 percent. In 1996

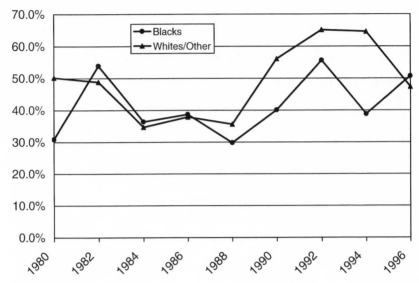

Figure 8.1. Percentage by race of those approving of the way Congress has handled its job, 1980–2000. *Source*: 1980–2000 ANES.

both groups were approximately split between approval and disapproval of the U.S. Congress.

John R. Hibbing and Elizabeth Theiss-Morse's (1995) explanation for why Congress as a political institution systematically lags behind other institutions in the public's eye establishes a link between knowledge, interest, political involvement, and approval. Simply put, the more one knows about Congress, the less impressed one is, while the less one knows, the more favorable one is toward Congress. This relationship between knowledge and approval for Congress is complicated by other attitudinal factors, of course. Those surveyed who felt that Congress was run by special interests, for example, expressed the most consistently negative attitudes toward Congress. Hibbing and Theiss-Morse conclude that the public contempt for the legislative process in Washington is the underlying cause of the public's negative attitude toward Congress as an institution. As much as many Americans dislike parties even though they remain highly partisan, they are also paradoxical in that they staunchly support democratic processes while condemning such processes in action. According to Hibbing and Theiss-Morse, the "media's eagerness to report any and all events makes it possible for citizens to view democratic processes with all blemishes revealed . . . features [that are] extremely unpopular with the vast majority of citizens, who yearn for simple government and visibly equitable representation" (159).

Blacks in those surveys had slightly less negative views of Congress than did Whites. This could be based on two factors. First, until 1995, the House of Representatives had a Democratic majority. Since most Blacks are Democrats, this could explain the higher ratings of Congress by their racial group. Research by Hibbing and Theiss-Morse (1995), among others, establishes that Republicans are less approving of Congress, which for the past forty years until the 1994 elections, was dominated by Democrats. At the same time, as discussed in chapter 7, Blacks are generally less knowledgeable about congressional politics than are Whites, in almost every instance. In 1994, for example, more than three-quarters (76 percent) of Whites were correct in identifying Democrats as the majority in the House of Representatives in 1993 compared to only about one-half or 54 percent of Blacks. More Whites than Blacks knew that Thomas Foley was Speaker of the House in 1993 and that the Democrats were the Senate majority in 1993. It turns out that politically knowledgeable and involved Americans tend to be the most critical of Congress. Blacks may be somewhat more approving of Congress because of their lower levels of political information. Blacks, however, were just as likely as Whites to favor twelve-year term limits for members of Congress. Three-quarters of Blacks and 79 percent of Whites endorsed term limits, while roughly only 20 percent of Blacks opposed it.

Dislike of Congress is the logical extension of the public's general distrust of government. Since the 1970s, trust in government and confidence in its ability to "do what is right" has sharply fallen off. In 1996 there was not a significant difference in trust in government between Blacks and Whites. However, this was not always the case. Blacks generally have expressed lower levels of trust in government than Whites since the question first appeared in the 1958 American National Election. When asked "How much of the time do you think you can trust the government in Washington to do what is right—just about always, most of the time, or only some of the time?" roughly 10 to 20 percent fewer Blacks than Whites felt that government could be trusted "most of the time." The results are shown in figure 8.2. While in a few years such as 1964 and 1968 the racial gap narrows significantly, it expands again during the 1970s. It is only in 1990 that we see an emerging trend suggesting that Blacks are becoming no more distrustful of government than are Whites. This trend of decreasing racial differences in political trust is mostly based on the continued decrease in the ranks of Whites expressing trust, not a rise in the percentage of Blacks expressing greater trust.

Much research and debate has focused on the exact meaning of this dramatic decline in trust of government in the United States, which followed the great wave of civil rights protest, the Vietnam War, and Presi-

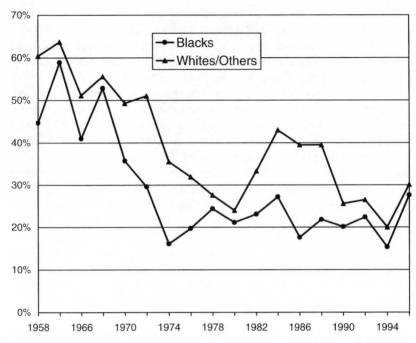

Figure 8.2. Percentage by race of those trusting government "most of the time," 1958–96. *Source:* 1958–96 ANES.

dent Nixon's resignation. On the one side, there is the view that the great loss of faith in government signaled deep alienation among the American people and represented a political crisis (Miller 1974). On the other hand, writes Jack Citrin (1974), the decline in trust was a logical reaction to the political turbulence of the 1960s and 1970s akin to disgruntled baseball fans shouting "Kill the umpire." This debate is rooted in David Easton's (1965) seminal distinction between two forms of political trust, diffuse and specific. Political support that is diffuse is an evaluation of the political system as a whole and its political community, while specific support is based on citizens' evaluations of political actors and their performance. Dissatisfaction with the political authorities, and even key authoritative institutions, such as Congress, is not as serious as a widespread loss of confidence in the regime.

In the end, public opinion researchers grappling with this question reject a "crisis in democracy" perspective, even as they advocate reforms to restore the public's faith in government. The crisis perspective is rejected because the public still exhibits strong faith in the democratic process. Decades of public surveys find no great loss of confidence in the nation. Data reported by Roper analysts Everett Carll Ladd and Karlyn H. Bowman (1998), for example, show that the overwhelming majority (approximately 90 percent) of Americans would not want to move and settle in another country, even if they were "free to do so." In a 1997 survey, 83 percent agreed with the statement that the "United States is the greatest nation on earth." People, however, are fundamentally dissatisfied with the way government is actually run.

Another reason why the alarmist perspective is rejected is that dissatisfaction with the performance of government is not related to other forms of mass participation. Voter turnout has declined over the last forty years, but again, this decline is not interpreted as a rejection of the democratic process. As reported in Ladd and Bowman (1998), 87 to 89 percent of Americans surveyed think that government can have a positive impact on people's lives (91). When asked to rate the job that the federal government does in running its programs, more than half (53 percent) gave the government "only fair" marks as opposed to 2 percent who said "excellent." Another 23 percent said "good," while 21 percent said "poor."

Trust in government has declined not only because of the negative characterization of government in the media and because many politicians campaign against government and as outsiders to Washington, but because the scope of the problems that Washington must "solve" has multiplied. Clearly the federal government has expanded in size because its political agenda has expanded.

All in all, low ratings of Congress, support for term limits, and the absence of great trust in the political system are not symptoms of widespread alienation or frustration with American democracy. Political trust, according to William Gamson (1968), is "the probability . . . that the political system (or some part of it) will produce preferred outcomes even if left untended" (54). Americans believes in the integrity of the democratic process, but still accord little trust to their government. The survey data show that Blacks in the 1950s and 1960s were less trusting of government than Whites were as a group, and no doubt this racial difference existed because of these groups' different political experiences. Today, however, both groups express little trust in government, in spite of Blacks' ability to elect more Blacks to Congress.

THE LINKS AMONG BLACK REPRESENTATION, ATTITUDES TOWARD CONGRESS, AND TRUST IN GOVERNMENT

In a preliminary analysis (not shown here), being descriptively represented in Washington was unrelated to Blacks' attitudes toward Congress, opinion toward term limits, and their feelings of political trust.

TABLE 8.1
The Effect of Descriptive Representation on Respondents' Approval Rating of Congress and Support for Term Limits (OLS Estimates)

	R's Approval Rating of Congress (1–5)		R's Level of Trust in Government (1–4)		R's Level of Political Efficacy (1–5)	
	b	Sig. Level	b	Sig. Level	b	Sig. Level
Independent variable						
Constant	2.061	.000	1.963	.000	2.723	.000
Sex (male)	−.115	.356	.011	.801	.056	.600
Education	−.015	.709	−.031	.033	.029	.397
Income	−.023	.361	.005	.602	.039	.073
Party identification (Rep-Dem)	.033	.464	.013	.427	−.016	.666
Ideology (Con-Lib)	−.041	.181	−.020	.077	−.033	.207
Knowledge Scale	−.076	.067	−.005	.745	.050	.154
Efficacy	.109	.021	.080	.000		
Media Use	−.021	.473	.024	.025	−.004	.875
Percent Congress is Black	.023	.000	.005	.002	.005	.195
Represented by Black	.085	.502	.008	.854	−.010	.928
N	587		630		631	
Adjusted R-squared	.073		.061		.007	

Note: The low and high values of the dependent variables are shown in parentheses.
Source: 1996 NBES.

Thus while Blacks trust Black representatives to be more responsive to their political needs than White members, this trust does not translate into expressing greater confidence in government always to do what is right.

But when the measure of how well Blacks were descriptively represented in Congress were added to the regression models, a different picture emerged. The multivariate analysis results are shown in table 8.1. None of the predictor variables turned out to be statistically related to Black support for term limits, and thus, its results are not shown. In the survey, however, Black respondents were asked what percent of the members of Congress do they think is Black? Blacks who had high estimations of Black representation in Congress were significantly less critical of Congress and more trusting of government. At the same time, Blacks represented by Blacks in Congress were no more approving of Congress or trusting.

While Hibbing and Theiss-Morse (1995) found that income, sex, party identification, and external political efficacy were important determinants of public attitudes toward Congress, only political efficacy was statistically related to Black approval or disapproval ratings. Contrary to what one might expect, politically knowledgeable Blacks, those who could identify their senators and representatives in Washington by name, party, or race, did not have significantly more negative opinions of Congress than less knowledgeable Blacks. Blacks who reported spending a lot of time reading the newspaper and watching television were also no more likely than low media users to disapprove of Congress.

More variables turned out to predict Blacks' level of political trust. College-educated Blacks and self-described political conservatives expressed significantly lower levels of political trust than Black high-school graduates and self-identified liberals. As in the case of attitudes toward Congress, politically efficacious Blacks were more trusting than Blacks who reported low levels of efficacy. High media users were also more trusting of government than lower media users.

In the end, however, while being descriptively represented in Congress did not improve Blacks' attitudes toward Congress or levels of political trust, believing Blacks to be numerically well represented there did. How well do Blacks feel represented in Congress? When asked directly, following the battery of questions pertaining to their attitudes toward the representatives in Washington, what percentage of representatives in Congress is Black, the average response was 13 percent. This is more than the 7 percent that Blacks currently make up, but not grossly in error. The standard deviation of the average guess to this question was 13 percent, which means that two-thirds of the sample estimated the percentage of Blacks in Congress to be somewhere between zero and slightly over one-quarter! Figure 8.3 presents the distribution of Blacks' estimates of the percentage of Congress that is Black.

Compounding this problem is the respondents' estimation of what percentage of the country is Black, which was asked just prior to the question of what percentage of Congress is Black. Whereas the average guess of 13 percent for Congress was only 6 percentage points higher than the truth, Black estimations of their percentage in the population were significantly higher than the truth. The average response to the question "What percent of the United States is Black" was 40 percent. The 1990 U.S. Census estimates the Black U.S. population to be 12 percent. The standard deviation for this measure was 22 percent, so that two-thirds of the sample estimated the Black U.S. population to be somewhere between 18 percent and 62 percent. Whereas no one estimated Congress to be 100 percent Black, some of the respondents guessed that the U.S. population is 70, 80, 90, or even 100 percent Black.

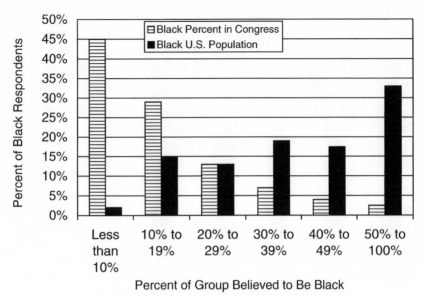

Figure 8.3. Blacks' estimations of what percentage of the U.S. Congress and the U.S. population is Black. *Source*: 1996 NBES.

The consequence of Blacks' grossly inflated views of their representation in the country is that most Blacks think that Blacks are more underrepresented in Washington as elected officials than they actually are. The scores range from 0 (zero) — indicating that regardless of their numbers in the population, no Black is presently serving in Congress — to 1.0, which means that regardless of their numbers in the population, a matching proportion of Blacks is elected to Congress. The average estimation of Black representation is far less than proportional. Based on the average guess for the proportion of the United States and the Congress that is Black, results indicate that one-third of the Black population is proportionately represented in Congress, while in reality the figure is closer to 60 percent. Most Blacks feel numerically very underrepresented in national government, and based on the estimates provided in the survey, more so than they actually are. This perception of underrepresentation in Congress is translated into greater disapproval of Congress and less trust of government among Blacks.

While Blacks' estimations of their proportion in Congress are on average not bad, their estimations of their proportion within the overall population are extremely inflated. To determine what type of Black respondent gave the highest estimates of the Black U.S. population, regression analysis was performed. The results are shown in table 8.2. As

TABLE 8.2

Regression Analysis of Black Estimations of the Percentage of the U.S. Population That Is Black

	R's Estimation of the U.S. Black Population (0–100%)	
	b	Sig. Level
Independent variable		
Constant	67.379	.000
Sex (male)	−8.768	.000
Education	−4.121	.000
Income	−.855	.002
Political knowledge scale	−1.475	.009
Media use	−.097	.774
Age	−.037	.450
South	2.905	.026
Represented by Black	5.080	.000
N	939	
Adjusted R-squared	.205	

Source: 1996 NBES.

one might expect, education was strongly related to these estimations of the Black population. Having a college degree resulted in significantly lower estimations of the size of U.S. population. High-income Blacks were also more likely to give better estimates than low-income Blacks. Black men also gave estimates were roughly 8 percent lower in contrast to those supplied by Black women. Southern Blacks gave more inflated estimates than those made by Blacks living outside of the South. Neither age nor media use impacted on the estimates Blacks gave. Finally, Blacks represented by Blacks in Washington gave estimates that were 5 percentage points higher than those given by Blacks represented by Whites.

CONCLUSION

Being descriptively represented in Congress had no bearing on whether Congress was doing a good job or not. Nor was descriptive representation related to support for political reform and trust in government more broadly. Still, Blacks who believed Blacks to be numerically strong in Congress had more positive views of Congress and greater trust than those Blacks who felt Blacks were numerically weak. Because, as Chapter 6 established, Blacks believe Black legislators are generally better representatives than are Whites, having more Blacks in Congress is logically going to translate into a "better" Congress. Still, Blacks who overestimated their proportion of the U.S. population may be less knowledgeable about government and therefore, under Hibbing and Theiss-Morse's model, less critical of Congress.

In the end, it is not clear that having more Blacks added to Congress would truly improve Blacks' evaluations of Congress's performance or truly raise their levels of trust in government. Descriptive representation, however, may still affect citizens' perceptions of the system's legitimacy and their commitment to the political system. More will be said about this in the next and final chapter.

V. Conclusion

CHAPTER 9

The Future of Black Faces in the U.S. Congress

> But we cannot deduce what is politically fair from abstract
> principles of political equality: we have to draw on empirical
> judgements of what is likely to happen as well as what seems
> in principle to be fair.
>
> — Anne Phillips, in *The Politics of Presence*

THIS BOOK BEGAN with a simple question: Do Blacks need to be descriptively represented in Congress to be fairly represented? Carol M. Swain
(1993) and Stephan Thernstrom and Abigail Thernstrom's (1997) contention that race doesn't matter is consistent with the opinion of most
congressional scholars who claim that the social characteristics of members have little bearing on their capacity to represent. Most gender
scholars reject this view, however. And now a new group of empirically
minded congressional scholars, notably Kenny J. Whitby (1998) and
David T. Canon (1999), finding that Black members of Congress are
more likely to push successfully for legislation that addresses the racial
concerns of Blacks, argue that Blacks need to be numerically part of
representative government if their group is to be fully represented. The
findings that I report in chapters 4 and 5 further corroborate and ex-
pand on the work of these scholars. Thus, while U.S. legislators are
capable of speaking for a "divergent rank" of social groups, the overwhelming empirical evidence indicates that with respect to Blacks, at
least, they normally don't. Black members in Congress have been the
most consistent spokespersons for and champions of Black interests. In
light of the unique features of the U.S. Congress whereby members advance national as well as particularistic concerns, for Blacks to be fully
represented, their interests must be understood as symbolic as well as
substantive.

I also substantiate the view that race matters in the political representation from the other side of the representative-legislator equation. Race
matters to Black constituents. All things being equal, Black constituents
believe that they are better represented in Congress when their representative is Black. Black constituents recognize that Black members strive
to represent the interests of Blacks more so than White members do.
They, therefore, credit Black members with doing more for them be-

cause of their race than legislators who represent them solely on the basis of their political party. Having shown through empirical means that race is related both in the behavior of legislators and in the opinions of their Black constituents, the question that I turn to in the last chapter of my book is appropriately normative. Race matters, but should it in a representative democracy? And should the government, either through the extension and enforcement of the Voting Rights Act or through electoral reform, see to it that Blacks and other minorities are descriptively represented? I base my answers to these questions on the empirical findings reported in this book. As the quote from political theorist Anne Phillips suggests, fair representation must be based, not only on our principles, but on what we know about the empirical or actual quality of political representation in the United States.

Mirror Representation: The Normative Debate

In a recently published article, Jane Mansbridge (1999) begins her case for the descriptive representation of women and minorities by noting, "Descriptive representation is not popular among normative theorists." Theorists opposed to descriptive representation assert that it does not guarantee substantive representation, which acts in the interest of the represented. Consequently, in their view, those advocating descriptive representation are guilty of "essentialism," falsely assuming that members of these groups have an essential identity that no others can represent. While a case for the political cohesiveness of Blacks can be empirically made, it is still often stretched too far. And, indeed, even scholars seeking ways to open the political process to more minority groups find it problematic when the focus becomes only that of electing more minority officeholders. Thus, Lani Guinier (1994) worries that the push for "numbers" has replaced the concern for ensuring that Black political interests are fully represented, and for this reason advocated proportional representation systems. In *The Boundaries of Blackness*, Cathy J. Cohen (1999) establishes how multiple, cross-cutting identities within the Black community, notably those of Black gays and lesbians, have not been equally reflected in the politics of Blacks but rather marginalized.

It is also essentialism that Stephan Thernstrom and Abigail Thernstrom (1997) object strongly to as well, but for quite another reason. The argument that Blacks can only be represented in government by Blacks, they contend, reinforces the social and political significance of racial group membership in society:

Racial classifications deliver the message that skin color matters—profoundly. They suggest that whites and blacks are not the same, and that race and ethnicity are the qualities that really matter. They imply that individuals are defined by blood — not by character, social class, religious sentiments, age, or education. By no demographic or other measures are African Americans truly a people apart. . . . And yet if both they and whites believe they are, it may well come true (492).

In the minds of critics, those pushing for the descriptive representation of Blacks and other social groups exaggerate the political distinctiveness of Blacks and therein contribute to the racial divide. It is this fear of "Balkinization of the races" that Associate Justice Sandra Day O'Connor in the 1993 Shaw ruling used to invalidate a North Carolina plan that had sent that state's first two Blacks to Congress since Reconstruction. Such reasoning suggests, in short, that advocating greater numerical representation for Blacks contributes rather than ameliorates the race problem in the United States.

A further criticism springs out of the republican view that government ought to consist of individuals with a higher level of talent and interest in politics than the average person. Rather than mirroring the public demographically, representatives belong to a "select" group of citizens. Logically, one should expect certain groups not to be ruling government, such as J. Roland Pennock's (1979) famous group of "morons." Members of the political and social elite — as opposed to the average individual — serving in government will in theory be more likely to produce the best public policies and laws even as they actively represent the will of the people. This was the dominant view, in fact, at the time of the nation's founding among federalists.

But, even if the talent pool is acknowledged to be broader than the groups presently reflected in government (and indeed, on this point of political equality there exists wide consensus, as Anne Phillips points out, although there is little agreement on the matter of social or economic equality [1995, 30]), it is not clear which groups ought to be affirmatively represented. Language minorities were added as groups protected under the Voting Rights Act in its 1975 extension. The basis for the inclusion of "language minorities" such as Latinos and Asian Americans, for example, was wholly unjustified according to Abigail Thernstrom (1987). For her, the history of Latinos and Asians in the United States is not at all comparable the history of state-sanctioned discrimination against Blacks. And no law exists to augment the numbers of women serving in elected government, although women are vastly numerically underrepresented in government.

Theorists who champion the cause of descriptive representation, such as Jane Mansbridge, Anne Phillips, Melissa Williams, and Iris Marion

Young, do often counter criticisms by presenting their own lists of costs to society imposed by the numerical underrepresentation of political minorities in government. The very first cost is to the deliberative function of a representative democracy. In a deliberative system, policies are discussed and debated among all segments of the society before the majority's opinion on the matter is determined. In this system, Mansbridge (1999) writes, "Although a representative need not have shared personally the experiences of the represented to facilitate communication and bring subtlety to a deliberation, the open-ended quality of deliberation gives communicative and informational advantages to representatives who are existentially closest to the issues."

It is not enough that a few minorities take part in deliberation, but their members must constitute a "critical mass" so that they become willing enough to enunciate minority positions. Minorities must also be interspersed across the wide array of committees and subcommittees and other levels of government. Descriptive representation advances the substantive representation of minorities such as Blacks through the deliberative function of democracy. Minority groups must be able to articulate and defend their own interests in a democracy (Williams 1998). Thus James Fishkin (1995) advocates the full and equal participation of all groups as a necessary component of his plan for deliberative democracy.

Mansbridge overturns the argument that by advancing the cause of descriptive representation society essentializes groups. The numerical underrepresentation of groups, she contends, is an underlying cause of essentialism in that token representatives are forced to represent all members despite their groups' internal differences. When more members of these underrepresented groups get elected, their groups' internal differences are exposed and a broader view of these groups can form. In this way, she writes,

> The appointment of Clarence Thomas to the Supreme Court of the United States may have served as a milestone in the evolution of the process in the Black community, as some African American organizations . . . opposed Thomas's nomination in spite of his descriptive characteristics. . . . The decision of many women's groups not to support all women candidates for election represented a similar milestone among U.S. feminists.

The accumulated empirical evidence fully supports Mansbridge's claims. As Canon (1999) and my work show, Black legislators are not a monolithic voting bloc in the U.S. House of Representatives. In the 106th, two Blacks are members of the Blue Dog coalition, a group of conservative Democrats. They represent the interests of economic conservatives. Other Blacks represent women, farmers, and small-business owners. And, in fact, Barbara Lee's (D-CA) lone dissent from the House resolution authorizing the use of armed force against the terrorists who attacked America on September 11, 2001, will remain historic. Lee had no support in her dissent from any member of the CBC. This political and policy diversity would not be quite as evident among only five or ten Black legislators. This diversity can only come about as Black membership in Congress reaches a critical mass that permits Black members to defend their groups' interests broadly.

Blacks still believe that members of their own race do a better job of representing them than Whites. As critics of descriptive representation contend, Blacks' reliance on race as a political cue can mislead them. Once conservative Supreme Court nominee claimed that the Senate hearings on his confirmation had become a "high-tech lynching," Black opinion rallied to support Clarence Thomas's confirmation as retiring Thurgood Marshall's replacement (Mansbridge and Tate 1992). It was only once Associate Justice Thomas's conservative judicial record on affirmative action and legal rights emerged that the opinion of the liberal Black majority became appropriately negative. At the same time, Blacks have rejected Black candidates in favor of White candidates and incumbents. In 1990, Peter Rodino of New Jersey managed to win re-election in a racially divisive election in which his Black opponent had the endorsement of the popular and nationally known Black civil rights figure Jesse Jackson. As part of Rodino's reelection strategy, however, he promised to retire if elected to one more term. Moreover, cities that are solidly Black that had previously elected Black mayors have since elected Whites.

The criticism that descriptive representation may not improve the policy representation of Blacks finds some empirical support in my study of the 104th Congress. Black legislators in the 104th did not vote on issues in the manner most directly representative of their Black constituents' views on key issues. As shown in chapter 4, the majority of Blacks who favored the five-year lifetime limit on welfare benefits wrongly believed that their Black representative in the House voted in favor of welfare reform. The vast majority of Black House-legislators opposed welfare reform.

The dyadic model of representation developed in the pioneering study by Miller and Stokes (1963) considered only the Burkean components of political representation—that representatives were either delegates or trustees, followers of their constituents' will or independent agents. New work in public opinion suggests strongly that representatives will always be both. This reconceptualization of public opinion complicates the model of political representation, giving it a dynamic quality, according to Kuklinski and Segura (1995). Public opinion and legislative policymaking "play on and reinforce each other." This new understanding of political representation as a dynamic process gives greater meaning to the long-standing republican views that representation should "enlarge and refine" the electorate. Because I don't have over-time panel study data, I cannot directly assess how much political leaders lead citizens and how much they themselves are responding to their constituents' collective will. Black members of Congress defend and act on a set of interests that most other members of Congress don't take up. As political leaders, they have the opportunity not only to pass legislation that benefits Blacks but also to change public opinion in ways favorable to their group. Radical Republicans during Reconstruction advocating Black officeholding, in fact, understood this. Not only would Blacks in government best be able to defend their newly won political rights, but their presence in government would very powerfully and symbolically represent the cause of racial equality.

Perfect policy congruency, therefore, can be considered the elusive "Holy Grail," the chalice used by Christ that has never been found. No one will ever attain it, especially given America's weak party structure. Policy congruency is attainable only in the aggregate in a dynamic process whereby leaders simultaneously persuade and follow.

Constituents still feel fully represented despite the lack of perfect policy congruency because of all the other activities that representatives undertake in order to represent their constituents. Representation, after all, is more than substantive, policy representation. It is also powerfully symbolic. Members of Congress, as I show in chapter 5, seek to represent their constituents symbolically through resolutions that give recognition or voice to groups. Because the United States has a district-based system, citizens expect to see their groups represented in government. Only Black legislators were found to be the most likely to seek the symbolic representation of African Americans. Finally, to all of this, I add my "power of one" argument. As Mayhew (2000) argues, Congress's historical legacy and continuing impact in the United States is not only the product of its collective will but springs forth by the actions undertaken by its individual members. There can be no substitute, therefore, for descriptive representation if outcomes in Congress also critically depend upon individual actors.

The evidence that descriptive district-based representation empowers Blacks is slight. Blacks are more knowledgeable about their representatives when that representative is Black, but they are neither more efficacious nor more likely to vote than Blacks represented by Whites. Finally, those who are most concerned about the numerical underrepresentation of Blacks in government have long argued that descriptive representation is an important component of political trust. Jane Mansbridge (1999) argues that descriptive representation enhances the relationship between the representative and constituent and contributes to the government's political legitimacy. Numerically underrepresented groups who see themselves in government are more likely to feel included in the polity, empowered, and more valued in society, she argues. Descriptive representation also enhances the legitimacy of government policies in the eyes of the underrepresented group. She writes, "Having had a voice in the making of a particular policy, even if that voice is through one's representative and even when one's views did not prevail, also makes that policy more legitimate in one's eyes." My study found only partial confirmation of this claim. While Blacks represented in Washington by Blacks were more knowledgeable about their representatives, they were no more active in politics than Blacks represented by Whites. Nor did I find in my analysis of the 1996 NBES a direct relationship between the trust in government and the descriptive representation of Blacks in Congress. Blacks, however, expressed higher levels of trust in government when they believed that Blacks constituted a large percentage of Congress. As I explain in chapter 8, while most Blacks' estimates of that percentage in the U.S. Congress were fairly accurate, their estimates of their own percentage in the U.S. population were not. Blacks believing that Congress is made up of a very high (20, 30, 40 percent) percent of Blacks, and who also tended to rate Congress more favorably and exhibit higher levels of political trust, may be the least familiar and most removed from Congress. I therefore argue that in the end, it is not clear that having more Blacks added to Congress would truly improve Blacks' evaluations of Congress's performance or truly raise their levels of trust in government.

Seymour Martin Lipset claims that groups will accept a political system as legitimate if that system is founded on the values that they support. Blacks, in spite of their terrible history in the United States, accept the values on which this country was founded. They also believe in the constitutional devices that were adopted to ensure their rights as minorities in a majority-rule system. The Constitution's Bill of Rights and its separation of powers powerfully affirmed their faith in the democratic process because in the end the courts did finally extend the Constitution to Black citizens, albeit two centuries late. There is a promise of democracy contained in the Constitution, and the mechanism of the separation of powers ultimately forced Congress and the states to fulfill that promise. Independent sources of powers — checks and balances — made this promise believable. Other systems lacking alternative sources of power are not as credible. Thus, my failure to find a direct link between legitimacy and descriptive representation is mostly likely unique to the

United States alone. Other democracies that are not fully representative of their population base may not win the trust and faith from its excluded minorities, as found in the U.S. case. The United States might constitute the "deviant" case in the absence of a link between descriptive group-based political representation and legitimacy.

THE VOTING RIGHTS CONTROVERSY

The data suggest that Blacks, however, are willing to accept being numerically underrepresented in American government without this lack of descriptive representation undermining their faith in the democratic process. Blacks remain confident that they will be able to see themselves reflected in Congress. Is this confidence misplaced? J. Morgan Kousser in *Colorblind Injustice* (1999) writes about how this country failed Blacks in the first Reconstruction and is possibly failing them again in the second Reconstruction. Race has clearly been this country's severest test of its political integrity. The irony is that Blacks want it both ways, as does the White majority, in that they want color-blindness—a desire based on the belief that they will continue to be descriptively represented in government regardless.

Whether Black officeholding in the House will remain high is an open question as the principal mechanism used to achieve their current high rates, the Voting Rights Act (VRA), will expire in 2007 unless Congress acts to renew it. My 1996 survey reveals, however, that liberal support in the Black community for racial redistricting and minority-majority districts is weak. The 1996 National Black Election Study (NBES) carried three items that measured Black attitudes toward majority-minority districts and racial redistricting. The three questions highlighted different aspects of the debate over minority-majority districts. At its core is one's acceptance or aversion to color-conscious policies. In *Whose Votes Counts?*, Thernstrom (1987) denounces the extended use of the VRA as the basis for creating majority-minority districts because it violates the American constitutional ideal of "color-blindness." The law is, in her opinion, just another form of affirmative action in the political arena. Supporters of the Voting Rights Act argue that color-conscious redistricting is the only way that Blacks and Latinos can win election. The first question of the 1996 NBES explicitly raises the "color consciousness" issue by asking if districts should be drawn "without regard to race." It reads,

Some people think that districts should be drawn so that Blacks, Hispanics, and Whites all have their own representatives in government. Other people think that districts should be drawn without regard to race. Which one do you think is best — districts drawn so that Blacks, Hispanics, and Whites all have their own representatives in government, or districts should be drawn without regard to race?

The second question does not explicitly draw attention to the race-conscious means of creating majority-minority districts to the respondent. It asks more simply instead whether Blacks and Hispanics should be voting majorities or spread evenly across all of the districts. It taps the degree to which having some majority-minority districts is worthwhile to the respondent. It reads,

Some people think that Black and Hispanic voters should be the voting majority in at least some congressional districts. Other people think that Black and Hispanic voters should be spread evenly across all congressional districts. Which do you think is best — Blacks and Hispanics should represent majorities in some congressional districts, or Blacks and Hispanics should be spread evenly across all congressional districts?

The problem of racial redistricting is more complicated than the juxtaposition of race-conscious redistricting versus the social good of having a few districts where minorities are voting majorities and where minorities can win elections. It is widely believed that the numerical representation of Blacks and Hispanics would be enhanced under a different electoral system — if the United States switched from a single-member plurality system (SMP) to one where seats were allocated proportionately to vote (Amy 1993; Guinier 1994). Changing to a proportional representation system would have the advantage of being race-neutral while still advancing the cause of increasing the numerical representation of minorities. Thus, a third consideration is whether one is wedded to the current electoral system or willing to cast it aside for one that would enhance minority descriptive representation. It reads,

Some people think that election rules should be changed so that the number of Blacks and Hispanics in Congress is equal to their population in the country. Other people think that election rules should remain as they are. Which one do you think is best — election rules should be changed so that the number of Blacks and Hispanics in Congress is equal to their population in the country, or that election rules should remain as they are?

Blacks in this survey emphatically rejected a race-conscious redistricting process. As shown in table 9.1, a whopping 79 percent of Blacks felt that districts should be drawn "without regard to race," rejecting the idea that some districts should drawn so that Blacks and Hispanics have their own representatives in Washington. A full 69 percent thought that

TABLE 9.1
Black Opinion on Majority-Minority Districts

Congressional districts are redrawn every ten years by state legislatures, but how they should be drawn has become very controversial. Please tell me, if you were choosing, which type of district do you think is best?	
1) Some people think that Black and Hispanic voters should be the voting majority in at least some congressional districts. Other people think that Black and Hispanic voters should be spread evenly across all congressional districts. Which do you think is best — Blacks and Hispanics should represent majorities in some congressional districts, or Blacks and Hispanics should be spread evenly across all congressional districts?	
Majorities in some	25%
Spread evenly	69
Don't know	6
2) Some people think that districts should be drawn so that Blacks, Hispanics, and Whites all have their own representatives in government. Other people think that districts should be drawn without regard to race. Which one do you think is best — districts drawn so that Blacks, Hispanics, and Whites all have their own representatives in government, or districts should be drawn without regard to race?	
Minorities have own representatives	18%
Districts drawn without regard to race	79
Don't know	3
3) Some people think that election rules should be changed so that the number of Blacks and Hispanics in Congress is equal to their population in the country. Other people think that election rules should remain as they are. Which one do you think is best — election rules should be changed so that the number of Blacks and Hispanics in Congress is equal to their population in the country, or that election rules should remain as they are?	
Election rules that favor minorities	60%
Election rules remain as they are	35
Don't know	5

Source: 1996 NBES.

minorities should be spread evenly across congressional districts instead of concentrated so that some contained Black and Hispanic majorities. At the same time a large majority (60 percent), when asked if election rules should change to favor the election of minorities, endorsed change. This latter opinion suggests that a Black majority would have supported voting rights activist Lani Guinier's (1994) efforts to turn away from minority-minority districting in favor of a proportional representation system if she had been confirmed by the Senate to head the Justice Department's Civil Rights Division.

At the same time, Black attitudes on racial redistricting and electoral reform as methods of achieving greater Black descriptive representation were very unstable. While only 5 percent or fewer expressed no opinion on these measures, suggesting that most people could answer the questions and weren't confused, when given follow-up information and asked if their position would change, many changed their minds. Changing one's position in response to a counterargument indicates one's emotional or intellectual attachment to the issue. In addition, one's susceptibility to the counterargument can reveal the reasons why opinion can change. Regardless of the position taken—color-blind versus color-conscious, pro-minority descriptive representation or not—about half or more of the respondents said that they would change their position in light of the counterargument.[1]

Table 9.2 shows the rate of change for Blacks taking the liberal or conservative side on the racial redistricting items. This table reveals that an asymmetry exists among Blacks on this issue as well. Whereas Sniderman and Piazza (1993) found that it was harder to talk White conservatives out of their opposition to affirmative action, here it is somewhat harder to talk Black liberals out of their support for minority-majority districts. The results reveal that 43 percent of liberals would change positions in response to the counterargument, versus 57 percent of conservatives; and on the second measure, 41.5 percent versus 50 percent. The exact opposite was true, however, for Black opinion on the third measure. On this issue, conservatives who wanted to keep the election rules as they are were significantly less impressed by the counterargument ("that minorities in Congress would always be less than their population in the country") and stayed firm compared to the liberals. Although in the minority on this last question, 63 percent of minorities who took the conservative position and didn't want the election rules to change stayed firm.

For groups intending to seek the Voting Rights Act's renewal, the study's findings should cause alarm bells to ring. Those in favor of the act's renewal, however, have an advantage over their rivals insofar as Black liberal support is stronger and more certain than is Black opposition. Blacks opposed to racial redistricting practices and minority-majority districts, after all, were found to be most susceptible to the counterarguments in contrast to liberals on two of the three measures. Thus finding an appealing frame for the act's extension will have larger political payoffs than it will for the groups actively seeking its demise. Another advantage that liberals have over conservative groups is the

Table 9.2
Blacks' Willingness to Change Position on Racial Redistricting Items

	Liberal Position Originally Taken	Conservative Position Originally Taken
Those Who Said Their Position Would Change in Light of the Counterargument		
Minorities in Some Districts vs. Minorities Spread Evenly	41.5%	50%
Minorities Have Own Representatives vs. Draw Districts Without Regard to Race	43	57
Election Rules That Favor Minorities vs. Election Rules Remain as They Are	51	37

Source: 1996 NBES.

role that racial identification plays in support for racial redistricting and majority-minority districts. Making renewal a civil rights cause will therefore dramatically boost support in the Black community.

The ability of Black leaders to present a strong and unified force in favor of extending the Voting Rights Act is an open question. Big civil rights organizations have deteriorated to a point where their own survival is at stake. The NAACP had suffered from the revelation that a former president had used the organization's funds to keep a former female employee from filing a sexual harassment lawsuit against him. Black civil rights organizations also suffer from not only a financial crisis but also a political one. As the controversy over the nomination of Clarence Thomas to fill Thurgood Marshall's place on the Supreme Court illustrated, Black organizations are not ready to speak with a united front on new emerging issues. Given that this is an issue greatly dividing White and Black Democrats, some Black civil rights groups may choose to remain silent on the question for their own strategic purposes. The Congressional Black Caucus (CBC), however, is clearly going to aggressively push for the VRA's renewal as though its members' lives depended on it. The fiscal and political state of the CBC as 2007 approaches is also questionable, depending on whether the Democrats regain political control of the House.

As public opinion scholars have argued (Zaller 1992; Page and Shapiro 1992), political leaders can exert a large influence on public opinion. The president's position on renewing the Voting Rights Act will be pivotal here. Opposition to its renewal by a Republican president could help mobilize Blacks politically in favor of its extension, since Blacks remain staunchly loyal to the Democratic party, and debate would become highly partisan. Opposition by a Democratic president, at the same time, might win Blacks' approval in a manner not unlike the debate over welfare reform. A majority of Blacks (60 percent) in the 1996 NBES favored the new welfare law guaranteeing only five years of lifetime support to families in poverty. Black support for it, given their liberal profile as a group and given that most Blacks and many Democrats in the House voted against the welfare reform legislation, was surprising. President Clinton's wholehearted pursuit and backing of welfare reform, taken together with his strong popularity in the Black community, is a principle factor that explains that Black support (Barker, Jones, and Tate 1998). Had a Republican president sought a similar reform of the welfare program, his or her legislation would have likely met with deep skepticism and serious opposition from Blacks.

Blacks still value descriptive representation, even if they don't favor race-conscious means toward achieving descriptive representation. One other question in the 1996 NBES survey illustrates the majority's preference for descriptive representation. Blacks were asked how strongly they agreed or disagreed to the following statement: "It is not important for the president to appoint an additional Black person to serve as a justice on the Supreme Court." A majority of Black respondents disagreed, with 41 percent voicing strong disagreement. In contrast, 13 percent of the respondents strongly endorsed this statement while 18 percent somewhat agreed with it.

POLITICAL REFORM, THE COURTS, AND THE FUTURE OF BLACK FACES

The United States has a system of political representation that encourages the view that Americans should see themselves reflected in government. Not virtually, but actually. America's weak party system means that political parties will never fully provide perfect representation since Democrats are not all alike in their interests and voting records. Because members of the House are elected from districts, the policies that they promote reflect not only universal concerns but strongly particularistic ones. So distinctive is the American national legislature that David Mayhew considers the term legislature as applied to the U.S. Congress "unfortunate," arguing that the Congress is actually a "representative assembly" (1974, 8). Implied in this statement is that Congress is an aggregation of independent deputies, whose allegiances cross over a wide array of interests, from those of their parties to their own stake in reelection and political advancement. The American system is a "mixture," concludes Miller and Stokes, "to which the Burkean, instructed delegate, and responsible party models all can be said to have contributed elements" (1963, 56). Race obtains its profound significance in the political representation of Americans not only because of its societal impact but also institutional one as well. Because members of Congress are much more than "instructed delegates," Black faces become necessary for their fair and equal political representation in government.

Will Blacks be able to obtain actual political representation if the Voting Rights Act is not enforced or renewed? The Supreme Court in a series of 5–4 decisions has recently already rendered the act less effective, first in the *Shaw v. Reno* decision, which has made it difficult to maximize Black and minority officeholding without jeopardizing Democratic incumbents. Then in January 2000, the high court in a 5–4 decision limited the power of the U.S. Justice Department under the Voting Rights Act to force states to increase the number of districts in which minorities represented voting majorities. Previously, under the act, the Justice Department could deny preclearance to states whose electoral plans it deemed racially discriminatory. The only recourse left for states denied that preclearance was to submit a new plan or appeal their case to the D.C. Federal Court of Appeals. In the majority decision written by the Chief Justice, the U.S. Attorney General and judges can only block redistricting plans that weaken the voting strength of minorities. The case arose in Bossier Parish, Louisiana, where a school board refused to adopt a redistricting plan that would have contained two Black-majority districts. The legally contested plan had twelve districts, none with a Black majority. The Court's decision sided with the school board. The implications for the round of redistricting in 2000 that began for congressional districts is that regardless of what the census figures reveal, the Justice Department and courts cannot compel states to create additional opportunities for minorities to win seats. Furthermore, some of the existing majority-minority districts might retroactively be held to violate the *Shaw v. Reno* test and thus may be held ineligible for use as a baseline standard for retrogression. This area of law is likely to remain unclear until cases involving Section 5 preclearance denials are resolved in the next round of redistricting.

As Mark E. Rush points out, "As long as single-member districts remain the remedy of choice in implementing the Voting Rights Act (VRA), gerrymandering controversies will abound" (1998, 261). The alternative to renewing the Voting Rights Act is changing the electoral system. In general, a proportional-representation (PR) electoral system is seen as a way to advance minority descriptive representation and get out of the "political thicket" of court litigation over racial gerrymandering. The biggest advantage of switching to PR is that it offers a "race-neutral" way in which minority descriptive representation can be advanced. PR is not panacea as there are numerous versions of PR systems, some of which could limit minority officeholding. However, while PR may not yield absolute proportional representation, it offers a more secure basis of descriptive representation in government for political minorities than possible under district-based forms of political representation. One must, in fact, question the real motives of those who oppose majority-minority districts because it is rooted in a color-conscious practice, but then who also oppose PR as a color-blind alternative to increasing the rates of minority political officeholding.

The political empowerment of marginalized ethnic and racial groups under different electoral systems has not been researched as thoroughly as it could be, especially since it requires cross-national data on minorities. In contrast, there is ample scholarship on the effects of different electoral systems on rates of female officeholding. By having to prepare candidate lists, political parties are given more incentives to strive for gender balance, and they place more women on their tickets. As normative theorists point out, however, the problem of race and ethnicity in democratic states is quite distinct from that of gender (Phillips 1995). Certainly in the United States, for example, the political divisions between Whites and Blacks are significantly greater than those between men and women, even while there exists a well-documented gender gap in U.S. political behavior. All this is to argue that even if the system were to be reformed to one less biased in favor of the status quo and entrenched interests, but more reflective of all interests, racial and ethnic conflict would still make penetrating the democratic systems difficult for Blacks and other marginalized minority groups.

In the 1996 NBES survey, a full 60 percent of Blacks endorsed electoral reform as a means of advancing their descriptive representation in Congress. There is ready-made Black support for reform. Contrary to what one might expect, some Black members of Congress, including James Clyburn of South Carolina, the Chairman of the CBC in the 106th, strongly favor moving from a winner-take-all district system to a PR or cumulative voting system. Building a movement for reform, however, would run steeply uphill against a history and tradition in favor of keeping single-member districts. And prospects for reforming the electoral system to PR are extremely low. As Richard Engstrom explains, for political and not constitutionally required purposes, "The American experience with electoral systems has been severely truncated" (1998, 242). Thus law professor Lani Guinier's written advocacy of PR systems, based on sound empirical evidence as well as the principle of "race neutrality" and fairness, cost her an appointment by President Clinton to head the Justice Department's Civil Rights Division. The idea of scrapping the continuously litigated Section 2 of the Voting Rights

Act for a national switch to PR was denounced as too radical not only by U.S. Senators but by a majority within the media as well.

District-based representative democracy promulgates the belief that government should mirror the population, when it, effectively, does not. And the value of grouping interests into a single entity—the district—over other methods of representing citizens is not empirically well supported. Although a long line of theorists suggest that district-based representation is empowering, Black descriptive representation was not, as results in chapter 7 bear out. But, in fact, partisan control instead can significantly raise or lower Blacks' rates of voter participation. Under a PR system, fewer groups would feel unrepresented ideologically in government as more parties would serve in government. Rates of political participation would likely increase under a PR system. Blacks as a politically cohesive numerical minority would be able to enjoy higher levels of descriptive representation in a PR system.

In the end, arguments made by numerically underrepresented groups such as Blacks and women that reforms should be adopted to insure their actual presence are rejected, less by the long-standing claims of virtual representation (which empirically have been shown to be false for these groups) than by the notion that elections guarantee their representation. Elections historically have been a poor mechanism to guarantee the representation of Blacks because of key features of the American electoral system. As such, as long as White candidates can play on racial fears and win on the basis of racial-bloc voting, the only available means Blacks have to secure their descriptive representation is through the courts. While the Supreme Court has repudiated majority-minority districts on the basis of "principle," it could sustain them on the basis of political pragmatism. As much as the Declaration of Independence established the principles guiding this nation, the country was founded on the basis of political pragmatism. Blacks are not likely to withdraw from politics and revolt if even fewer numbers of Blacks serve in the House and it begins to resemble Congress's lily-white upper chamber, the U.S. Senate.

Even without race continuing to exist as a political fault line within the United States, even without America's racial history or its legacy, our system creates a reasonable demand for descriptive representation for all in government. District-based political representation is the principle of homogeneity and consensus. America is a diverse nation and therefore we either change the system better to reflect its diversity, or the courts must fulfill their assumed constitutional role of protecting the interests of political minorities, including women. Such interests under the current political system can only be advanced in a national assembly that effectively mirrors the population.

The 1996 National Black Election Study

IN 1984, a national telephone survey of voting-eligible African Americans was conducted by the Program for Research on Black Americans at the University of Michigan under the direction of James S. Jackson. Modeled after the University of Michigan's landmark National Election Studies with its pre- and post-election interview components, the 1984 National Black Election Study (NBES) represented the first-ever national political survey of a racial minority group. In 1988, a reinterview of the original 1984 NBES respondents was conducted, but in 1992, a data set comparable to the 1984 NBES or its 1988 reinterview did not exist. With funds from Ohio State University and the National Science Foundation (SBR-9507469), a survey modeled after the original 1984 NBES was conducted in 1996 by Katherine Tate at Ohio State University. This 1996 Black telephone survey, called the National Black Election Study or NBES, was designed to provide the third of an ongoing time series of Black political attitudes and behavior during the 1996 national elections. To facilitate racial group comparisons as well, the survey also carried many items contained in the Center for Political Studies' 1996 National Election Study.

The telephone survey was carried out by Market Strategies in Southfield, Michigan. Telephone interviewing began July 19 and ended November 4, 1996. A total of 1,216 interviews with voting-eligible Blacks was completed. Immediately following the election, 854 respondents were reinterviewed; the post-election reinterviewing ended January 6, 1997. Like its 1984–88 NBES and 1996 NES counterparts, the 1996 NBES was designed to explore the electoral behavior and attitudes of Blacks in the presidential election. However, unlike the original NBES, the 1996 study also had an explicit congressional focus. Respondents were matched to their congressional districts and asked to evaluate their House representatives. A total of 252 House districts fell into the sample, including the districts of 34 of the 39 Black members of Congress. In all, 31 percent of the Black respondents were represented by these Black legislators.

A number of individuals participated in the design and implementation of the study. Katherine Tate was the principal investigator of the study. Fred Steeper and Judith Perry directed the pre- and post-election surveys at Market Strategies. Kevin Cooper, also of Market Strategies, designed the sample. Doctoral students Teresa Todd, Gloria Hampton, and Stefanie Chambers at Ohio State University assisted in the development and implementation of this survey. An advisory board was created at Ohio State University to provide input into the development of the study; its members were Paul Beck (chair of the Political Science Department), Janet Box-Steffensmeier, Gregory Caldeira, Aage Clausen, Thomas Nelson, William E. Nelson (Political Science and Black Studies), Samuel Patterson, and Herbert Weisberg (Director of the Polimetrics Lab). National Election Study researchers, most notably Steven Rosenstone, Virginia Sapiro, and Kathy Cirksena, shared information and their expertise. Special thanks also go to Karin M. Clissold of Market Strategies and Gary Jacobson at University of California-San Diego for their expertise and advice.

SAMPLE DESCRIPTION

Like the original 1984 NBES, the 1996 NBES is a full-coverage, disproportionate probability random-digit-dial telephone survey. However, there are two important differences between the two samples. First, while the 1984 study sampled from three strata, the 1996 survey was a stratified random sample with four strata. These four strata were

1. Metropolitan statistical areas with populations of one million or more and Black populations of 15 percent or more (n = 600, estimated incidence = 22%).
2. The Southern states (Alabama, Florida, Georgia, Louisiana, Mississippi, South Carolina, Texas and Virginia), excluding the MSAs that fall into Strata 1 (n = 400, estimated incidence = 23%).
3. Telephone exchanges serving the remaining continental United States with 5 percent or greater Black population (n = 175, estimated incidence = 17%).
4. All remaining telephone exchanges in the continental United States with Black populations less than 5 percent (n = 25, estimated incidence = 1.4%).

Strata 3 and 4 are essentially the 1984 NBES's third stratum split into two. Telephone exchanges serving in the above strata were pooled, and a random-digit dial sample was generated independently with each pool. This is not a self-weighing design, so the data set requires weighting. The basis for the strata weights is shown in table A.1.

The full-coverage design of the NBES surveys is unique; by comparison, for cost and efficiency reasons, nearly every other Black telephone survey sample today is targeted (limited in most instances to telephone exchange areas that are 15 to 25 percent or more Black (Clissold and

TABLE A.1
Strata Weights

	U.S. Black Population (N)	Percent of Total Pop.	Self-Weighting	Sample Size (n)	Weight
Strata Description					
Large MSAs	13,238,232	.43144357	519	606	0.86
Southern States	7,169,510	.23365952	280	410	0.68
Balance (5% Black or more)	8,677,847	.28281732	339	175	1.94
Balance (less than 5% Black)	1,597,988	.05207959	62	25	2.48

Tate 1997). Blacks living in predominantly White communities are automatically excluded in targeted samples as locating and securing interviews with Black respondents living in such communities is costly. For example, while interviews with Blacks from Strata 1 cost about $100 each to complete, interviews in Strata 4 (an area that was less than 5 percent Black) were four and one-half times more costly.

A second sample difference between the 1984 and 1996 NBES is that while the 1984 NBES generated numbers using the Mitofsky-Waksberg design, the 1996 survey was a list-assisted sample. The phone numbers sampled from the four strata underwent a series of screenings to increase the working number rate. The first stage of screening purged known business phone numbers. The remaining numbers were identified as either listed or unlisted. The unlisted numbers were screened for an operator intercept signifying a nonworking number. The screenings were performed in-house and the systems used were part of the GENESYS system.

After screening, the sample files were sent to the Marking Systems Group to have the 105th congressional district appended. (Definitions for the 105th Congress were appended to all states except Texas, where large-scale redistricting occurred. Because the new districts were not yet available at the time of the field starting date, the 104th Congress were appended to Texas.) This was done by first determining whether the phone number was listed. If it was listed, the census block was determined and an "exact" match was made. If the number was not listed, the congressional district serving the plurality of the exchange was appended. There is a flag included that distinguishes between exact matches and plurality-based matched.

Members of telephone households were eligible to participate in the study if a member was Black and at least 18 years or age or older. The race of the household member was determined using this screener: "Because we are interested in the opinions of different demographic groups in the country, the first question I need to ask is: Is there an adult 18 years of older living in your household who is a Black American?" While the 1984 NBES used the Kish selection method, Black respondents were chosen from eligible telephone households on the basis of having had the most recent birthday. Using the last-birthday method as a means of selection is less intrusive than the Kish grid, which requires the complete enumeration of the household, from which one person is randomly selected. Salmon and Nichols (1983) found that samples drawn using the last-birthday method were just as representative as those whose respondents were chosen by the Kish selection method. Because potentially sensitive questions are not asked in the screening, some believe that the next-birthday method improves the cooperation rate, although previous research found that differences in the response rates between the two methods are not statistically significant (Oldendick et al. 1988). The 1996 NBES Pilot utilized a random-split of both selection methods and found that the last-birthday technique yielded a slightly higher, although not statistically significant, response rate than the Kish grid method.

RESPONSE RATES AND THE REPRESENTATIVENESS OF THE SAMPLE

Response rates can be calculated a number of different ways. Table A.2 presents the dispositions of attempted calls in the preelection survey so that any formula can be applied to calculate the study's response rates for comparative purposes. The overall response rate for the preelection study was 65 percent. This response rate adjusts for the proportion of respondents whose eligibility for the study was undetermined. It was estimated through screening that roughly 15 percent of those contacted were Black households. Thus, only 15 percent of the 1,446 respondents of undetermined status (those who refused to answer the race screening item, those too busy to participate, or households with answering machines) were included in the denominator of the refusal rate estimate as potential Black respondents who were lost. Strata 4 had the lowest response rate of 57 percent. Because the incidence rate was less than 2 percent in this stratum, and Blacks were difficult to find through a random-digit dial sample, eligible Black respondents who initially refused to participate in the study were offered $50 for completing the interview.

TABLE A.2
Pre-election Survey Final Disposition Codes and Response Rates

	Strata 1	Strata 2	Strata 3	Strata 4	Total
Completed Interviews	606	412	175	25	1,218
Determined Status:	227	144	54	14	439
Refusals	181	106	47	11	345
Callbacks	46	38	7	3	94
Undetermined Status:	600	361	179	306	1,446
Callbacks	45	38	25	25	133
Refusals	352	210	91	121	774
Non-contacts	203	113	63	160	539
Unanswered Numbers	855	501	274	410	2,040
Noneligible Numbers	4,080	3,187	1,568	2,807	11,642
Noneligible Respondents	5,732	4,395	1,963	4,200	16,290
Total Records	12,100	9,000	4,213	7,762	33,075
Incidence or Screening Rate	.208	.178	.184	.015	.153
Response Rate	63%	66%	67%	57%	65%

Note: The study's total response rate is calculated as completed interviews/[completed interviews + determined status + (incidence*undetermined status summed for strata 1 through 4)]

Phone numbers were determined to be "unanswered" if, after at least six attempts, no contact was made. "Unanswered" numbers were attempted at least once on the weekend, weekdays between 8 a.m. and 5 p.m., and weekdays after 5 p.m. There was no limit to the number of callbacks to "live" numbers. A number was considered live if contact was made, that is, if at any time the call was answered. Thus, for example, answering machines belonging to households were considered live numbers.

In the postelection survey, 70 percent of the 1,218 original preelection respondents were reinterviewed for a total of 854 interviews. The recontact rate across the four strata was 70 percent for Strata 1, 73 percent for Strata 2, 64 percent for Strata 3, and 63 percent for Strata 4. Of those we were unable to recontact, 194 had telephones that were disconnected or out of service, or the individual no longer lived there, or was permanently unavailable. The remaining 170 were refusals or callbacks.

THE REPRESENTATIVENESS OF THE SAMPLE

Because the 1984 and 1996 NBES surveys were conducted by telephone, Black respondents were not as representative of the general Black adult population as a face-to-face survey would have been. For comparison purposes, table A.3 presents the demographic characteristics of both the 1984 and 1996 NBES respondents and the March Current Population Survey data from the U.S. Census, which is a face-to-face survey. While CPS is designed to track employment and unemployment patterns in the United States, a second stated purpose of the CPS is to collect monthly information on the demographic status of the population. Based on interviews with 40,000 or more households, the CPS samples therefore, are designed to be highly representative of the U.S. population. The CPS data shown in table A.3 are for Black respondents 18 years of age or older, yielding 10,313 respondents in 1984 and 8,723 respondents in 1996.

The poor and least educated are generally found in households without telephones. As expected, then, low-income and less-educated Blacks are generally underrepresented in the NBES surveys. In addition, both the 1984 and 1996 surveys overrepresent Black women by 3 to 5 percent. Black women are generally overrepresented in surveys, including face-to-face surveys, because men are less likely than women to be attached to Black households. Thus, the overrepresentation of Black women in the NBES telephone samples is likely compounded by different response rates for Black men and women in telephone surveys. The NBES samples are comparable to the CPS studies for age, although in the NBES, respondents 55 years of age and older are somewhat overrepresented. Again, as in the case for women, the elderly may be more cooperative when asked to participate in phone surveys than those in the middle-two age categories.

The 1996 NBES sample is very similar to the original 1984 sample. Both overrepresent Black women, middle-income and educated Blacks, and working Blacks. The 1996 NBES, however, may be slightly less representative than the 1984 sample in its overrepresentation of middle-income Blacks and the Black elderly.

THE RACE-OF-INTERVIEWER EFFECT

The 1996 NBES used White, Black, and Asian telephone interviewers. The actual race of the interviewer was self-coded (see table A.4). About half of the preelection interviewing (49%) was performed by White interviewers, while Black conducted 44 percent of the interviews. Hispanic and Asian interviewers who coded themselves as belonging to an-

TABLE A.3
The Representativeness of the 1984 and 1996 NBES Weighted Samples

	1984 NBES	1984 CPS	1996 NBES	1996 CPS
Gender:				
Male	37.8%	42.8%	37.4%	40.7%
Female	62.2	57.2	62.6	59.3
Age:				
18–24	20.2	19.8	15.9	15.4
25–34	28	24.6	25.1	21.8
35–54	29.6	30.1	41.6	38.6
55+	22.2	25.4	17.4	24.2
Educational Attainment[1]:				
Elementary: 0–8 years	13.1	17.8	2.5	8.8
High school: 1–3 years	14.8	17.9	9.1	18.4
High school: 4 years	31.1	36.8	29.4	34.3
College: 1–3 years	23.7	17.3	37.4	26.4
College: 4+ years	17.4	10.2	21.7	12.2
Family Income[2]:				
less than $10,000	29.7	37.3	11.6	22.0
$10,000–29,999	49.7	42.6	43.0	36.0
$30,000–49,999	20.6	20.1	25.1	21.5
$50,000 or more	—	—	20.4	20.4
Region[3]				
South	59.0	56.2	55.1	53.1
Non-South	41.0	43.8	44.9	46.9
Marital Status:				
Married (includes separated)	48.6	48.7	36.5	44.5
Never married	28.9	31.6	40.1	35.7
Widowed	11.8	10.4	5.5	8.3
Divorced	10.7	9.3	17.9	11.6
Labor Force Status:				
Working	60.0	53.1	72.8	57.1
Unemployed (includes laid off)	13.5	9.5	8.0	6.5
Not in labor force	25.4	37.4	18.7	36.5
Home-Ownership:				
Rent	45.2	44.3	44.1	47.5

Table A.3 (*Continued*)

	1984 NBES	1984 CPS	1996 NBES	1996 CPS
Own	48.8	53.7	53.3	50.8
Other[4]	6.0	1.9	2.6	1.7

[1]In contrast to the 1996 CPS, the 1984 CPS education categories did not indicate whether the respondents had actually graduated.

[2]The income categories in the 1984 NBES ranged from less than $10,000 to $40,000 or more at intervals of $10,000, while the income categories in the 1986 NBES ranged from less than $10,000 to $105,000 or more at intervals of $5,000 and $10,000.

[3]As defined by the U.S. Bureau of the Census, the South represents Alabama, Arkansas, Delaware, the District of Columbia, Florida, Georgia, Kentucky, Louisiana, Maryland, Mississippi, North Carolina, Oklahoma, South Carolina, Tennessee, Texas, Virginia, and West Virginia.

[4]The other category for the census represents those not paying "cash rent."

other racial or ethnic group completed 8 percent of the interviews. The use of both Black and White interviewers in the 1996 NBES is consistent with that for the 1984 NBES, although none of the interviewers in the 1984 preelection study coded themselves as belonging to another group that was neither White nor Black. In the 1984 preelection study, 46 percent of the interviews were conducted by Whites and 53% by Blacks. The remaining 1 percent of the preelection interviews in 1984 were conducted by interviewers whose race was not coded.

Respondents were asked, however, a final question at the end of the 1996 survey to gauge whether they had placed interviewers in a racial category or not. This question read, "We'd like to know what kind of

Table A.4

Cross-tabulation of Perceived Race of Interviewer by Actual Race of Interviewer in 1996 NBES (Numbers Shown in Parentheses)

	Self-coded Race of Interviewer		
	White	Black	Other
Perceived Race of Interviewer			
White	71.5 (411)	22.0 (116)	63.4 (61)
Black	9.8 (56)	62.9 (333)	10.7 (10)
Other	8.2 (47)	4.6 (24)	5.4 (5)
Don't Know	10.1 (58)	9.6 (51)	18.2 (17)
Refused/NA	0.4 (2)	0.9 (5)	2.3 (2)
	100%	100%	100%

things people can tell just from listening to a person's voice over the telephone. During the interview, did you think I was White, Black, or someone of another group?" Examining the issue for the first time for a Black telephone survey, Gurin, Hatchett, and Jackson (1989) found that the actual race of the interviewer is less important than what the respondent perceives the race of that interviewer to be. Thus, the perceived-race-of-interviewer measure (as opposed to the actual race of the interviewer) should be introduced into the analysis of the data as a potential control measure for response bias.

NAMES AND DISTRICTS OF REPRESENTATIVES WHO FELL INTO 1996 NBES SAMPLE

Finally, table A.5 presents the names of the U.S. House representatives whose districts fell into the 1996 NBES sample.

TABLE A.5
List of House Members Whose Districts Fell into 1996 Sample

State and District Codes	Representatives	State and District Codes	Representatives
1.01	Callahan, Sonny	6.32	Dixon, Julian C.
1.02	Everett, Terry	6.33	Roybal-Allard, Lucille
1.03	Browder, Glen	6.34	Torres, Estaban E.
1.04	Bevill, Tom	6.35	Waters, Maxine
1.05	Cramer, Robert	6.37	Millender-McDonald, Juanita
1.06	Bachus, Spencer	6.38	Horn, Steve
1.07	Hillard, Earl F.	6.40	Lewis, Jerry
5.02	Thorton, Ray	6.42	Brown Jr., George E.
5.04	Dickey, Jay	6.50	Filner, Bob
6.01	Riggs, Frank	6.51	Cunningham, Randy
6.05	Matsui, Robert T.	8.01	Schroeder, Patricia
6.07	Miller, George	8.02	Skaggs, David E.
6.08	Pelosi, Nancy	8.05	Hefley, Joel
6.09	Dellums, Ronald R.	8.06	Schaefer, Dan
6.11	Pombo, Richard W.	9.01	Kennelly, Barbara
6.14	Eshoo, Anna	9.02	Gejdenson, Sam
6.18	Condit, Gary	9.03	DeLauro, Rosa
6.19	Randanovich, George	10.01	Castle, Al Michael N.
6.21	Thomas, Bill	11.01	Norton, Eleanor Holmes
6.23	Gallegly, Elton	12.01	Scarborough, Joe
6.26	Berman, Howard	12.02	Peterson, Pete
6.27	Moorhead, Carlos	12.03	Brown, Corrine
6.28	Drier, David	12.04	Fowler, Tillie

State and District Codes	Representatives	State and District Codes	Representatives
12.05	Thurman, Karen L.	17.16	Manzullo, Donald
12.06	Stearns, Cliff	17.18	LaHood, Ray
12.07	Mica, John L.	17.20	Durbin, Richard J.
12.08	McCollum, Bill	18.01	Visclosky, Peter J.
12.09	Bilirakis, Michael	18.03	Roemer, Tim
12.10	Young, C.W.Bill	18.04	Souder, Mark E.
12.11	Gibbons, Sam M.	18.10	Jacobs, Andrew Jr.
12.12	Canady, Charles T.	20.02	Brownback, Sam
12.13	Miller, Dan	20.03	Meyers, Jan
12.14	Goss, Porter J.	21.01	Whitfield, Edward
12.15	Weldon, Dave	21.02	Lewis, Ron
12.16	Foley, Mark	21.03	Ward, Mike
12.17	Meek, Carrie	22.01	Livingston, Robert
12.18	Ros-Lehtinen, Ileana	22.02	Jefferson, William J.
12.19	Johnston, Harry	22.03	Tauzin, W. J. Billy
12.20	Deutsch, Peter	22.04	Fields, Cleo
12.22	Shaw Jr., Clay	22.05	McCrery, Jim
12.23	Hastings, Alcee L.	22.06	Baker, Richard
13.01	Kingston, Jack	22.07	Hayes, Jimmy
13.02	Bishsop Jr., Sanford	24.01	Gilchrest, Wayne T.
13.03	Collins, Mac	24.02	Ehrlich, Robert L.
13.04	Linder, John	24.03	Cardin, Benjamin L.
13.05	Lewis, John	24.04	Wynn, Albert R.
13.06	Gingrich, Newt	24.05	Hoyer, Steny H.
13.07	Barr, Bob	24.06	Bartlett, Roscoe
13.08	Chambliss, Saxby	24.07	Cummings, Elijah
13.09	Deal, Nathan	24.08	Morella, Constance
13.10	Norwood, Charlie	25.02	Neal, Richard E.
13.11	McKinney, Cynthia A.	25.07	Markey, Edward J.
17.01	Rush, Bobby L.	25.09	Moakley, Joe
17.02	Jackson Jr., Jesse	26.03	Ehlers, Vernon J.
17.04	Gutierrez, Luis V.	26.07	Smith, Nick
17.05	Flanagan, Michael	26.09	Kildee, Dale E.
17.06	Hyde, Henry	26.10	Bonior, David E.
17.07	Collins, Cardiss	26.11	Knollenberg, Joe
17.09	Yates, Sidney	26.12	Levin, Sander M.
17.10	Porter, John Edward	26.14	Conyers Jr., John
17.11	Weller, Jerry	26.15	Collins, Barbara-Rose
17.12	Costello, Jerry F.	27.03	Ramstad, Jim
17.13	Fawell, Harris W.	27.04	Vento, Bruce
17.14	Hastert, Dennis	28.01	Wicker, Roger
17.15	Ewing, Thomas	28.02	Thompson, Bennie

State and District Codes	Representatives	State and District Codes	Representatives
28.03	Montgomery, G.V.	37.03	Jones, Walter B.
28.04	Parker, Mike	37.04	Heineman, Fred
28.05	Taylor, Gene	37.05	Burr, Richard
29.01	Clay, William L.	37.06	Coble, Howard
29.03	Gephardt, Richard	37.09	Myrick, Sue
29.05	McCarthy, Karen	37.10	Ballenger, Cass
29.06	Danner, Pat	37.12	Watt, Melvin
31.02	Christensen, Jon	39.01	Chabot, Steve
32.01	Ensign, John	39.03	Hall, Tony
34.01	Andrews, Robert E.	39.04	Oxley, Michael G.
34.02	LoBiondo, Frank A.	39.10	Hoke, Martin R.
34.04	Smith, Christopher H.	39.11	Stokes, Louis
34.07	Franks, Bob	39.13	Brown, Sherrod
34.08	Martini, Bill	39.16	Regula, Ralph
34.09	Torricelli, Robert G.	39.17	Traficant Jr., James
34.10	Payne, Donald M.	39.19	LaTourette, Steven C.
34.11	Frelinghuysen, Rodney	40.01	Largent, Steve
34.12	Zimmer, Dick	40.02	Coburn, Tom
36.01	Forbes, Michael J.	40.06	Lucas, Frank D.
36.03	King, Peter T.	42.01	Foglietta, Thomas M.
36.04	Frisa, Daniel	42.02	Fattah, Chaka
36.05	Ackerman, Gary	42.03	Borski, Robert A.
36.06	Flake, Floyd H.	42.07	Weldon, Curt
36.07	Manton, Thomas J	42.08	Greenwood, James C.
36.09	Schumer, Charles C.	42.09	Shuster, Bud
36.10	Towns, Edolphus	42.13	Fox, Jon D.
36.11	Owens, Major R.	42.14	Coyne, William J.
36.12	Velazquez, Nydia M.	42.16	Walker, Richard S.
36.15	Rangel, Charles B.	42.17	Gekas, George W.
36.16	Serrano, Jose	42.18	Doyle, Mike
36.17	Engel, Eliot L.	44.01	Kennedy, Patrick J.
36.18	Lowey, Nita M.	45.01	Sanford, Mark
36.19	Kelly, Sue W.	45.02	Spence, Floyd D.
36.20	Gilman, Benjamin A.	45.03	Graham, Lindsey
36.21	McNulty, Michael R.	45.04	Inglis, Bob
36.24	McHugh, John M.	45.05	Spratt Jr., John M.
36.26	Hinchey, Maurice D.	45.06	Clyburn, James E.
36.27	Paxon, Bill	47.03	Wamp, Zach
36.28	Slaughter, Lousie M.	47.05	Clement, Bob
36.30	Quinn, Jack	47.07	Bryant, Ed
37.01	Clayton, Eva	47.08	Tanner, John
37.02	Funderburk, David	47.09	Ford, Harold E.

State and District Codes	Representatives	State and District Codes	Representatives
48.01	Chapman, Jim	51.02	Pickett, Owen B.
48.03	Johnson, Sam	51.03	Scott, Robert C.
48.04	Hall, Ralph M.	51.04	Sisisky, Norman
48.05	Bryant, John	51.05	Payne Jr., L. F.
48.06	Barton, Joe L.	51.06	Goodlatte, Robert W.
48.07	Archer, Bill	51.07	Bliley Jr., Thomas J.
48.09	Stockman, Steve	51.08	Moran, James P.
48.10	Doggett, Lloyd	51.09	Boucher, Rick
48.11	Edwards, Chet	51.10	Wolf, Frank R.
48.18	Jackson-Lee, Sheila	51.11	Davis III, Thomas M.
48.22	Delay, Tom	53.06	Dicks, Norm
48.24	Frost, Martin	53.07	McDermott, Jim
48.25	Bentsen, Ken	54.02	Wise, Bob
48.26	Armey, Dick	54.03	Rahall II, Nick J.
48.27	Ortiz, Solomon P.	55.01	Neumann, Mark W.
48.29	Green, Gene	55.02	Klug, Scott L.
48.30	Johnson, Eddie Bernice	55.05	Barrett, Thomas M.
51.01	Bateman, Herbert H.	55.06	Petri, Tom

List of Black Members of the U.S. Congress

OVER THE COURSE of my research, I found that the numbers of Blacks elected to Congress varied slightly from source to source. This was highly frustrating because I didn't know which numbers were the correct ones. The inconsistency I think stems from whether one counts the number elected or the number who served. It also depends on whether one counts, as I do, the nonvoting delegate from the District of Columbia who first joined the 92nd Congress. So beginning with the 92nd Congress, my numbers are automatically elevated by one.

I count only those who served, not the number elected. In a few instances Blacks were elected but failed to serve in certain congresses. For example, Adam Clayton Powell was reelected to 90th Congress, but by a 365–64 vote, the House voted to exclude him. Some sources report that six Blacks served in the House of the 90th Congress, when in fact only five did. He would win re-election to the 91st Congress as well, and Congress would by a vote of 252–160 allow him to take office. (In 1969, in a 7–1 decision, the Supreme Court would rule that Powell had been unlawfully excluded from the 90th Congress.) Another example is the case of Andrew Young of Georgia, who would win his third term to the 95th Congress but resign in January to become the nation's first Black ambassador to the United Nations. Thus, I don't count Young as having served in the 95th Congress.

To support the numbers I report in chapter 2, I present the list of Black members whom I count as having served in each congress, starting with the 92nd Congress, in the tables below.

92ND CONGRESS, 1971–72:	BLACK REPRESENTATIVE
California	Ronald Dellums
	Augustus Hawkins
Illinois	Ralph Metcalfe
	George Collins
Maryland	Parren Mitchell
Michigan	John Conyers, Jr.
	Charles Diggs

Missouri	William Clay, Sr.
New York	Shirley Chisholm
	Charles B. Rangel
Ohio	Louis Stokes
Pennsylvania	Robert Nix
District of Columbia	Walter Fauntroy
SENATE:	Edward R. Brooke (R-MA)

93RD CONGRESS, 1973–74:	BLACK REPRESENTATIVE
California	Ronald Dellums
	Yvonne Burke
	Augustus Hawkins
Georgia	Andrew Young
Illinois	Ralph Metcalfe
Maryland	Parren Mitchell
	George Collins
Michigan	John Conyers, Jr.
	Charles Diggs
Missouri	William Clay, Sr.
New York	Shirley Chisholm
	Charles B. Rangel
Ohio	Louis Stokes
Pennsylvania	Robert Nix
Texas	Barbara Jordan
District of Columbia	Walter Fauntroy
SENATE:	Edward R. Brooke (R-MA)

94TH CONGRESS, 1975–76:	BLACK REPRESENTATIVE
California	Ronald Dellums
	Augustus Hawkins
	Yvonne Burke
Georgia	Andrew Young
Illinois	Ralph Metcalfe
	Cardiss Collins
Maryland	Parren Mitchell
Michigan	John Conyers, Jr.
	Charles Diggs

Missouri	William Clay, Sr.
New York	Shirley Chisholm
	Charles B. Rangel
Ohio	Louis Stokes
Pennsylvania	Robert Nix
Tennessee	Harold Ford
Texas	Barbara Jordan
District of Columbia	Walter Fauntroy
SENATE:	Edward R. Brooke (R-MA)
95TH CONGRESS, 1977–78:	**BLACK REPRESENTATIVE**
California	Ronald Dellums
	Augustus Hawkins
	Yvonne Burke
Illinois	Ralph Metcalfe
	Cardiss Collins
Maryland	Parren Mitchell
Michigan	John Conyers, Jr.
	Charles Diggs
Missouri	William Clay, Sr.
New York	Shirley Chisholm
	Charles B. Rangel
Ohio	Louis Stokes
Pennsylvania	Robert Nix
Tennessee	Harold Ford
Texas	Barbara Jordan
District of Columbia	Walter Fauntroy
SENATE:	Edward R. Brooke (R-MA)
96TH CONGRESS, 1979–80:	**BLACK REPRESENTATIVE**
California	Ronald Dellums
	Augustus Hawkins
	Julian Dixon
Illinois	B. Stewart
	Cardiss Collins
Maryland	Parren Mitchell
Michigan	John Conyers, Jr.
	Charles Diggs

Missouri	William Clay, Sr.
New York	Shirley Chisholm
	Charles B. Rangel
Ohio	Louis Stokes
Pennsylvania	William H. Gray III
Tennessee	Harold Ford
Texas	Mickey Leland
District of Columbia	Walter Fauntroy

97TH CONGRESS, 1981–82:	BLACK REPRESENTATIVE
California	Ronald Dellums
	Augustus Hawkins
	Julian Dixon
	Mervyn M. Dymally
Illinois	Gus Savage
	Harold Washington
	Cardiss Collins
Maryland	Parren Mitchell
Michigan	John Conyers, Jr.
	George Crockett
Missouri	William Clay, Sr.
New York	Shirley Chisholm
	Charles B. Rangel
Ohio	Louis Stokes
Pennsylvania	William H. Gray III
Tennessee	Harold Ford
Texas	Mickey Leland
District of Columbia	Walter Fauntroy

98TH CONGRESS, 1983–84:	BLACK REPRESENTATIVE
California	Ronald Dellums
	Augustus Hawkins
	Mervyn M. Dymally
	Julian Dixon
Illinois	Gus Savage
	Harold Washington
	Cardiss Collins
Indiana	Katie Hall

Maryland	Parren Mitchell
Michigan	John Conyers, Jr. George Crockett
Missouri	William Clay, Sr. Alan Wheat
New York	Ed Towns Major R. Owens Charles B. Rangel
Ohio	Louis Stokes
Pennsylvania	William H. Gray III
Tennessee	Harold Ford
Texas	Mickey Leland
District of Columbia	Walter Fauntroy

99TH CONGRESS, 1985–86:	BLACK REPRESENTATIVE
California	Ronald Dellums Augustus Hawkins Mervyn M. Dymally Julian Dixon
Illinois	Gus Savage Charles Hayes Cardiss Collins
Maryland	Parren Mitchell
Michigan	John Conyers, Jr. George Crockett
Missouri	William Clay, Sr. Alan Wheat
New York	Ed Towns Alton R. Waldon, Jr.* Major R. Owens Charles B. Rangel
Ohio	Louis Stokes
Pennsylvania	William H. Gray III
Tennessee	Harold Ford
Texas	Mickey Leland
District of Columbia	Walter Fauntroy

*Won special election in 1986 to fill seat created by death; he served only two months before his defeat by Flake in the regular November election.

100TH CONGRESS, 1987–88:	BLACK REPRESENTATIVE
California	Ronald Dellums
	Augustus Hawkins
	Mervyn M. Dymally
	Julian Dixon
Georgia	John Lewis
Illinois	Gus Savage
	Charles Hayes
	Cardiss Collins
Maryland	Kweisi Mfume
Michigan	John Conyers, Jr.
	George Crockett
Mississippi	Mike Espy
Missouri	William Clay, Sr.
	Alan Wheat
New York	Ed Towns
	Floyd Flake
	Major R. Owens
	Charles B. Rangel
Ohio	Louis Stokes
Pennsylvania	William H. Gray III
Tennessee	Harold Ford
Texas	Mickey Leland
District of Columbia	Walter Fauntroy

101ST CONGRESS, 1989–90:	BLACK REPRESENTATIVE
California	Ronald Dellums
	Augustus Hawkins
	Mervyn M. Dymally
	Julian Dixon
Georgia	John Lewis
Illinois	Gus Savage
	Charles Hayes
	Cardiss Collins
Maryland	Kweisi Mfume
Michigan	John Conyers, Jr.
	George Crockett
Mississippi	Mike Espy
Missouri	William Clay, Sr.
	Alan Wheat

New Jersey	Donald Payne
New York	Ed Towns
	Floyd Flake
	Major R. Owens
	Charles B. Rangel
Ohio	Louis Stokes
Pennsylvania	William H. Gray III
Tennessee	Harold Ford
Texas	Mickey Leland
District of Columbia	Walter Fauntroy

102ND CONGRESS, 1991–92:	BLACK REPRESENTATIVE
California	Ronald Dellums
	Maxine Waters
	Mervyn M. Dymally
	Julian Dixon
Connecticut	Gary Franks
Georgia	John Lewis
Illinois	Gus Savage
	Charles Hayes
	Cardiss Collins
Louisiana	William Jefferson
Maryland	Kweisi Mfume
Michigan	John Conyers, Jr.
	Barbara-Rose Collins
Mississippi	Mike Espy
Missouri	William Clay, Sr.
	Alan Wheat
New Jersey	Donald Payne
New York	Ed Towns
	Floyd Flake
	Major R. Owens
	Charles B. Rangel
Ohio	Louis Stokes
Pennsylvania	Lucien E. Blackwell
Tennessee	Harold Ford
Texas	Craig Washington
District of Columbia	Eleanor Holmes Norton

103RD CONGRESS, 1993–94:	BLACK REPRESENTATIVE
Alabama	Earl Hilliard
California	Ronald Dellums
	Maxine Waters
	Julian Dixon
	Walter R. Tucker III
Connecticut	Gary Franks
Florida	Corrine Brown
	Carrie Meek
	Alcee L. Hastings
Georgia	John Lewis
	Cynthia McKinney
	Sanford D. Bishop, Jr.
Illinois	Mel Reynolds
	Bobby L. Rush
	Cardiss Collins
Louisiana	William Jefferson
	Cleo Fields
Maryland	Albert R. Wynn
	Kweisi Mfume
Michigan	John Conyers, Jr.
	Barbara-Rose Collins
Mississippi	Bennie G. Thompson
Missouri	William Clay, Sr.
	Alan Wheat
New Jersey	Donald Payne
New York	Ed Towns
	Floyd Flake
	Major R. Owens
	Charles B. Rangel
North Carolina	Eva Clayton
	Melvin Watt
Ohio	Louis Stokes
Pennsylvania	Lucien E. Blackwell
South Carolina	James Clyburn
Tennessee	Harold Ford
Texas	Eddie Bernice Johnson
	Craig Washington
Virginia	Robert Scott

District of Columbia	Eleanor Holmes Norton
SENATE:	Carol Moseley Braun (D-IL)
104TH CONGRESS, 1995–96:	BLACK REPRESENTATIVE
Alabama	Earl Hilliard
California	Ronald Dellums
	Maxine Waters
	Julian Dixon
	Walter R. Tucker III*
Connecticut	Gary Franks
Florida	Corrine Brown
	Carrie Meek
	Alcee L. Hastings
Georgia	John Lewis
	Cynthia McKinney
	Sanford D. Bishop, Jr.
Illinois	Mel Reynolds**
	Bobby L. Rush
	Cardiss Collins
Louisiana	William Jefferson
	Cleo Fields
Maryland	Albert R. Wynn
	Kweisi Mfume***
Michigan	John Conyers, Jr.
	Barbara-Rose Collins
Mississippi	Bennie G. Thompson
Missouri	William Clay, Sr.
New Jersey	Donald Payne
New York	Ed Towns
	Floyd Flake
	Major R. Owens
	Charles B. Rangel
North Carolina	Eva Clayton
	Melvin Watt
Ohio	Louis Stokes
Oklahoma	Julius Caesar (J. C.) Watts
Pennsylvania	Chaka Fattah
South Carolina	James Clyburn
Tennessee	Harold Ford

Texas	Eddie Bernice Johnson
	Sheila Jackson-Lee
Virginia	Robert Scott
District of Columbia	Eleanor Holmes Norton
SENATE:	Carol Moseley Braun (D-IL)

*Resigned in October 1995 and Millender-McDonald elected.
**Resigned in October 1995 and Jackson, Jr. elected.
***Resigned in February 1996 and Cummings elected.

105TH CONGRESS, 1997–98:   BLACK REPRESENTATIVE

Alabama	Earl Hilliard
California	Julian Dixon
	Ronald Dellums*
	Juanita Millender-McDonald
	Maxine Waters
Florida	Corrine Brown
	Alcee L. Hastings
	Carrie Meek
Georgia	Sanford Bishop
	John Lewis
	Cynthia McKinney
Illinois	Danny Davis
	Jesse Jackson, Jr.
	Bobby L. Rush
Indiana	Julia Carson
Louisiana	William Jefferson
Maryland	Elijah Cummings
	Albert R. Wynn
Michigan	John Conyers, Jr.
	Carolyn Cheeks Kilpatrick
Mississippi	Bennie G. Thompson
Missouri	William Clay, Sr.
New Jersey	Donald Payne
New York	Floyd Flake
	Major R. Owens
	Charles B. Rangel
	Ed Towns
North Carolina	Eva Clayton
	Melvin Watt

Ohio	Louis Stokes
Oklahoma	J. C. Watts
Pennsylvania	Chaka Fattah
South Carolina	James Clyburn
Tennessee	Harold Ford, Jr.
Texas	Sheila Jackson-Lee
	Eddie Bernice Johnson
Virginia	Robert C. Scott
District of Columbia	Eleanor Holmes Norton
SENATE:	Carol Moseley Braun (D-IL)

*Resigned and Barbara Lee elected by special election April 7, 1998.

106TH CONGRESS, 1999–2000: BLACK REPRESENTATIVE

Alabama	Earl Hilliard
California	Julian Dixon
	Barbara Lee
	Juanita Millender-McDonald
	Maxine Waters
Florida	Corrine Brown
	Alcee L. Hastings
	Carrie Meek
Georgia	Sanford Bishop
	John Lewis
	Cynthia McKinney
Illinois	Danny Davis
	Jesse Jackson, Jr.
	Bobby L. Rush
Indiana	Julia Carson
Louisiana	William Jefferson
Maryland	Elijah Cummings
	Albert R. Wynn
Michigan	John Conyers, Jr.
	Carolyn Cheeks Kilpatrick
Mississippi	Bennie G. Thompson
Missouri	William Clay, Sr.
New Jersey	Donald Payne
New York	Gregory W. Meeks
	Major R. Owens

Charles B. Rangel
Ed Towns

North Carolina   Eva Clayton
Melvin Watt

Ohio   Stephanie Tubbs Jones

Oklahoma   J. C. Watts

Pennsylvania   Chaka Fattah

South Carolina   James Clyburn

Tennessee   Harold Ford, Jr.

Texas   Sheila Jackson-Lee
Eddie Bernice Johnson

Virginia   Robert C. Scott

District of Columbia   Eleanor Holmes Norton

107TH CONGRESS, 2001–2002:   BLACK REPRESENTATIVE

Alabama   Earl Hilliard

California   Diane Edith Watson*
Barbara Lee
Juanita Millender-McDonald
Maxine Waters

Florida   Corrine Brown
Alcee L. Hastings
Carrie Meek

Georgia   Sanford Bishop
John Lewis
Cynthia McKinney

Illinois   Danny Davis
Jesse Jackson, Jr.
Bobby L. Rush

Indiana   Julia Carson

Louisiana   William Jefferson

Maryland   Elijah Cummings
Albert R. Wynn

Michigan   John Conyers, Jr.
Carolyn Cheeks Kilpatrick

Mississippi   Bennie G. Thompson

Missouri   William Clay, Jr. (son of William Clay, Sr.)

New Jersey	Donald Payne
New York	Gregory W. Meeks
	Major R. Owens
	Charles B. Rangel
	Ed Towns
North Carolina	Eva Clayton
	Melvin Watt
Ohio	Stephanie Tubbs Jones
Oklahoma	J. C. Watts
Pennsylvania	Chaka Fattah
South Carolina	James Clyburn
Tennessee	Harold Ford, Jr.
Texas	Sheila Jackson-Lee
	Eddie Bernice Johnson
Virginia	Robert C. Scott
District of Columbia	Eleanor Holmes Norton

*On December 2000, Dixon died of a heart attack. In a special election, Diane Edith Watson won his district to join the 107th Congress.

Notes

Chapter 1
THE PUZZLE OF REPRESENTATION

1. North Carolina's last Black representative actually served until 1901.

Chapter 2
BLACK MEMBERS OF CONGRESS

1. Swain based her conclusions on historian Terry Seip's *The South Returns to Congress* (Baton Rouge: Louisiana State University Press, 1983), pp. 27–29.
2. This figure was reported in "Capital Questions," with C-Span scholar Ilona Nickels (website: http://www.c-span.org/questions/week151.htm).

Chapter 3
THE ELECTIONS OF BLACKS TO CONGRESS

1. The legislative history and the racial demographics of the districts that sent the first northern Blacks to Congress are difficult to piece together. In addition to Lublin's (1997) account, I've largely relied on information published in various editions of Congressional Quarterly's *Politics in America* and historical accounts.

Chapter 4
LEGISLATIVE STYLES AND VOTING RECORDS

1. Janet Box-Steffensmeier and Tobin Grant graciously provided me with these data for the 103rd Congress.

Chapter 9
THE FUTURE OF BLACK FACES IN THE U.S. CONGRESS

1. In the Sniderman and Piazza (1993) thought-experiment study on which these items were based, the rate of change to the counterarguments on affirmative action were comparatively low, about 20 percent.

References

Abramowitz, Alan I. 1984. "National Issues, Strategic Politicians, and Voting Behavior in the 1980 and 1982 Congressional Elections." *American Journal of Political Science* 28:710–21.

Alt, James E. 1994. "The Impact of the Voting Rights Act on Black and White Voter Registration in the South." In *Quiet Revolution in the South: The Impact of the Voting Rights Act, 1965–1990.* Edited by C. Davidson and B. Grofman. Princeton: Princeton University Press.

Amy, Douglas J. 1993. *Real Choices/New Voices: The Case for Proportional Representation Elections in the United States.* New York: Columbia University Press.

Anderson, Eric. 1981. *Race and Politics in North Carolina, 1872–1901* Baton Rouge: Louisiana State University Press.

Arnold, R. Douglas. 1990. *The Logic of Congressional Action.* New Haven: Yale University Press.

Barber, Kathleen L. 2000. *A Right to Representation.* Columbus: Ohio State University.

Barker, Lucius J., Mack H. Jones, and Katherine Tate. 1998. *African Americans and the American Political System.* 4th ed. Englewood Cliffs, N.J.: Prentice Hall.

Barnett, Marjorie Ross. 1982. "The Congressional Black Caucus: Illusions and Realities of Power." In *The New Black Politics.* Edited by M. B. Preston, L. J. Henderson Jr. and P. Puryear. New York: Longman.

Barrett, Edith J. 1995. "The Policy Priorities of African American Women in State Legislatures." *Legislative Studies Quarterly* 20:223–247.

Binder, Sarah A., Forrest Maltzman, and Lee Sigelman. 1998. "Senators' Home-State Reputations: Why Do Constituents Love a Bill Cohen So Much More Than an Al D'Amato?" *Legislative Studies Quarterly,* 23:545–560.

Blair, Daine D., and Jeanie R. Stanley. 1991. "Personal Relationships and Legislative Power: Male and Female Perceptions." *Legislative Studies Quarterly* 16:495–47.

Bobo, Lawrence, and Franklin D. Gilliam Jr. 1990. "Race, Socioeconomic Status, and Black Empowerment." *American Political Science Review* 84:377–394.

Bositis, David A. 1994. *The Congressional Black Caucus in the 103rd Congress.* Washington, D.C.: Joint Center for Political and Economic Studies.

Bratton, Kathleen A., and Kerry L. Haynie. 1999. "Agenda-Setting and Legislative Success in State Legislatures: The Effects of Gender and Race." *Journal of Politics* 61, no. 3, pp. 658–79.

Brischetto, Robert, David R. Richards, Chandler Davidson, and Bernard Grofman. 1994. "Texas." In *Quiet Revolution in the South.* Edited by C. Davidson and B. Grofman. Princeton: Princeton University Press, pp. 233–70.

Browning, Robert P., Dale Rogers Marshall, and David H. Tabb. 1984. *Protest Is Not Enough*. Berkeley and Los Angeles: University of California Press.

Button, James, and David Hedge. 1997. "Legislative Life in the 1990s: A Comparison of Black and White State Legislators." *Legislative Studies Quarterly*, 21:199–218.

Cain, Bruce, John Ferejohn, and Morris Fiorina. 1987. *The Personal Vote*. Cambridge: Harvard University Press.

Cameron, Charles, David Epstein, and Sharyn O'Halloran. 1996. "Do Majority-Minority Districts Maximize Substantive Black Representation in Congress?" *American Political Science Review* 90, no. 4, pp. 794–812.

Canon, David T. 1999. *Race, Redistricting, and Representation: The Unintended Consequences of Black Majority Districts*. Chicago: University of Chicago Press.

Carmines, Edward G., and James A. Stimson. 1989. *Issue Evolution: Race and the Transformation of American Politics*. Princeton: Princeton University Press.

Caul-Kittilson, Miki. 2001. "Political Parties and the Adoption of Candidate Gender Quotas: A Cross-National Analysis." *Journal of Politics* 63, no. 4 (Nov.): 1214–29.

Champagne, Richard, and Leroy N. Rieselbach. 1995. "The Evolving Congressional Black Caucus: The Reagan-Bush Years." In *Blacks and the American Political System*. Edited by Huey L. Perry and Wayne Parent. Gainesville: University of Florida Press, pp. 130–161.

Chapman, Valeria Sinclair. 1996. "Symbols and Substance." Paper presented at the annual convention of the 1996 American Political Science Association, San Francisco.

———. 2002. "Presence, Promise, and Progress: Black Representation in the U.S. Congress." Unpublished manuscript, Ohio State University.

Chisholm, Shirley. 1973. *The Good Fight*. New York: Harper & Row.

Christopher, Maurine. 1971. *America's Black Congressmen*. New York: Thomas Y. Crowell.

Clay, William L. 1992. *Just Permanent Interests: Black Americans in Congress, 1870–1991*. New York: Amistad Press.

Clissold, Karin M., and Katherine Tate. 1997. "Methodological and Design Considerations in Telephone Surveys of Black Americans." Manuscript, The Ohio State University.

Cohen, Cathy J. 1999. *The Boundaries of Blackness: AIDS and the Breakdown of Black Politics*. Chicago: University of Chicago Press.

Cohen, Philip N. 2001. "Choice and Access in Black and White Women's Employment." Paper under review. University of California, Irvine.

Darcy, R., and Charles D. Hadley. 1988. "Black Women in Politics: The Puzzle of Success." *Social Science Quarterly* 69 (Sept.): 629–45.

Darcy, R., Susan Welch, and Janet Clark. 1994. *Women, Elections, and Representation*. 2nd ed. Lincoln: University of Nebraska Press.

Davidson, Chandler, ed. 1984. *Minority Vote Dilution*. Washington, D.C.: Howard University Press.

Davidson, Chandler and Bernard Grofman, eds. 1994. *Quiet Revolution in the South: The Impact of the Voting Rights Act, 1965–1990*. Princeton: Princeton University Press.

Davidson, Roger H. 1969. *The Role of the Congressman*. New York: Pegasus.

Davidson, Roger H., and Walter J. Oleszek. 1981. *Congress and Its Members*. Washington, D.C.: Congressional Quarterly Press.

Dawson, Michael C. 1994. *Behind the Mule*. Princeton: Princeton University Press.

Deering, Christopher J., and Steven S. Smith. 1997. *Committees in Congress*. 3rd ed. Washington, D.C.: Congressional Quarterly Press.

Easton, David. 1965. *A Systems Analysis of Political Life*. New York: Wiley.

Edelman, Murray J. 1964. *The Symbolic Uses of Politics*. Urbana: University of Illinois Press.

Engstrom, Richard L. 1998. "Minority Electoral Opportunities and Alternative Election Systems in the United States." In *Voting Rights and Redistricting in the United States*. Edited by M. E. Rush. Westport, Conn.: Greenwood Press.

Erikson, Robert S., and Gerald C. Wright. 2001. "Voters, Candidates and Issues in Congressional Elections." In *Congress Reconsidered*. 7th ed. Edited by Lawrence C. Dodd and Bruce I Oppenheimer. Washington, D.C.: Congressional Quarterly Press.

Eulau, Heinz, and Paul Karps. 1978. "The Puzzle of Representation: Specifying Components of Responsiveness," In *The Politics of Representation*. Edited by Heinz Eulau and John Wahlke. Beverly Hills, Calif.: Sage, pp. 55–71.

Feingold, Beth. 1992. "Concepts of Representation Among Female and Male State Legislators." *Legislative Studies Quarterly* 4:509–37.

Fenno, Richard F., Jr. 1978. *Home Style: House Members in Their Districts*. Boston: Little, Brown.

———. 1997. *Learning to Govern, An Institutional View of the 104th Congress*. Washington, D.C.: Brookings Institution Press.

Fiorina, Morris P. 1974. *Representatives, Roll Calls, and Constituencies*. Lexington, Mass.: Lexington Books.

———. 1989. *Congress: Keystone of the Washington Establishment, 2nd ed.* New Haven : Yale University Press.

Fiorina, Morris P., and Douglas Rivers. 1989. "Constituency Service, Reputation, and the Incumbency Advantage." In *Home Style and Washington Work*. Edited by Morris P. Fiorina and David W. Rohde. Ann Arbor: University of Michigan Press.

Fishkin, James S. 1995. *The Voice of the People: Public Opinion and Democracy*. New Haven: Yale University Press.

Foner, Eric. 1990. *A Short History of Reconstruction, 1863–1877*. New York: Harper & Row.

———. 1996. *Freedom's Lawmakers: A Directory of Black Officeholding During Reconstruction*. Baton Rouge: Louisiana State University Press.

Friedman, Sally. 1996. "House Committee Assignments of Women and Minority Newcomers, 1965–1994." *Legislative Studies Quarterly* 1:73–81.

Froman, Lewis A. 1963. *Congressmen and Their Constituences*. Chicago: Rand McNally.

Frymer, Paul. 1999. *Uneasy Alliances: Race and Party competition in America*. Princeton: Princeton University Press.

Gamson, William A. 1968. *Power and Discontent*. Homewood, Ill.: Dorsey Press.

Gay, Claudine. 2001. "The Effect of Black Congressional Representation on Political Participation." *American Political Science Review* 95, no. 3: 589–602.

Gill, LaVerne McCain. 1997. *African American Women in Congress: Forming and Transforming History.* New Brunswick, N.J.: Rutgers University Press.

Grady, Robert C. 1993. *Restoring Real Representation.* Urbana: University of Illinois Press.

Grimshaw, William J. 1992. *Bitter Fruit: Black Politics and the Chicago Machine, 1931–1991.* Chicago: University of Chicago Press.

Grofman, Bernard, and Chandler Davidson, eds. 1992. *Controversies in Minority Voting: The Voting Rights Act in Perspective.* Washington, D.C.: Brookings Institution Press.

Grofman, Bernard, Lisa Handley, and Richard Niemi. 1992. *Minority Representation and the Quest for Voting Equality.* New York: Cambridge University Press.

Guinier, Lani. 1994. *The Tyranny of the Majority: Fundamental Fairness in Representative Democracy.* New York: Free Press.

Gurin, Patricia, Shirley Hatchett, and James S. Jackson. 1989. *Hope and Independence: Blacks' Response to Electoral and Party Politics.* New York: Russell Sage Foundation.

Hall, Richard L. 1996. *Participation in Congress.* New Haven: Yale University Press.

Hamilton, Charles V. 1991. *Adam Clayton Powell, Jr.: The Political Biography of an American Dilemma.* New York: Atheneum.

Haynie, Kerry L. 2001. *African American Legislators in the American States.* New York: Columbia University Press.

Hibbing, John R., and Elizabeth Theiss-Morse. 1995. *Congress as Public Enemy.* New York: Cambridge University Press.

Holt, Thomas. 1977. *Black Over White.* Champaign and Urbana: University of Illinois Press.

Jackson, James S. 1993. National Black Election Panel Study, 1984 and 1988 [computer file]. Ann Arbor: University of Michigan, Research Center for Group Dynamics, Institute for Social Research [producer], 1997; Inter-university Consortium for Political and Social Research [distributor].

Jacobson, Gary C. 1987. "The Marginals Never Vanished: Incumbency and Competition in Elections to the U.S. House of Representatives, 1952–82." *American Journal of Political Science* 31, No. 1 (Feb.): 126–41.

Johnson, James B. and Philip E. Secret. 1996. "Focus and Style Representational Roles of Congressional Black and Hispanic Caucus Members." *Journal of Black Studies,* 26(3):245–273.

Kahn, Kim Friedkin. 1996. *The Political Consequences of Being a Woman: How Stereotypes Influence the Conduct and Consequences of Political Campaigns.* New York: Columbia University Press.

Killian, Linda. 1998. *The Freshmen: What Happened to the Republican Revolution?* Boulder, Colo.: Westview Press.

Kingdon, John W. 1981. *Congressmen's Voting Decisions,* 2nd ed. New York: Harper & Row.

Kousser, J. Morgan. 1974. *The Shaping of Southern Politics: Suffrage Restriction and the Estblishment of the One-Party South, 1880–1910.* New Haven: Yale University Press.

———. 1999. *Colorblind Injustice: Minority Voting Rights and the Undoing of the Second Reconstruction.* Chapel Hill: University of North Carolina Press.

Kuklinski, James H., and Gary M. Segura. 1995. "Endogeneity, Exogeneity, Time, and Space in Political Representation" *Legislative Studies Quarterly* 1:3–21.

Ladd, Everett Carll, and Karlyn H. Bowman. 1998. *What's Wrong: A Survey of American Satisfaction and Complaint.* Washington, D.C.: AEI Press.

Lublin, David. 1997. *The Paradox of Representation.* Princeton: Princeton University Press.

Lublin, David, and Katherine Tate. 1995. "Racial Group Competition in U.S. Mayoral Elections." In *Classifying by Race.* Edited by P. E. Peterson. Princeton: Princeton University Press.

Mann, Thomas E. 1978. *Unsafe at Any Margin: Interpreting Congressional Elections.* Washington, D.C.: American Enterprise Institute for Public Policy Research.

Mansbridge, Jane J. 1986. *Why We Lost the ERA.* Chicago : University of Chicago Press.

———. 1999. "Should Blacks Represent Blacks and Women Represent Women? A Contingent 'Yes.'" *Journal of Politics* 61, no. 3 (Aug.): 628–57.

Mansbridge, Jane J., and Katherine Tate. 1992. "Race Trumps Gender: Black Opinion on the Thomas Nomination." *PS: Political Science and Politics* 25, no. 3.

Mayhew, David R. 1974. *Congress: The Electoral Connection.* New Haven: Yale University Press.

———. 2000. *America's Congress: Action in the Public Sphere, James Madison Through Newt Gingrich.* New Haven: Yale University Press.

McAdam, Doug. 1982. *Political Process and Development of Black Insurgency, 1930–1970.* Chicago: University of Chicago Press.

McClain, Paula D., and Joseph Stewart Jr. 1998. *Can We All Get Along? Racial and Ethnic Minorities in American Politics* 2nd ed. Boulder, Colo.: Westview Press.

McDonagh, Eileen Lorenzi. 1993. "Constituency Influence on House Roll-Call Votes in the Progressive Era, 1913–1915." *Legislative Studies Quarterly* 18, no. 2 (May): 185–210.

Mezey, Michael L. 1993. "Legislatures: Individual Purpose and Institutional Performance." In *Political Science: The State of the Discipline II.* Edited by Ada W. Finifter. Washington, D.C.: American Political Science Association, pp. 335–64.

Miller, Warren, and Donald Stokes. 1963. "Constituency Influence in Congress." *American Political Science Review* 57, no. 1 (Mar.): 45–46.

Monroe, James A. 1990. *The Democratic Wish, Popular Participation and the Limits of American Government.* New York: Basic Books.

Morrow, William L. 2000. *A Republic If You Can Keep It, Constitutional Politics and Public Policy.* Upper Saddle River, N.J.: Prentice Hall.

Niemi, Richard, and Herbert F. Weisberg. 1993. *Controversies in Voting Behavior,* 3rd Ed. Washington, D.C.: Congressional Quarterly Press.

Oldendick, Robert W., George F. Bishop, Susan B. Sorenson, and Alfred J. Tuchfarber. 1988. "A Comparison of Kish and Last Birthday Methods of Respondent Selection in Telephone Surveys." *Journal of Official Statistics* 4, no. 4: 307–18.

Ornstein, Norman, Thomas E. Mann, and Michael J. Malbin. 1998. *Vital Statistics on Congress, 1997–98.* Washington, D.C.: Congressional Quarterly Press.

Page, Benjamin I. 1981. *Choices and Echoes in Presidential Elections: Rational Man and Electoral Democracy.* Chicago: University of Chicago Press.

Page, Benjamin I., and Robert Y. Shapiro. 1992. *The Rational Public.* Chicago: University of Chicago Press.

Parker, Frank R. 1990. *Black Votes Count.* Chapel Hill: University of North Carolina Press.

Patterson, Samuel C., and Gregory A. Caldeira. 1983. "Getting Out the Vote: Participation in Gubernatorial Elections." *American Political Science Review* 77:675–89.

Payne, Donald L. 1997. "Introduction, the 104th Congress—The Perspective of the Chairman of the Congressional Black Caucus." In *African American Power and Politics* by Hanes Walton Jr. New York: Columbia University Press.

Pennock, J. Roland. 1979. *Democratic Political Theory.* Princeton: Princeton University Press.

Perkins, Jerry. 1986. "Political Ambition among Black and White Women: An Intragender Test of the Socialization Model." *Women & Politics* 6, no. 1, pp. 27–40.

Phillips, Anne. 1995. *The Politics of Presence.* NewYork: Oxford University Press.

Pinderhughes, Dianne M. 1995. "Black Interest Groups and the 1982 Extension of the Voting Rights Act." In *Blacks and the American Political System.* Edited by Huey L. Perry and Wayne Parent. Gainesville: University of Florida Press, pp. 203–24.

Pitkin, Hanna F. 1967. *The Concept of Representation.* Berkeley: University of California Press.

Poole, Keith T. 1999. "Changing Minds? Not in Congress!" Unpublished paper, Carnegie-Mellon University.

Poole, Keith T., and Howard Rosenthal. 1991. "Patterns of Congressional Voting." *American Journal of Political Science* 35 (Feb.): 235–43.

Popkin, Samuel L. 1991. *The Reasoning Voter: Communication and Persuasion in Presidential Campaigns.* Chicago: University of Chicago Press.

Pressman, Jeffrey L., and Aaron Wildavsky. 1984. *Implementation.* 3rd ed. Berkeley and Los Angeles: University of California Press.

Reed, Adolph L., Jr. 1986. *The Jesse Jackson Phenomenon: The Crisis of Purpose in Afro-American Politics.* New Haven: Yale University Press.

Reeves, Keith. 1997. *Voting Hopes or Fears? White Voters, Black Candidates, and Racial Politics in America.* New York: Oxford University Press.

Rohde, David W. 1991. *Parties and Leaders in the Postreform House*. Chicago: University of Chicago Press.

Rosenstone, Steven J., and John Mark Hansen. 1993. *Mobilization, Participation, and Democracy in America*. New York: Macmillan.

Rush, Mark E. 1998. "Postscript: The Promise of Electoral Systems and the Perils of Electoral Reform." In *Voting Rights and Redistricting in the United States*. Edited by M. E. Rush. Westport, Conn.: Greenwood Press.

Sacks, Kevin. 1995. "Louisiana's Governor's Race Will Be a Study in Contrasts." *The New York Times*, 23 October, p. A10.

———. 2000. "PUBLIC LIVES; He Has Reason to Ponder the Shape of Things to Come." *The New York Times*, 29 April, p. A8.

Sanbonmatsu, Kira. 2002. *Democrats, Republicans, and the Politics of Women's Place*. Ann Arbor, MI: University of Michigan Press.

Salmon, Charles T. and John Spicer Nichols. 1983. "The Next-Birthday Method of Respondent Selection." *Public Opinion Quarterly* 47:270–276.

Schwartz, Nancy L. 1988. *The Blue Guitar: Political Representation and Community*. Chicago: University of Chicago Press.

Shepsle, Kenneth A. 1978. *The Giant Jigsaw Puzzle: Democratic Committee Assignments in the Modern House*. Chicago: University of Chicago Press.

Sinclair, Barbara. 1983. *Majority Leadership in the U.S. House*. Baltimore: The Johns Hopkins University Press.

———. 1997. *Unorthodox Lawmaking, New Legislative Processes in the U.S. Congress*. Washington, D.C.: Congressional Quarterly Press.

Singh, Robert. 1998. *The Congressional Black Caucus, Racial Politics in the U.S. Congress*. Thousand Oaks, Calif.: Sage.

Smith, Eric R.A.N. 1989. *The Unchanging American Voter*. Berkeley: University of California Press.

Smith, Robert C. 1981. "Black Power and the Transformation from Protest to Politics." *Political Science Quarterly* 96:431–43.

Smith, Rogers M. 1997. *Civic Ideals: Conflicting Visions of Citizenship in U.S. history*. New Haven: Yale University Press.

Sniderman, Paul M. "The New Look in Public Opinion Research." In *Political Science: The State of the Discipline II*. Edited by Ada W. Finifter. Washington, D.C.: American Political Science Association, pp. 219–45.

Sniderman, Paul M., and Thomas Piazza. 1993. *The Scar of Race*. Cambridge: Harvard University Press.

Swain, Carol M. 1993. *Black Faces, Black Interests: The Representation of African Americans in Congress*. Cambridge: Harvard University Press.

———. 1997. "Women and Blacks in Congress: 1870–1996." In *Congress Reconsidered*. 6th ed. Edited by Lawrence C. Dodd and Bruce I. Oppenheimer. Washington, D.C.: Congressional Quarterly Press.

Swers, Michele. 1998. "Are Women More Likely to Vote for Women's Issue Bills Than Their Male Colleagues?" *Legislative Studies Quarterly* 3:435–88.

Tate, Katherine. 1994. *From Protest to Politics: The New Black Voters in American Elections*. Enlarged ed. Cambridge: Harvard University Press and the Russell Sage Foundation.

———. 1997. "African American Female Senatorial Candidates: Twin Assets or

Double Liabilities?" In *African American Power and Politics*. Edited by Hanes Walton, Jr. New York: Columbia University Press.

———. 1998. "National Black Election Study, 1996" [computer file]. ICPSR version. Columbus: Ohio State University [producer], 1997. Ann Arbor: Interuniversity Consortium for Political and Social Research [distributor].

Thernstrom, Abigail. 1987. *Whose Votes Count? Affirmative Action and Minority Voting Rights*. Cambridge: Harvard University Press.

Thernstrom, Stephan, and Abigail Thernstrom. 1997. *America in Black and White*. New York: Simon & Schuster.

Thomas, Sue. 1994. *How Women Legislate*. New York: Oxford University Press.

Thomassen, Jacques. 1994. "Empirical Research into Political Representation: Failing Democracy or Failing Models." In *Elections At Home and Abroad*. Edited by M. Kent Jennings and Thomas E. Mann. Ann Arbor: University of Michigan Press, pp. 237–64.

Verba, Sidney, and Norman H. Nie. 1972. *Participation in America: Political Democracy and Social Equality*. New York: Harper & Row.

Verba, Sidney, Kay Lehman Schlozman, and Henry E. Brady. 1995. *Voice and Equality: Civic Voluntarism in American Politics*. Cambridge: Harvard University Press.

Walters, Ronald W. 1988. *Black Presidential Politics in American: A Strategic Approach*. Albany: State University of New York Press.

Walton, Hanes, Jr. 1997. *African American Power and Politics, The Political Context Variable*. New York: Columbia University Press.

Wattenberg, Martin P. 1996. *The Decline of American Political Parties, 1952–1994*. Cambridge: Harvard University Press.

Weissberg, Robert. 1976. *Public Opinion and Popular Government*. Englewood Cliffs, N.J.: Prentice-Hall.

Whitby, Kenny J. 1998. *The Color of Representation: Congressional Behavior and Black Constituents*. Ann Arbor: The University of Michigan Press.

Williams, Linda F. 1989. "White/Black Perceptions of the Electability of Black Political Candidates." *National Political Science Review* 2:45–64.

Williams, Melissa S. 1998. *Voice, Trust, and Memory: Marginalized Groups and the Failings of Liberal Representation*. Princeton: Princeton University Press.

Wolfinger, Raymond E., and Steven J. Rosenstone. 1980. *Who Votes?* New Haven: Yale University Press.

Wood, Gordon S. 1998 [1969]. *The Creation of the American Republic, 1776–1787*. Chapel Hill: University of North Carolina Press.

Young, Iris Marion. 1990. *Justice and the Politics of Difference*. Princeton: Princeton University Press.

Zaller, John R. 1992. *The Nature and Origins of Mass Opinion*. New York: Cambridge University Press.

Index